Lecture Notes in Public Budgeting and Financial Management

World Scientific Lecture Notes in Economics

ISSN: 2382-6118

Series Editor: Ariel Dinar *(University of California, Riverside, USA)*

The World Scientific Lecture Notes in Economics (WSLNE) series is aimed to produce lecture note texts for a wide range of economics disciplines, both theoretical and applied at the undergraduate and graduate levels. Contributors to WSLNE are highly ranked and experienced professors of economics who see in publication of their lectures a mission to disseminate the teaching of economics in an affordable manner to students and other readers interested in enriching their knowledge of economic topics.

Published:

Vol. 5: *Lecture Notes in Public Budgeting and Financial Management*
by William Duncombe

Vol. 4: *Lecture Notes in Urban Economics and Urban Policy*
by John Yinger

Vol. 3: *Econometric Models for Industrial Organization*
by Matthew Shum

Vol. 2: *Economics of the Middle East: Development Challenges*
by Julia C. Devlin

Vol. 1: *Financial Derivatives: Futures, Forwards, Swaps, Options, Corporate Securities, and Credit Default Swaps*
by George M. Constantinides

Forthcoming:

Lectures in Neuroeconomics
edited by Paul Glimcher and Hilke Plassmann

Economics, Game Theory and International Environmental Agreements: The Ca' Foscari Lectures
by Henry Tulkens

Lecture Notes in Microeconomics: Modeling Strategic Behavior
by George J. Mailath

World Scientific Lecture Notes in Economics – Vol. 5

Lecture Notes in Public Budgeting and Financial Management

William Duncombe
Syracuse University, USA

World Scientific

NEW JERSEY • LONDON • SINGAPORE • BEIJING • SHANGHAI • HONG KONG • TAIPEI • CHENNAI • TOKYO

Published by

World Scientific Publishing Co. Pte. Ltd.
5 Toh Tuck Link, Singapore 596224
USA office: 27 Warren Street, Suite 401-402, Hackensack, NJ 07601
UK office: 57 Shelton Street, Covent Garden, London WC2H 9HE

Library of Congress Cataloging-in-Publication Data
Names: Duncombe, William, author.
Title: Lecture notes in public budgeting and financial management /
William Duncombe (Syracuse University, USA).
Description: New Jersey : World Scientific, 2018. |
Series: World Scientific lecture notes in economics ; Volume 5
Identifiers: LCCN 2016033509| ISBN 9789813145894 (hc : alk. paper) |
ISBN 9789813145900 (pbk : alk. paper)
Subjects: LCSH: Finance, Public--United States. | Fiscal policy--United States. |
Taxation--United States. | Nonprofit organizations--United States--Finance.
Classification: LCC HJ141 .D86 2016 | DDC 352.4/80973--dc23
LC record available at https://lccn.loc.gov/2016033509

British Library Cataloguing-in-Publication Data
A catalogue record for this book is available from the British Library.

For any available supplementary material, please visit
http://www.worldscientific.com/worldscibooks/10.1142/10177#t=suppl

Desk Editors: Herbert Moses/Philly Lim /Sylvia Koh

Typeset by Stallion Press
Email: enquiries@stallionpress.com

Printed in Singapore

Foreword

If there was ever a case of the teacher learning from the student, then the relationship between William (Bill) Duncombe and me epitomized that situation. I first learned of Bill when I met his father at an American Society for Public Administration annual conference in Detroit, Michigan. I was a professor in the Department of Public Administration, The Maxwell School of Citizenship and Public Affairs, Syracuse University. Sydney Duncombe was a well-known and respected former state budget director and professor of political science at the University of Idaho and alumnus of the Maxwell School. We has just awarded a full scholarship to Bill. At the time, Bill was working as an analyst for the Boeing Corporation in Seattle, Washington. Not long after that chance meeting with Professor Duncombe, Bill was a student in my public budgeting class. He did not say much and, in retrospect, I know why. That was when MY education in budgeting, public finance, and financial management began — and I had already taught the course for several years both at Michigan State University and at Syracuse University.

Bill was a student not like any other. Soft spoken and mild mannered, he had a keen intellect and was driven to succeed. While there are 24 hours in a day, Bill seemed to work 26 hours. He never stopped. For Bill this was normal and, while he was almost always diplomatic, he often wondered why others did not work as hard as he did — but he never said that openly and his criticisms were always thoughtful and gentle. Through his doctoral education and then as a member of the faculty, Bill would follow this pattern — long hours with commitment to learning and mastery of new material and social science methods.

After completing his doctoral degree, Bill took a faculty position at the University of Georgia, teaching budgeting and public finance. But he did not stay there very long because our department hired him. It was perhaps the best faculty hire that we ever made. Bill helped to reshape the required public budgeting class that had a political science orientation modeled after the research of academics such as Aaron Wildavsky and Allen Schick. This tradition at the Maxwell School made sense at the time since the profession, especially at the federal and state budget offices, had so many Maxwell School graduates. But times changed and, in Bill's view, public budgeting was more than the budget process, it included detailed analysis of the revenue side of the budget and a basic understanding of financial management including topics such as borrowing, debt, accounting, and auditing. So, Bill proceeded to methodically change the course and these notes reflect much of what he did. A few highlights in the form of stories to honor Bill are in order.

As a teacher, Bill Duncombe was methodical, comprehensive, and patient. He wanted to give students enough information so that they can learn the subject and practice the concepts and tools. His idea of public budgeting is that if you were going to actually do it, you needed to develop some basic skills. We naturally created a syllabus for the course. I say we because Bill and I took the position that all of the MPA students should have the same syllabus, assignments, and examinations. While we naturally differed based on our areas of specialization and personalities, we stuck to this idea of one common syllabus and this practice, started by Bill Duncombe in the late 1980s, is still true at the Maxwell School. This is where the lecture notes come in. Over the years, we often assigned a required text along with additional readings and case studies. We also created a few short case exercises. (More on this below.) But Bill developed lecture notes for each topic on the syllabus. The notes varied by topic. Some were comprehensive with illustrative data from the federal government or state and local governments. The notes defined and illustrated major concepts. In addition, the notes had exercises. Although we always told the students that the notes should not replace the required readings, the dirty little secret is that Bill's notes (with some of my additions to them) were viewed by the students as superior to the required readings and hence more valuable. Bill would periodically update the notes and add to them as appropriate. In fact, in the late 1990s, Bill and I seriously considered doing a public budgeting and financial management textbook that would use his lecture notes as the core materials to be supplemented by additional writing. We did not follow through with that idea because of more pressing professional obligations for both of us, but this collection of Bill's notes signifies the fact that the spirit of that idea lived on and I am pleased to see it come to fruition, albeit in a somewhat different form.

Bill Duncombe believed that concepts and skills can be learned through patience and practice. If students were willing to try, Bill would work for them for hours. For me, a funny remembrance comes from the cost analysis case study in the book, The Heartland County Road Budget. The case is deceptively simple. When Bill taught this case he started slowly, shortly after nine in the morning. We combined all of the sections so that he had about 125 students. He filled up the board with cost allocation data methodically going through the case. Naturally as the morning rolled into the afternoon, the case became more and more intricate. Sometimes, there were quite sighs coming from the students. Some started to glaze over. But Bill was undaunted and by about two in the afternoon, he ended the case. I am smiling as I write this because Bill was simply a master at it and I am convinced that most of the students learned the basics of cost analysis that day.

Another example comes from the Maxwell School's famous day care budget case which is available from the Electronic Hallway. I got that case many years ago from Robert Berne who, at the time, was a professor at the Wagner School of Public Service, New York University. The case is quite brief. I used it a couple of times when a student in my class said that it was not a realistic portrait of the structure of a typical day care center. Bill's wife, who also worked in a day care center, agreed. Bill proceeded to complicate the case quite a bit and it became a substantial required exercise in the course. Students prepared a "flexible" budget in Excel, did some cost allocations and forward projections. They ran a few scenarios and submitted their work along with a detailed memorandum. In my judgment, this day care budget exercise, which has been going on now for about 25 years, is a hallmark of the public budgeting course at the Maxwell School.

I miss Bill Duncombe. His passing was untimely and the Maxwell School lost one of its finest. His work in public finance, financial management, and educational finance will be reviewed for years to come. His meticulous collection of finance data will similarly be analyzed by doctoral students under the guidance of his former colleagues. Yet, for me — a former teacher but more important, student of Bill Duncombe — these notes represent part of Bill's legacy — first and foremost a teacher of future professionals who, with the appropriate knowledge and skills, will modestly make the world a better place. Bill Duncombe never said that this was his objective, he was too modest for that, but this is what he was all about.

Jeffrey D. Straussman
Professor

Department of Public Administration and Policy
Rockefeller College of Public Affairs and Policy
University at Albany
State University of New York

Preface

Bob Bifulco
Syracuse University, Syracuse, NY, USA

These lecture notes are used as part of a course entitled Public Budgeting offered at the Maxwell School of Citizenship and Public Affairs at Syracuse University. Although the course and these lecture notes have been updated continually over the last two decades, the course has been taught very close to its current form since the early 1990s. The late Bill Duncombe, a Professor of Public Administration at the Maxwell School from 1991 to 2013, is the primary developer of the course and author of these notes. The course and the thousands of students who have benefitted from it are an important legacy of Professor Duncombe's career, a career marked by tireless dedication to the field of public finance, the Maxwell School, and his students.

This course provides an overview of budgeting and financial management in the public and non-profit sectors. Fundamental concepts and practices of budgeting, financial management, and public finance are introduced, with special emphasis on state and local government budgeting and financial management in the US.

The objectives of the course are to learn the basic concepts and nomenclature of public finance, to develop an understanding of budget processes as well as the sources and uses of public revenues, and to make relatively simple, but useful computations in an intelligent way. Key course learning outcomes include the abilities to:

- explain and assess key elements of government budgeting processes,
- apply concepts of cost accounting and analysis to understand agency expenditure needs,
- design and produce a flexible budget for a government agency, and
- apply concepts and measures of efficiency, equity, and adequacy to the evaluation of government revenue policies.

If I had to specify one innovation of this course, it would be the emphasis on analysis. Professor Duncombe's strong view was that students should leave a course like this one with the conceptual tools and specific skills required to prepare and justify budgets. Although the politics of the budgeting process are touched upon, a much stronger emphasis is placed on the work that analysts in budgeting offices actually do. Many of Professor Duncombe's students went on to work as budget analysts, either as entry to their public sector careers or in some cases on their way to becoming budget directors. Many of these students can testify and have testified to just how useful the concepts and skills covered in this course have been in their work.

Professor Duncombe was last involved in tweaking the course and these lectures in the summer of 2012. The lectures are presented in the order that they have been covered in the versions of the course taught since that summer.

LECTURE 1. Introduction to Budgeting and Public Finance
LECTURE 2. The Basics of Budget Preparation
LECTURE 3. The Use of Cost Accounting to Improve Budgeting
LECTURE 4. Getting Control of Your Budget: The Use of Cost Analysis in Budgeting
LECTURE 5. Budget Review and Approval
LECTURE 6. Federal Budgeting Process
LECTURE 7. Budget Execution and Control
LECTURE 8. Capital Budgeting and Debt Management
LECTURE 9. Revenue Forecasting and Evaluation Criteria

LECTURE 10. Consumption Taxes
LECTURE 11. Local Property Taxes
LECTURE 12. User Fees and Charges
LECTURE 13. State Government Lotteries

Topics covered in past versions of the course that have been dropped from the most recent version, and this book, include government financial accounting, cash management, debt management, revenue forecasting, and income taxes. These topics fit well with the topics covered in these lectures; however, they have been removed from the most recent version of the course to ensure appropriate coverage and pacing for the other topics in the course, which has proven to be particularly important when the course is offered in an intensive 3 weeks format. Some of these topics could easily be added to those covered in these lectures in a semester long version of the course, or could be substituted for some of the topics covered in these lectures.

The course is intended as an introduction to public finance and budgeting for MPA students. In many years, the course has been the first course taken by students in the Maxwell MPA program, and taught in an intensive three-week format. However, the course has been taught equally well over a full semester. The course works nicely as an introduction to public administration because of the central role that the budgeting process plays, particularly in state and local governments, and because it raises important issues concerning the relationship of the bureaucracy, executive, and legislature. Also, the way tax evaluation is covered provides a useful paradigm to help students grasp standard approaches to policy analysis.

There are no indispensable pre-requisites for the course, and it has been designed for students from a wide variety of backgrounds and undergraduate majors. However, it can be helpful in covering some of the key concepts in tax evaluation if students have taken an intermediate level undergraduate course in microeconomics. When students have such a background, issues of tax incidence and the effect of taxes on economic efficiency can be covered in greater depth. Thus, although the course works well as an introduction to a broader public administration curriculum, it also can make sense for students to take after some more basic courses in economics, policy analysis, and public organizations.

Although Professor Duncombe was the driving force in the development of this course, and the author of the overwhelming bulk of these notes, he has taught the course with several other faculty members and instructors at the Maxwell School, each of whom has contributed to the course and in some cases these lecture notes in their own way. In addition to myself, these individuals include Jeffrey Straussman, Lloyd Blanchard, Wilson Wong, Ross Rubenstein, Cynthia Searcy, Sharon Kioko, and Yilin Hou. As Professor Straussman, his first partner in arms, so nicely captures in his foreword, Professor Duncombe's influence on us, is another of his many legacies.

About the Author

William D. Duncombe was a Professor of public administration at the Maxwell School of Citizenship and Public Affairs at Syracuse University. He was a dedicated teacher, renowned scholar, and a devoted friend. Duncombe received his MPA in 1987 and his PhD in public administration in 1989, both from the Maxwell School. His first academic job was teaching public administration at the University of Georgia, but he returned to Maxwell in 1991, where he stayed until his untimely death in 2013 at the age of 57. During his 22 years at Maxwell, Duncombe taught public budgeting and statistics to hundreds of MPA students and was well known for his dedication to his students. He was the first recipient of the Birkhead–Burkhead Teaching Excellence Award and Professorship given by Maxwell's Department of Public Administration and International Affairs in 2001, and he received the Excellence in Graduate Education Faculty Recognition Award from Syracuse University as well as the Leslie A. Whittington Excellence in Teaching Award from the National Association of Schools of Public Affairs and Administration, both in 2006. He has also mentored dozens of PhD students, many of whom now teach public budgeting and financial management in public administration departments around the world. Duncombe had an international reputation for his research on education finance, property taxes, public budgeting, and financial management. He was selected as the editor of *Public Budgeting and Finance* in 2011, elected as a fellow in the National Academy of Public Administration in 2010, and given the Aaron Wildavsky Award for lifetime achievement in budgeting and financial management scholarship by the Association of Budgeting and Financial Management in 2009. He also received the Richard A. Musgrave Prize for the best article in the *National Tax Journal* in 2011. His many acts of kindness and selflessness will long be remembered.

Contents

Lecture 1

Introduction to Budgeting and Public Finance

1.1 Setting Priorities in Chongoria

Chongoria, a country of 40 million people, is a country in transition. It is trying to develop democratic institutions and a market-oriented economy. Prior to 2005, Chongoria had an authoritarian political system that was governed by a single political party. The economy was largely controlled by the state. There was little private property and employees worked for the central government, local governments, or the state-owned enterprises such as steel, coal, and natural gas companies.

The newly elected parliament of Chongoria is made up of nine different political parties. Three of the parties just formed a center-left coalition to govern the country. There is a prime minister and a cabinet comprising representatives from the three coalition partners. While the economy is industrialized, about 20% of the population still works in agriculture. The government is faced with several major policy challenges. The economy is experiencing negative growth and the unemployment rate is about 30% of the working age population. Approximately 40% of the population is below the poverty line as defined by standards set by the United Nations. Many of the large industrial companies are inefficient and several have already gone bankrupt. The older companies contributed to the country's environmental problems. A small, well-organized separatist group in the eastern part of the country poses a threat to the democratically elected government. Meanwhile, the country bordering Chongoria on the north has been making noises about "liberating" the four million people in northern Chongoria who come from the same ethnic group as Chongoria's northern neighbor.

While Chongoria has a work force that is skilled and literacy is over 90% of the population, a major challenge of the government is to generate employment for those workers who have lost their jobs because of plant closings. Meanwhile, the birth rate has been declining and the percent of those who are pensioners is growing. Under the previous regime, women retired at age 58 and men retired at age 60. Pensions represent a major cost to the government although they are not adjusted for inflation. The current annual inflation rate in Chongoria is 35%, down from the 42% in the previous year, and real income has dropped for the past 3 years. Health care, once adequate by international standards, is beginning to deteriorate as indicated by a decline in average life expectancy for males from 74 years to 68 years. Infant mortality is also on the increase.

The new government of Chongoria needs to establish national priorities as reflected in the budget. The prime minister has asked the cabinet, a 10-member body drawn from the governing coalition in the parliament, to identify what the major functions of government for Chongoria should be and then determine what percent of the total budget should be allocated to each function.

1.2 Budgets Set Priorities

If you were a member of the ruling body for Chongoria, what functions would you identify and how much would you allocate to each function? There are no correct answers to these questions. Yet, a cursory review of the paragraphs above reveals that Chongoria needs to spend money on national security, health care, economic development, social welfare, and environmental protection. Some functions are not referred to above but they are common in most countries such as justice and education. How much should be apportioned to each function? This is a political decision and is based on values held by the political leadership. The values may include ideas about social justice, the "fair" distribution of wealth in society and the appropriate roles of government in a market-oriented economy. Values are expressed when resources are allocated to competing purposes.

Consider the choices of three members of the cabinet who have the authority to make the allocation decisions. The first person identifies the following priorities:

Function	Percent of budget
National security	30
Economic development	20
Health	15
Internal security and justice	15
Education	10
Infrastructure	10

The second person has a different distribution. This person's allocation is as follows:

Function	Percent of budget
Social welfare	40
National security	20
Economic development	30
Environmental protection	10

The third person has yet a different distribution of resources. This allocation is as follows:

Function	Percent of budget
Social well-being	35
Internal and external security	25
Social protection	20
Development	20

What do these allocations indicate? The three decision-makers seem to assess the needs of Chongoria differently. This difference is expressed in the variation in the functions selected and the weights assigned to the different functions. Yet, we need to probe the functions and the allocations a bit deeper. For instance, social well-being as expressed by the third decision-maker may include education that is identified as a separate function by the first decision-maker. It is important to go beyond simply the category of the government function to find out what it actually includes. When we look at actual budgets, it is important to look beyond the functional categories and the corresponding allocation to understand what exactly is being financed by government, that is, what activities and services are being included in the government functions identified by the decision-makers? The budget of Chongoria, like budgets in all governments, is a political document that frames the major values that permeate the society.

1.3 Stylized Facts about Government Growth

Budgets reflect the changing priorities for government programs. A brief overview of government spending in the US illustrates this point. First, government, as expressed in budgetary expenditures, has experienced steady growth especially since 1940, even when account is taken for inflation. In constant (inflation adjusted) dollars, outlays by the federal government have grown from $139.2 billion in 1940 to over $3,234 billion in 2013 (see Table 1.1 from FY 2015 federal budget). Federal outlays (in constant dollars) grew by 6.3% per year from 1940 to 1980, but slowed down to an annual rate of 2.5% from 1980 to 2008.

When we compare the growth in government expenditures to the economy as a whole, however, a different picture emerges. Relative to the economy as measured by gross domestic product (GDP), federal government outlays increased steadily from 1940 to 1990. During the 1990s, however, federal outlays decreased as a percent of GDP, and were lower in 2008, on the eve of the great recession, than they were 30 years earlier. Federal government expenditures, however, rose

Table 1.1. Summary of receipts, outlays, and surpluses or deficits (–) in current dollars, constant (FY 2009) dollars, and as percents of GDP: 1940–2015. (dollar amounts in billions).

	In Current Dollars			In Constant (FY 2009) Dollars			As Percents of GDP		
Fiscal Year	**Receipts**	**Outlays**	**Surplus or Deficit (–)**	**Receipts**	**Outlays**	**Surplus or Deficit (–)**	**Receipts**	**Outlays**	**Surplus or Deficit (–)**
1940	6.5	9.5	–2.9	96.3	139.2	–42.9	6.7	9.6	–3.0
1950	39.4	42.6	–3.1	392.1	423.1	–31.0	14.1	15.3	–1.1
1960	92.5	92.2	0.3	656.0	653.7	2.1	17.3	17.2	0.1
1970	192.8	195.6	–2.8	1,016.4	1,031.4	–15.0	18.4	18.6	–0.3
1980	517.1	590.9	–73.8	1,309.5	1,496.4	–187.0	18.5	21.1	–2.6
1990	1,032.0	1,253.0	–221.0	1,657.5	2,012.5	–355.0	17.4	21.2	–3.7
2000	2,025.2	1,789.0	236.2	2,543.6	2,246.9	296.7	19.9	17.6	2.3
2005	2,153.6	2,472.0	–318.3	2,371.8	2,722.4	–350.6	16.7	19.2	–2.5
2006	2,406.9	2,655.0	–248.2	2,562.1	2,826.3	–264.2	17.6	19.4	–1.8
2007	2,568.0	2,728.7	–160.7	2,663.1	2,829.7	–166.7	17.9	19.0	–1.1
2008	2,524.0	2,982.5	–458.6	2,529.0	2,988.5	–459.5	17.1	20.2	–3.1
2009	2,105.0	3,517.7	–1,412.7	2,105.0	3,517.7	–1,412.7	14.6	24.4	–9.8
2010	2,162.7	3,457.1	–1,294.4	2,137.5	3,416.8	–1,279.3	14.6	23.4	–8.8

(*Continued*)

Table 1.1. (*Continued*)

	In Current Dollars			In Constant (FY 2009) Dollars			As Percents of GDP		
Fiscal Year	**Receipts**	**Outlays**	**Surplus or Deficit (−)**	**Receipts**	**Outlays**	**Surplus or Deficit (−)**	**Receipts**	**Outlays**	**Surplus or Deficit (−)**
2011	2,303.5	3,603.1	−1,299.6	2,232.7	3,492.4	−1,259.7	15.0	23.4	−8.4
2012	2,450.2	3,537.1	−1,087.0	2,331.0	3,365.2	−1,034.1	15.2	22.0	−6.8
2013	2,775.1	3,454.6	−679.5	2,597.9	3,234.0	−636.1	16.7	20.8	−4.1
2014 estimate	3,001.7	3,650.5	−648.8	2,768.9	3,367.3	−598.5	17.3	21.1	−3.7
2015 estimate	3,337.4	3,901.0	−563.6	3,022.2	3,532.5	−510.3	18.3	21.4	−3.1

Source: Office of Management and Budget, FY 2015 Budget of the US, Table 1.3.

dramatically in 2009 in response to the great recession (Table 1.1). State and local expenditures have grown steadily relative to GDP between 1948 and 1970 (from just above 5% of GDP to just above 10% of GDP), and have remained around 10 and 12% of GDP since 1970.

Approximately one-fifth of federal expenditures are in national defense (Table 1.2), while 66% are in the broad category "human resources." Social security outlays constitute approximately one-third of human resources outlays, with the next largest shares for income security programs (23%) and Medicare (20%). You can see that there have been dramatic changes in the distribution of the federal budget since 1960, when over 50% was spent on defense and only 28% on human resources.

At the state level, 35% of direct general expenditure is for public welfare, 18% is for higher education, and 9% is for highways (Table 1.3). Over 87% of state and local welfare spending is done by state governments (Table 1.4). Besides public welfare, state governments do the majority of spending for higher education, health, highways, corrections, and natural resources.

For local governments, education represents 44% of their total spending. The vast majority of this spending is done by independent school districts. Another spending category for local governments is public utilities, which are particularly important for municipal government and special districts. They are reflected in the higher percent for utilities spending under special district government.

Municipalities and special districts are also the main financers of airports and seaports (Table 1.4). The provision of environmental services such as water and sewer treatment and solid waste management is also the principal financial responsibility of municipal governments, as is public safety. While the provision of many vital services has been decentralized to the local government level in the US, there is significant variation in the amount of decentralization across the states. New York state has a particularly decentralized system with county governments providing significant financing for the medical entitlement program, Medicaid, for example.

Table 1.2. Outlays by superfunction and function: 1940–2015.

Superfunction and Function	**1940**	**1950**	**1960**	**1970**	**1980**	**1990**	**2000**	**2010**	**2014 Estimate**	**2015 Estimate**
					As percentages of outlays					
National defense	17.5	32.2	52.2	41.8	22.7	23.9	16.5	20.1	17.0	16.2
Human resources	43.7	33.4	28.4	38.5	53.0	49.4	62.4	69.0	71.8	70.7
Physical resources	24.4	8.6	8.7	8.0	11.2	10.1	4.7	2.6	2.7	3.7
Net interest	9.5	11.3	7.5	7.4	8.9	14.7	12.5	5.7	6.1	6.5
Other functions	8.2	18.7	8.4	8.8	7.6	4.8	6.4	5.0	4.9	5.4
Undistributed offsetting receipts	−3.4	−4.3	−5.2	−4.4	−3.4	−2.9	−2.4	−2.4	−2.5	−2.5
Total, Federal outlays	100.0	100.0	100.0	100.0	100.0	100.0	100.0	100.0	100.0	100.0
(On-budget)	100.2	98.8	88.2	85.9	80.7	82.0	81.5	84.0	80.5	80.6
(Off-budget)	−0.2	1.2	11.8	14.1	19.3	18.0	18.5	16.0	19.5	19.4
					As percentages of GDP					
National defense	1.7	4.9	9.0	7.8	4.8	5.1	2.9	4.7	3.6	3.5
Human resources	4.2	5.1	4.9	7.2	11.2	10.5	11.0	16.1	15.1	15.1
Physical resources	2.4	1.3	1.5	1.5	2.4	2.1	0.8	0.6	0.6	0.8
Net interest	0.9	1.7	1.3	1.4	1.9	3.1	2.2	1.3	1.3	1.4
Other functions	0.8	2.9	1.5	1.6	1.6	1.0	1.1	1.2	1.0	1.1
Undistributed offsetting receipts	−0.3	−0.7	−0.9	−0.8	−0.7	−0.6	−0.4	−0.6	−0.5	−0.5
Total, Federal outlays	**9.6**	**15.3**	**17.2**	**18.6**	**21.1**	**21.2**	**17.6**	**23.4**	**21.1**	**21.4**
(On-budget)	9.7	15.1	15.2	16.0	17.1	17.4	14.4	19.6	17.0	17.3
(Off-budget)	(−*)	0.2	2.0	2.6	4.1	3.8	3.3	3.8	4.1	4.2

*0.05% or less.

Source: Office of Management and Budget, FY 2015 Budget of the US, Table 3.1.

Table 1.3. Percent distribution of state and local direct general expenditure by function 2005–2007.

			Local Governments					
Description	**State and Local Governments**	**State Government**	**Total**	**County Government**	**Municipal Government**	**Township Government**	**Special District Government**	**School District Government**
Education	34.8%	22.2%	44.1%	16.1%	13.0%	29.2%	3.1%	97.2%
Higher education	9.1%	17.7%	2.6%	1.6%	0.3%			5.9%
Elementary and secondary	23.7%	0.9%	40.7%	13.6%	11.6%	27.8%	0.4%	91.3%
Public welfare	17.0%	34.9%	3.7%	11.5%	3.1%	0.6%	0.4%	
Hospitals	5.3%	5.0%	5.5%	9.6%	3.6%	0.1%	26.2%	
Health	3.3%	3.9%	2.9%	8.2%	2.2%	1.0%	2.7%	
Highways	6.4%	9.2%	4.4%	6.7%	7.9%	12.3%	1.7%	
Air transportation (airports)	0.9%	0.2%	1.4%	0.8%	2.6%	0.1%	6.2%	
Water transport and terminals	0.2%	0.2%	0.3%	0.1%	0.3%	0.0%	1.9%	
Police protection	3.7%	1.2%	5.6%	7.1%	12.8%	9.2%	0.1%	
Fire protection	1.6%		2.8%	1.9%	6.5%	5.6%	4.8%	
Correction	3.0%	4.6%	1.9%	6.3%	1.1%		0.2%	

(*Continued*)

Table 1.3. (*Continued*)

			Local Governments					
Description	**State and Local Governments**	**State Government**	**Total**	**County Government**	**Municipal Government**	**Township Government**	**Special District Government**	**School District Government**
Natural resources	1.3%	2.0%	0.7%	1.1%	0.2%	0.4%	4.3%	
Parks and recreation	1.7%	0.5%	2.5%	2.0%	5.5%	3.6%	4.2%	
Housing and community development	2.0%	0.9%	2.9%	1.1%	4.6%	0.7%	16.0%	
Sewerage	1.0%	0.2%	1.6%	1.9%	3.2%	4.0%	1.3%	
Solid waste management	1.0%	0.2%	1.6%	1.9%	3.2%	4.0%	1.3%	
Governmental administration	5.3%	5.1%	5.4%	11.6%	8.2%	9.2%	0.0%	
Interest on general debt	4.1%	4.3%	4.0%	3.6%	5.2%	2.7%	7.1%	2.8%
Utilities	8.1%	2.5%	12.3%	2.4%	22.8%	5.4%	63.8%	

Source: US Bureau of the Census, 2007 *Census of Government*.

Table 1.4. Percent of state and local direct general expenditure by government type and spending function.

		Local Governments					
Description	**State Government**	**Total**	**County Government**	**Municipal Government**	**Township Government**	**Special District Government**	**School District Government**
Direct expenditure	44.2%	55.8%	12.4%	17.5%	1.6%	6.5%	17.7%
Education	27.6%	72.4%	6.2%	5.5%	1.5%	0.1%	59.1%
Higher education	83.4%	16.6%	2.5%	0.5%			13.5%
Elementary and secondary	1.6%	98.4%	8.0%	7.8%	2.1%	0.1%	80.4%
Pubic welfare	87.5%	14.3%	75.1%	31.3%	2.0%	196.8%	
Hospitals	40.3%	59.7%	25.6%	10.9%	0.0%	23.1%	
Health	50.3%	49.7%	34.7%	10.6%	0.6%	3.8%	
Highways	61.0%	63.8%	37.3%	19.7%	17.6%	36.2%	
Air transportation (airports)	8.0%	92.0%	12.5%	47.0%	0.2%	32.3%	
Water transport and terminals	31.2%	68.8%	5.7%	21.3%	0.4%	41.4%	

(*Continued*)

Table 1.4. (*Continued*)

		Local Governments					
Description	**State Government**	**Total**	**County Government**	**Municipal Government**	**Township Government**	**Special District Government**	**School District Government**
Police protection	13.5%	86.5%	26.8%	55.1%	4.5%	0.1%	
Fire protection		100.0%	15.9%	64.2%	6.2%	13.7%	
Correction	64.6%	35.4%	29.4%	5.6%		0.3%	
Natural resources	68.8%	31.2%	12.1%	3.0%	0.5%	15.6%	
Parks and recreation	13.8%	86.2%	17.1%	53.3%	3.9%	11.9%	
Housing and community development	19.0%	81.0%	7.5%	36.2%	0.7%	36.6%	
Sewerage	3.1%	96.9%	12.5%	59.8%	4.3%	20.3%	
Solid waste management	9.8%	90.2%	26.2%	51.0%	7.1%	5.9%	
Governmental administration	41.2%	58.8%	30.7%	24.9%	3.1%		
Interest on general debt	44.4%	55.6%	12.1%	20.2%	1.2%	8.0%	14.0%
Utilities	13.4%	86.6%	4.1%	44.9%	1.2%	36.4%	

Source: US Bureau of the Census, *2007 Census of Government*.

1.4 Budgeting Overview

The public budgeting process is the main mechanism by which much of the money spent by governments gets distributed to government agencies that then spend funds in order to achieve their goals. This is true whether the country is Chongoria or the US. Not all public expenditures are reflected in a public budget. Government "businesses" such as utilities, government-owned golf courses, or national airlines may not be included in the government budget. These expenditures are often referred to as "off-budget" entities. It is likely that the traditional budget process determines at least half of the public expenditures of this country. Since the budget process is an important part of government, it is likely that you will get involved in the process at some point in your career. You are likely to be involved either in preparing, reviewing, or auditing budgets.

1.4.1 What are the objectives of the budget process?

The most obvious response to this question is that we have budgets because we need to *allocate the scarce resources of government.* The budget acts as a counterpart to markets in the private sector. However, while private markets operate on their own without much coordination, the budget processes at each level of government involve a complicated process of coordinating the actions of many government officials.

There are several *economic justifications* for government involvement in the economy. Specifically, the budget plays a central role in *stabilizing* the economy (fiscal policy). The deficit can be used as a tool to promote or slow down economic growth by increasing or decreasing spending. The budget can be used to improve *equity* across groups in the society and across generations. This is done through spending on social programs, such as money for low-income individuals and families, and through tax policy by determining who pays taxes and who does not. The budget is also used to improve the *efficiency* of the economy. A private economy needs the intervention of government to operate efficiently. The budget is one of the principal tools for correcting "market failures".

Stabilization, equity, and efficiency can be thought of as macro dimensions of budgeting. Political decision-makers in the central government make major choices on the appropriate allocation of the country's resources to government versus the private sector, the timing of spending and the benefits that will be provided to different groups in society.

The government budget is also important in managing resources. Allen Schick (1966) has identified three major functions of budget processes.[1] First, budgets are used to *control* spending. The budget is one of the principal mechanisms for guaranteeing that the expenditures of government agencies conform to legislative intent and legal restrictions. In other words, did the agency spend the money the way it was supposed to spend it? This entails reviewing government spending in light of the legal restrictions and ensuring that spending is in line with the intent of elected representatives and the chief executive. Controlling expenditures was probably one of the major driving forces behind the development of executive budget processes in the US at the beginning of the twentieth century. Expenditure control has continued to be a central function of budget systems throughout the world.

Another important role of a budget is as a *management* tool to help public administrators improve the management of their agency. Specifically, the management function of budgeting focuses on finding the most efficient or cost effective methods of providing public services. This became an important objective of budgets particularly during the 1930s as the federal governments expanded enormously and federal managers needed better tools for managing their departments. Some of the techniques that will be described in Lectures 3 and 4 pertain to the management function of budgeting.

Budgets have also been used as a device for a government organization to lay out long-range objectives, present alternative methods for achieving objectives and decide on "the best" alternative, in other words, *planning*. Budgeting, by its very nature, is prospective.

[1]Allen Schick. 1966. "The Road to PPB: The Stages of Budget Reform." *Public Administration Review* 26 (December): 243–258.

Budgets are statements about the future; therefore, every budget process has elements of planning. Many of the reforms in budgeting are intended to get managers to consider the multi-year implications of programs and their requisite resources needs.

The three functions of budgeting — control, management, and planning — can be found in all budget processes. The relative emphasis among the functions will vary from one government to another. Developing countries, new non-profit organizations, and governments that have problems with corruption need to emphasize the control function of budgeting. Once control mechanisms are well established, the management and planning functions should receive more attention.

1.4.2 What is different about public budgeting?

All organizations, whether they are public, private, or non-profit organizations, have to budget their resources. Decisions have to be made about adding new personnel, whether to invest in capital resources and what type, and how to reduce photocopying, telephone, and utility expenditures. Private managers often have to prepare quarterly or annual budgets that they have to defend to their boss or the finance department. However, despite some similarities between budgeting in the public and private sectors, there are also some significant differences that make public budgeting distinctive and in many ways more difficult than budgeting in private organizations.

A variety of actors: There are many actors that participate in the public budgeting process. Consider the following list that is by no means all-inclusive[2]:

Managers of government programs, who are in charge of programs and units within large bureaucracies, have budgetary responsibility. Managers must prepare budgets and are usually responsible for spending funds to achieve public purposes. Managers represent the

[2]This section draws from the discussion in Irene S. Rubin. 2009. The Politics of Budgeting: Getting and Spending, Borrowing and Balancing. Washington, D.C., CQ Press, pp. 11–16.

"front line" when it comes to budgeting. They need to have a basic understanding of how budgets work, the law governing public spending in their jurisdiction, and the political environment that shapes budget choices.

The *central budget office* is the executive branch agency that is directly responsible to the chief executive of the government. The budget office reviews budget requests prepared by managers and then submitted by the department heads in the government. Budget examiners (sometimes called budget analysts) review budget requests for accuracy, persuasiveness, and consistency with the chief executive's fiscal and policy priorities.

Once the budget review is completed, the executive budget is prepared. The *chief executive* submits the executive budget to the legislature for approval. Governmental tradition as well as constitutional and statutory guidelines may shape the timing and presentation of the chief executive's budget. In Great Britain, for example, the Chancellor of the exchequer makes an annual speech before parliament laying out spending priorities for this year's budget.

The influence of the *legislature* on the budget cannot be separated from the political authority of the legislative branch in a country's political system. While the Congress of the US exerts considerable influence on the federal budget, national legislatures in most countries do not have such power. In the US, the authority of the legislature at the state and local levels varies considerably from one government to another. There are several ways that legislators may have an effect on the budget.

Interest groups are an important element in the budget process. As a rule of thumb, interest groups try to influence budget decisions so that programs or revenue decisions reflect the collective interests of the members of the groups. Consider the example described below of the efforts of Pew Charitable Trust on the environment. Interest groups can choose to use different tactics to influence policy and budgets.

Citizens have an indirect impact on budgeting through the election of the legislature and the election of the chief executive in countries that have direct election of the chief executive. Citizens also participate in the budget process by putting pressure on their elected representatives to allocate budgetary resources in a desired direction. Sometimes citizen input into the budget process may be more direct as the article from governing.com demonstrates.

The courts may also be an important player when it comes to the budget process. In the US, federal courts have required remedial action by defendant government agencies charged with custodial responsibilities in schools, prisons, and facilities for the mentally disabled. When local government agencies are the defendants, they must eliminate unconstitutional conditions such as overcrowding in local jails or racial segregation in public schools and public housing. In these cases, courts have issued orders that, in part, dictate the administrative actions that must be followed by the defendant executive agencies. For example, courts have set staffing ratios, the amount of space required in prison cells and even the temperature range that is permissible in custodial institutions.

Other levels of government may also influence the budgeting decisions of a government. State governments in the US receive significant amounts of intergovernmental aid from the federal government, particularly for social programs, such as Medicaid. Local governments also receive significant revenue from state governments. School districts in many states receive over half of their revenue from a variety of state education grants. Decisions for lower-level governments about the administration of programs can also affect the budgets of higher-level governments. A major area of contention between states and the federal government is over the administration of the Medicaid program. The federal government pays a significant share of the costs, but state governments administer the program. The key thing to remember about governance in the US is that decision-making in many policy areas is spread across all three levels of government (federal–state–local), and that budgets are often interdependent across these levels. Table 1.5 from the *2007 Census of Government* shows how many governmental units exist in the US.

An open environment: As the variety of actors imply, the budgeting process in the public sector is much more open than budgeting in

Table 1.5. Government units: 1977–2007.

Type of Government	2007	2002	1997	1992	1987	1982	1977
Total	89,476	87,900	87,504	86,743	83,237	81,831	79,913
Federal government	1	1	1	1	1	1	1
State governments	50	50	50	50	50	50	50
Local governments	89,425	87,849	87,453	86,692	83,186	81,780	79,862
General purpose:							
County	3,033	3,034	3,043	3,043	3,042	3,041	3,042
Subcounty	36,011	35,937	36,001	35,962	35,891	35,810	35,684
Municipal	19,492	19,431	19,372	19,296	19,200	19,076	18,862
Township	16,519	16,506	16,629	16,666	16,691	16,734	16,822
Special purpose:							
School district	13,051	13,522	13,726	14,556	14,721	14,851	15,174
Special district	37,381	35,356	34,683	33,131	29,532	28,078	25,962

the private sector. Public organizations, either by law or custom, need to be accountable to a variety of actors. Citizens, interest groups, and the courts can and often do intervene in the process. Not surprisingly, this changes the focus of the public budgeting and accounting system from recording profits to assuring accountability to the public (and more directly to the legislative body). This mission affects the type of information collected in the budget, what it is used for and how financial information is recorded.

Multiple objectives: Public organizations often have complex and sometimes contradictory objectives. For example, it is not unusual in health regulatory bureaus within state health departments to have a "mission" of both assuring good care for low-income patients, funded by state and federal dollars, while, at the same time, trying to hold costs down. While organizations within a private business certainly have different short-term objectives, their overall objective is to improve the profitability of the firm. Rarely is a similar unambiguous objective found in public organizations.

The New York Times June 28, 2001

Charity is New Force in Environmental Fight

Unlike many philanthropies that give to conservationist groups, Pew has been anything but hands-off, serving as the behind-the-scenes architect of highly visible recent campaigns to preserve national forests and combat global warming. Though some of its money goes to long-established groups, Pew has also created its own organizations, with names like the National Environmental Trust and the Heritage Forest Campaign.

Over the last decade, financing by wealthy foundations has swollen the budgets of environmental groups that depend heavily on donations for things like land acquisition and scientific research. But with its deep pockets and focus on aggressive political advocacy, Pew is not only the most important new player but also the most controversial, among fellow environmentalists and its opponents in industry.

"I don't think you make social change happen on the basis of paid staff in Washington and paid ads anywhere," Carl Pope, the executive director of the Sierra Club, said, referring to the Pew groups' reputation for top-down management. The Sierra Club, still the largest environmental organization, has applied for Pew grants but has never been successful and has stopped trying, Mr. Pope said. The reason has less to do with substance — the groups are more or less united on the issues — than with style. With 700,000 members, the Sierra Club has many grass-roots constituents to please, while Pew's approach is focused on the issues that the managers in Philadelphia deem ripe for intervention.

Pew's executives and their supporters dismiss the griping as sour grapes, saying that traditional organizations fear being eclipsed by Pew and that the other foundations that contribute to conservationist causes feel threatened by its willingness to jump into the political fray. "If you ride the ridges, you get shot at more often than if you stay in the valleys," Joshua W. Reichert, Pew's powerful director of environmental programs, said. With $52 million to spend on environmental causes this year, Pew tries to articulate a single voice — that of the trust and, in particular, Mr. Reichert.

Pew, as a non-profit organization, stops short of lobbying and supporting candidates for office, something that some other environmental groups, like the Sierra Club and the League of Conservation Voters, which do not have non-profit status, are permitted to do. But Pew is free to advocate specific causes, and its organizations have done so in many ways, including buying full-page advertisements in newspapers.

Doug Crandall, staff director of the Republican-controlled House subcommittee on forests, called the Pew groups "the 800-pound gorilla" on environmental issues "because they focus and target these issues quite effectively."

Study: Citizen Budgeting Related to Better Outcomes

BY: J.B. Wogan | April 15, 2013

Mary Bunting, the city manager of Hampton, Va., knows firsthand the importance of engaging citizens in the budget process.

A few years ago, in the throes of the recession, Bunting noticed a frustrating trend in the budgeting process. Her staff would painstakingly prepare a budget using careful cost-benefit analysis -- only to see it derailed in the final hours when an interest group would complain about a cut.

So in 2010 Bunting set out to gather public input early in the budget process. Each year since then, she's added new ways for citizens to get engaged. Today, she hosts 800-person live events with keypad polling, in addition to conducting online polls, telephone surveys and smaller town hall meetings. Her staff even routinely visits community events, such as soccer club meetings, to connect with citizens who don't normally attend city meetings.

"I wanted [the public] to understand the complexity of the budget and the tradeoffs," Bunting said. "The biggest thing I was trying to do was to build a body of evidence, so that [the council] understood that there was a larger group of residents that supported the cuts."

Apparently, Bunting was onto something. Inviting public comment early in the budget process, and doing so in multiple ways, is closely associated with better performance outcomes, according to a new study in *The American Review of Public Administration.*

State and local government meetings, from a state agency to a county board, are notoriously low in attendance. Some governments have reacted with experiments to spur better public involvement, especially in drafting budgets. Since 2008, Chicago Alderman Joe Moore has invited residents of his ward to vote on how to spend about $1 million of the city's budget on a menu of community infrastructure projects. (The 2012 *winners* were sidewalk repairs, a new playground, neighborhood murals and more than 100 tree plantings.) Last year in Seattle, Mayor Mike McGinn's office used an interactive *online game* to gauge public support on spending areas, such as public safety and human services.

Despite this patchwork of efforts to involve citizens, public administrators still don't know exactly when to seek public input and how it might affect the day-to-day work of governing. So Hai Guo and Milena Neshkova, both assistant professors in the Department of Public Administration at Florida International University, set out to study the relationship between citizen participation in budgeting and measurable performance outcomes. Their analysis relied on 2005 survey data on state transportation agencies and their civic engagement strategies (focus groups, for example) across four stages in the budget process.

Because their research focused solely on transportation agencies, they looked at transportation-related outcomes that governments value: fewer road-related fatalities and fewer poor-quality roads. They took into account external factors, such as level of funding, that might account for differences in fatality rates or road conditions. They found that not only is there an inverse relationship (more attempts at civic engagement mean fewer fatalities and low-quality roads), but that the relationship is statistically significant. In other words, the result isn't due to chance.

More importantly, the association was strongest at the earliest stage in the process. "You need to engage them early. I think that's the point we're trying to make," Guo said. Since the analysis was specific to state transportation departments, Guo says he'd like to see if the same pattern would emerge at other levels of government.

Bunting's own experience in Hampton aligns largely with the findings of the study. Since reaching out to the public at the beginning of the budget cycle, and doing so in multiple ways, she says she hasn't heard the same level of outcry when budgets arrive at the council's desk; and to the degree that criticism still exists, it's only part of a much larger public discussion already informing the budget. Last September the White House *recognized* Bunting as an "innovation champion of change" for her work in promoting open government in her city.

This article was printed from: **http://www.governing.com/blogs/view/gov-study-citizen-budgeting-related-to-better-performance.html.**

1.5 Budget Cycle

The budget cycle has four broad phases: executive preparation, legislative review, implementation, and audit. These phases pertain to most *executive budget* processes in the US and many countries around the world. The budget cycle is linked to the length of the fiscal period-most frequently 1 or 2 years. The cycle is predictable in the sense that the basic activities described below repeat themselves with regularity from one fiscal period to the next. Indeed, one of the most important features of budgeting is its repetitive nature. Roles of the major participants in budgeting are well established and predictable. In addition, there is a sequence to most budget systems so that the major phases of the budget cycle occur at the same time one cycle after another.

At the federal level in the US, the budget process is a very complex series of activities that determine how much to spend and tax each year. The process involves the executive branch agencies, the president and Congress. The president's budget is really just a plan for spending. It represents proposals that Congress may, and almost certainly will, change over the course of its deliberations on the president's submission. After Congress passes its appropriation bills and they are signed by the president, we can say that there is a federal budget. The major steps in the federal budget process are outlined in Table 1.6.

Countries differ in the way they formulate their budgets so there is no reason to assume that the practices in the US are followed elsewhere.

1.5.1 Preparation/review

This stage primarily involves the actions of executive branch agencies. This is the process of preparing the budget for submission to the legislature. For example, for the budget for the fiscal year 2017 (July 1, 2016–June 30, 2017 for most state governments), the preparation process begins as early as the spring of 2015. Generally, the preparation process will begin in the spring for an agency and

Table 1.6. Major steps in the federal budget process.

Formulation of the President's Budget for 2015	Executive Branch agencies develop requests for funds and submit them to the Office of Management and Budget. The president reviews the requests and decides what to include in his budget.	February 2013–January 2014
State of the Union Address	The president speaks to the country about his priorities for the year ahead.	Late January/ Early February 2014
Budget preparation and submission	The budget documents are completed by the OMB and sent to Congress.	January 2014–February 2014
Congressional action	Congress reviews the president's budget, develops its own, and eventually approves spending and revenue bills.	March 2014–September 2014
President's final approval	President signs spending and revenue bills to make them law.	Late September 2014
Fiscal year begins		October 1, 2014
Budget implemented	Agency program managers begin to spend (and raise) the money approved by the Congress and the president.	October 1, 2014–September 30, 2015

Source: Department of Education and Public Programs, John F. Kennedy Presidential Library and Museum, "Understanding the Federal Budget" Table 3. Available at: http://www.jfklibrary.org/Education/Teachers/Civic-Education-Programs-and-Materials/Federal-Budget-Simulation-Lesson-Plan.aspx. Accessed July 20, 2010. Adapted from the Office of Management and Budget online publications, *A Citizen's Guide to the Federal Budget, FY 2001* and *FY 2002* (http://www.gpoaccess.gov/usbudget/fy01/pdf/guide.pdf and http://www.gpoaccess.gov/usbudget/fy02/pdf/guide.pdf).

end in December of that year when the chief executive finalizes the budget to be sent to the legislative body.

Fiscal year: You will often see the term "fiscal year" used in reference to the budget (and government financial statements). Government budgets often do not begin on January 1 of each year. The most commonly used fiscal year is July 1–June 30. However, many governments use different fiscal years (e.g., federal government: October 1–September 30; New York: April 1–March 30). Fiscal years are commonly labeled FY 2013–2014 or FY 2014 (fiscal year from July 1, 2013 to June 30, 2014). You want to make sure you know when the fiscal year begins as you are reading a budget.

Generally the preparation stage involves three distinct parts:

(1) *Budget call/Guidelines*: The first step in the budget is initiated by the chief executive and the central budget agency. The budget agency helps the chief executive to develop written guidelines to be sent to the agency to guide their budget activity. These guidelines usually contain:

    — list of chief executives priorities,
    — limits on expenditure growth which are usually driven by revenue forecasts,
    — instructions on how to prepare the budget.

    The budget "call" is where the chief executive lays out the ground rules under which the agencies are to prepare their budget.

(2) *Agency budget preparation*: The greatest time in this phase (summer to late fall) is spent by agencies developing their budget requests. This is based on estimates of anticipated needs, on growth in costs, and on the restrictions imposed by the chief executive on overall expenditure growth. Large agencies may have a complicated review process before their final budget request is submitted.

(3) *Budget review/Submission*: The central budget office assimilates all the requests from the individual agencies and begins the process of fitting these requests into the fiscal limitations and priorities of the chief executive. Since total agency submissions generally exceed the desired expenditure level, this process generally involves a process of carefully reviewing agency requests to find "room to cut." This process involves the close interaction of the budget office with the agency. Finally, the chief executive is brought in to settle any major disputes and to finalize the *executive budget*. The final budget is submitted to the legislature generally at the beginning of the calendar year.

1.5.2 Legislative approval

The second phase of the process begins when the legislative body receives the budget from the executive branch. The legislature generally reviews, modifies, and approves the executive budget. This process will generally run from the beginning of the calendar year until the beginning of the fiscal year. For most state governments, this is July 1 and for the federal government it is October 1.

(1) First, the legislature will divide the budget into its revenue components that are sent off to "Ways and Means Committee" or "Finance Committee." The expenditure parts of the budget are sent off to appropriation committees. Usually, the lower house will first evaluate appropriations and then pass to the upper house when they have been approved. Committee reviews and hearings represent the "guts" of the legislative review.
(2) Once the appropriations and finance committees have reported out their recommendations, then it is up to the full legislature to amend and/or approve these bills. This is where final reconciliation of any differences between projected revenues and expenditures occurs.
(3) The final appropriation and revenue bills once approved by the legislature usually pass to the chief executive for final approval. At the federal level, the president only has the choice of accepting or vetoing the whole bill. In some states, governors have line item *vetoes* where they can "surgically remove" certain parts of these acts.

As you might imagine the approval process is highly politicized, we will examine approval in the context of the "politics of the budgetary process." We will also devote separate attention to the federal process that has undergone a major transformation in the last several decades.

1.5.3 Execution

Once the budget is passed, then the process turns back to the executive agencies and the budget office. This is the process of actually executing the public programs that have been funded. The vast majority of appropriations are for ongoing programs that are receiving funding for another year. For new programs, there is the process of developing the new administrative codes, hiring a new staff, setting up new facilities, etc.

Just because a program has received an appropriation does not mean that it will automatically get a check for the full appropriation that it can spend during this year. There is generally an elaborate control system that is put in place to control when the agency receives the appropriation, and how it can spend the money.

(1) Once an appropriation is approved, then the agencies must submit to the central budget office some plan for *apportionment and allotment*, which lays out when they want the money dispersed. These are usually on a monthly or quarterly basis, and are used to help keep agencies from overspending.
(2) Once the apportionment plan has been approved, then each agency determines the *allotments* to subunits in its organizations.
(3) Agencies then will incur *obligations* or legal commitments for expenditures of the appropriation. It is likely that the central budget office will have to approve certain obligations.
(4) Once the good arrives, then the agency will authorize the central budget office to make an *outlay* to the supplier in payment.
(5) Finally, the agency will actually use the good or service in the process of carrying its function, which is recorded as part of the *cost* of providing public services.

1.5.4 Audit/evaluation

The final stage of the process begins when the fiscal year ends. For example, for the fiscal year 2015 budget, this stage will begin in July of 2015 in many governments. Basically, this is the part of the process that is used to make sure that the budget execution accomplished the objectives of the budget. Several types of audits that may be used in this stage:

(1) *Financial audit*: This is a detailed review of the financial records to determine if the funds were spent legally. This audit is

used to assure that the *control objectives* of the budget were accomplished.

(2) *Management audit*: This type of audit is directed to the *performance* of the agency, specifically were the agency objectives accomplished as efficiently as possible. This audit focuses on the *management* objectives of the budget.

(3) *Program audit/evaluation*: This is an evaluation of the success of the agency in accomplishing program objectives and whether there may be better alternatives for accomplishing these objectives. This is used to guide *planning* in future budgets.

Generally, the first of these audits has received the most attention; however, agencies such as the US general accountability office (GAO) are carrying out an increasing number of management and program audits.

An agency may be involved in several elements of the budget process at once. For example, an agency in July 2014 in the federal government may be:

— beginning preparation of the FY 2015–2016 budget,
— in the execution phase of the FY 2014–2015 budget,
— and being audited with regard to the FY 2013–2014 budget.

This overlap of budget cycles is sometimes referred to as *scrambled budget cycles* to represent the "juggling act" that agencies have to go through. This may cause particular problems for a new program because it may be several years after execution before an agency has a clear evaluation of the program. In the meantime, they have had to prepare several additional budgets without the benefit of this knowledge.

1.6 The Budget Cycle in Non-profit Organizations

The budget process of non-profit organizations varies substantially depending on their size and complexity. Consider a small religious organization with 300 family members known as the new covenant society (NCS). NCS has a building that is financed by a conventional mortgage by a lending institution, a full time, paid spiritual leader, and a full time secretary. Other paid employees work part time and are paid on an hourly basis. The main income of NCS comes from the families who make voluntary contributions. Income also comes from renting the space to other non-profit organizations, interest earned on accounts held by NCS, bequests, selected income producing sales from the thrift shop and periodic assessments for special services such as religious school education, weddings, and funerals.

NCS will likely have committees for various activities such as the youth committee, the spiritual committee, the social action committee, and the finance committee. Each committee will have a chair. The financial vice president may head the finance committee. The governing body of NCS is the board of directors.

The budget cycle of NCS begins when the financial vice president asks committee chairs to provide the finance committee with a budget request for the forthcoming year. The finance committee will review the requests and make adjustments to them based on income projections as well as judgments about the assumptions underlying each request. In addition, the committee will forecast next year's income and costs such as the mortgage payment on the property, utility costs and salary increase. The budget will be submitted to the board of directors for review. The board may change parts of the budget. In some non-profit organizations, the budget may be put to the membership for a vote. Once the fiscal year starts, spending will take place. The board of directors will typically make adjustments to the budget.

1.7 The Budget Document

There is no uniform way to prepare and present budget documents although professional organizations such as the government finance officers association (GFOA) provide guidelines for public officials to follow when preparing and submitting budget documents. It is more and more common to use the internet to store and transmit budgetary information. Nevertheless, basic patterns tend to be followed by governments when they prepare and transmit their documents. What makes for a good budget presentation? GFOA suggests four broad criteria.

(1) Budgets should be a *policy document.* The budget should convey the government's major public policy initiatives so residents know how and where their money is being spent. Consequences of changes should be highlighted and the fiscal burden of policy changes should be identified.
(2) The budget should be an *operations guide.* This means that the budget should include information that facilitates comparisons with prior years and also provides managers with information on costs and measures of performance.
(3) The budget should be a *financial plan.* This means that the budget should account for all financial activities in the government including all funds that support various activities.
(4) The budget should be a vehicle for *communication.* This means that the budget, including the chief executive's budget message, the summary tables and the departmental budgets as reflected in the chief executive's budget, should be understandable to the taxpayers and residents of the government.

1.7.1 The transmittal letter

The executive budget is usually accompanied by a transmittal letter from the chief executive to the legislature. Below is an example of a *transmittal letter* by governor Schwarzenegger for the 2010–2011 budget. Notice that the governor did two things in this message. He summarized the economic climate, which is still "struggling to recover." This provided a signal both to people in government and to the residents in the state of California that budget cuts are going to be necessary to balance the budget. He also identified the one program area that may experience the least cuts — education. He also wants to work with Washington "to give California both the flexibility and fairness that is needed to better manage critical state programs." He is referring most likely to Medicaid, a major federal entitlement program, which has grown very rapidly and requires a state contribution. Transmittal letters vary based on the amount of detail that the chief executive prefers to include in the letter, the number of pressing fiscal and policy issues at the time the letter is written and the governing style of the chief executive.

1.7.2 Summary tables

There is no single preferred way of displaying budgetary information. Budgets may be presented in highly aggregated formats summarizing only the budget totals by organizational units. More detail would include the *objects of expenditures* such as personnel, non-personnel expenditures, and contracts. *Line item* detail is also included in some budgets to break down spending into more detailed information.

GOVERNOR
ARNOLD SCHWARZENEGGER

January 8, 2010

To the Senate and the Assembly of the California Legislature:

In accordance with Article IV, Section 12 of the California Constitution, I submit to you the Governor's Budget for 2010-11.

Last year, we confronted what history will record as "The Great Recession." Working together, we made profoundly difficult decisions necessary to close a $60 billion budget gap, the largest in our state's history. Because of your efforts and the diligent work of the Treasurer and Controller, we averted both a budget crisis and a cash crisis

With our national economy still struggling to recover, California, like most other states, must confront an additional budget gap of nearly $20 billion. In many ways, the decisions that will be necessary to close this gap will be even more challenging – and far more difficult. However, failure is not an option and we must do what is necessary to keep our state solvent and maintain critical services.

My budget calls for even greater reductions in nearly every aspect of state government than were necessary in 2009. With these reductions, we make every effort to maintain essential services for Californians who need them the most in the midst of this fiscal crisis. In particular, my budget proposal protects education, including higher education, from additional deep cuts. I believe strongly that additional reductions below current year funding levels would leave a permanent scar on our children and on the greatest university system in the world. In fact, I intend to propose a re-prioritization of funds away from administration and into the classroom, and away from prisons and into our universities. I ask you to join me in setting these new priorities for the future of our great state

My budget proposal also calls for a far greater engagement than ever before with our counterparts in Washington — to give California both the flexibility and fairness that is needed to better manage critical state programs, achieve substantial savings, and avoid even deeper and more painful budget reductions. Working with the Obama Administration, with our congressional delegation, and with other states, I believe we can build on the progress we have made in 2009.

We must begin our work immediately. If we fail to take swift action in the Special Session that I have called, our problem will only grow, and the decisions that will be required to make up for lost savings will grow even more difficult than those now before us.

The work that lies ahead will be some the most difficult that you and I will ever be asked to undertake as public servants. Let us prove once again that we can meet this new and unprecedented challenge

Sincerely,

\s\ Arnold Schwarzenegger

Arnold Schwarzenegger

Economic and revenue forecasts: Budgets are built on assumptions. Budget processes begin with some assessment of the economy. Common economic indicators are employment growth, the unemployment rate, inflation, and revenue growth.

Detailed budgets by department: Most governments report budgetary detail for executive branch departments. The detail will include some narrative about the functions and services provided by the department, what the money is spent for such personnel, supplies, travel, etc., and information about activities performed by personnel. Sometimes the budget will also include indicators of performance.

Consider the FY 2014–2015 budget for the fire department of the city of Tallahassee, Florida. (Tallahassee's fiscal year is from October 1 to September 30.) The budget for the fire department is available on the web as part of a budget on public safety: http://www.talgov.com/Uploads/Public/Documents/dma/pdf/fy15/fy15-safetyandneighborhoodsvc.pdf. For full Tallahassee budget see, http://www.talgov.com/dma/dma-budget-fy15budget.aspx.

The summary contains an organization chart, operating budget, the budget narrative, performance indicators, and the capital improvement budget for the fire department. Notice that the narrative summary tells the reader the services the department provides, the "Trends and Issues" facing the department, and "Significant Changes from FY 2014." The fire department handles more than fire suppression, including emergency medical service, removal of hazardous material, search and rescue, and building inspections. The trends and issues section indicates the need to develop a new fee service in pursuit of a renegotiated agreement with the county.

As part of the narrative for the Tallahassee budget is a discussion of the budget process in the city, and where the public can have input in the process. You will notice looking at the process that the "capital budget process" is broken out separately. As we will discuss later in the course, separation of the capital, and operating budgets is a common practice. The budget process and calendar of budget process are available at the following website: http://www.talgov.com/Uploads/Public/Documents/dma/pdf/fy15/fy15-budgetpolicies.pdf.

In addition, the budget provides a summary of the organization of city services and the number of full-time equivalent

(FTE) positions available (http://www.talgov.com/Uploads/Public/Documents/dma/pdf/fy15/fy15-orgoverview.pdf) and presents a number of summary tables for the whole operating budget and by "fund." http://www.talgov.com/Uploads/Public/Documents/dma/pdf/fy15/fy15-operatingbudget.pdf. We will discuss in more detail later the use of "funds" in government budgeting and accounting.

The budget summary for Tallahassee's fire department is in the first website you were given, and is reproduced below.

City of Tallahassee
Fiscal Year 2015 Adopted Budget

Safety and Neighborhood Services

Fire

Operating Budget

Budgetary Cost Summary	FY 2013 Actual	FY 2014 Estimated	FY 2015 Proposed	FY 2015 Approved
200101 Fire Administration	8,890,021	8,480,429	10,786,498	10,742,717
200201 Fire Prevention	635,976	640,926	661,352	633,640
200301 Training	624,462	926,862	684,894	661,240
200401 General Operations	20,152,513	21,027,425	20,932,668	20,425,341
200403 Hazardous Materials	6,010	5,276	11,122	11,078
200415 Station #15	851,397	915,662	989,497	969,196
200416 Advanced Life Support	683,537	770,142	752,007	755,322
200501 Airport Operations	1,081,977	1,035,687	1,143,778	1,154,060
200701 Support Services	406,245	523,977	498,216	540,025
200801 Plans Review	381,579	422,182	394,508	391,151
Total Expenditures	33,713,717	34,748,568	36,854,540	36,283,770

Expenditure Category Summary	FY 2013 Actual	FY 2014 Estimated	FY 2015 Proposed	FY 2015 Approved
Personnel Services	22,428,014	23,782,598	24,190,403	23,677,878
Operating	1,335,061	1,453,088	1,571,120	1,531,575
Other Services & Charges	92,478	161,366	161,366	161,366
Capital Outlay	68,035	110,400	110,400	110,400
Allocated Accounts	6,624,627	6,690,018	7,244,464	7,244,464
Utilities and Other Expenses	307,443	315,698	367,422	367,422
Transfers	1,851,311	1,868,750	2,833,065	2,833,065
Contributions to Operations	352,906	366,650	376,300	357,600
Year End Adjustments	653,842	0	0	0
Total Expenditures	33,713,717	34,748,568	36,854,540	36,283,770

Funding Summary	FY 2013 Actual	FY 2014 Estimated	FY 2015 Proposed	FY 2015 Approved
Fire Services Fund	33,713,717	34,748,568	36,854,540	36,283,770
Total Funding	33,713,717	34,748,568	36,854,540	36,283,770

FTE Summary	FY 2013 Actual	FY 2014 Estimated	FY 2015 Proposed	FY 2015 Approved
200101 Fire Administration	7.00	7.00	7.00	7.00
200201 Fire Prevention	6.00	6.00	6.00	6.00
200301 Training	6.00	6.00	6.00	6.00
200401 General Operations	229.00	229.00	241.00	229.00
200415 Station #15	9.00	9.00	9.00	9.00
200416 Advanced Life Support	5.00	5.00	5.00	5.00
200501 Airport Operations	9.00	9.00	9.00	9.00
200701 Support Services	5.00	5.00	5.00	5.00
200801 Plans Review	4.00	4.00	4.00	4.00
Total FTE	280.00	280.00	292.00	280.00

Several aspects of the table are noteworthy. The top portion of the table displays the budget in *program* format. The fire department has several programs — administration, fire prevention, training, general operations, etc. The budget provides information on actual fiscal year 2012 (FY 2012) spending, estimated FY 2013 spending, as well a proposed and approved FY 2014 spending. Proposed spending is the amount requested by the chief executive and approved is the amount appropriated by the legislature. In this instance, the executive had proposed a budget of $36.85 million and the legislature approved a budget of $36.28 million.

The second panel of the budget provides summary information by expenditure category, or "objects of expenditure," such as personal services (salaries), operating costs, etc. As we will discuss over the next several classes, this is the most common type of budget presentation. In this case, the information is not presented in detail.

The third panel provides information on sources of revenues to fund this budget. In most cities, fire departments do not have their own source of revenue, but in Tallahassee, the city charges residences and businesses outside the city a fire service fee. This appears to be part of an "interlocal agreement" with Leon County.

The final panel provides information on how many FTE employees are assigned to each program. There were no changes in the number of FTE between FY 2013 and FY 2015, even though the executive's 2015 proposed budget had sought an increase of 12 FTEs. Because the number of approved FTEs is that same as in prior years, any changes in the personnel services budget reflects adjustments to salary and benefit costs rather than employment of additional staff. Note, some departmental budgets do provide additional information about personnel costs, particularly since they are usually the largest portions of an agency's budget. In this case, personnel services are 67% of the proposed operating budget for FY 2014.

FTE is a measure that reports the number of personnel assigned to an activity, service, or program. This is not the same as full time positions. An example should clarify the distinction. Assume that in Tallahassee's fire department, there is a firefighter named Jane Doe.

Jane works half time on the fire administration and half time in general operations. She would therefore be 0.5 FTE for budgetary purposes for each program. She is also a full time employee, therefore, her compensation will include her salary plus benefits such as vacation pay, sick days, health insurance, and pension. Part time employees work less than full time employees. They will be counted in FTE estimates for budgetary planning; however, they may not receive the non-wage benefits that full time employees receive. Overtime pay may also be included in departmental budget requests. The overtime rate is based on either statutory standards set by the legislature or established through collective bargaining agreements between the jurisdiction and bargaining units such as trade unions that negotiate such rates with the government or non-profit organization. Since departmental budgets are prospective, overtime costs can only be estimated based on historical trends or anticipated workload increases.

Many departmental budget submissions are also accompanied by information about the activities and outcomes of departmental programs. This trend has been going on for several decades and reflects, what the British call, "value for money." Governments want to show residents what they are getting for the money paid in taxes and fees for services. Within the fire department budget, there is a section for "Performance Measures."

The first part lists the program objectives for the department. The next part provides information on the actual performance measures themselves including: input measures, output measures, efficiency measures, effectiveness measures, and outcome measures. Do you think that the measures included in these tables are good measures of performance? Are they missing some important measures?

Historical tables: Some budget submissions include historical tables. This is especially true of large governments. The budget of the US includes historical tables that record long term trends. Many of the statistical series go back 70 years. These historical tables can be retrieved from the US Office of Management and Budget on the web site. http://www.whitehouse.gov/omb/budget/Historicals/.

1.7.3 Tax and spending bills: the real budget

Up to this point, we have concentrated on the chief executive's budget prior to legislative approval. Most budgetary processes require that a legislative body approves the budget prepared by the chief executive. The legislative body may be a parliament, a town council, and a village board of trustees, a city council or the US Congress. In many countries, the legislature has little real political power; consequently, the chief executive's budget will invariably be the real budget. In non-profit organizations, the board of directors will ordinarily approve the budget prepared by the executive director.

The legislative phase of the budget cycle in the federal government and most state governments ends with *appropriations bills* and *revenue bills.* In all important respects these are the real budget, because appropriations provide executive branch agencies with the authority to spend money. Legislative bodies inform themselves about the executive budget request by holding appropriations hearings with the senior management of the executive departments. As a general rule of thumb, the smaller and less complicated the government, the more likely that the legislature will appropriate the budget as a single decision. This is especially true for local governments. In many state governments, revenues and expenditures are reviewed by different committees before the full legislature votes on appropriations bill(s). Often the spending side of the budget is broken into several appropriations bills. Much of the revenue side of the budget is dictated by the tax bills that are passed by the legislature. These bills set tax rates, define the tax base, and may add revenue sources. One important thing to note here is that the spending and tax sides of the budget are often not part of the same legislation, and may not be carefully coordinated.

Lecture 2

The Basics of Budget Preparation

2.1 Taking Charge at the ORB

It is September 15, 2014, and Keppler begins preparation of her annual budget. Keppler was no stranger to the budget process. Six years earlier, she had started her public career as an analyst in the Budget Bureau of Crescent City, the largest city in the state of Okiana. She had developed a reputation as an astute and tough budget analyst specializing in health and welfare programs. Now, however, the shoe was on the other foot. After serving 2 years as the research director in the Okiana Department of Public Health, she was asked one month ago to take over as the Assistant Commissioner of the Okiana regulation bureau (ORB), which did health, safety and facility inspections of nursing homes and hospitals. The ORB had become a problem agency for the Okiana Department of Public Health. Sloppy record keeping and inconsistent quality control had gotten the ORB in trouble with the US Department of Health and Human Services, which threatened "serious action" if major improvements were not made. Keppler had been brought in to turn the agency around.

Her first major task is to prepare a realistic budget for next year that would provide the bureau adequate resources to improve record keeping and quality control. Given the projected slow growth in state revenues, any new personnel and significant increases in expenditures will require strong justification. Unfortunately, previous budgets were literally prepared on the back of an envelope, and what little justification existed had been "misplaced" by her predecessor. She was horrified at the lack of historical budget and cost information. As Kemper sat in her office surrounded by years of disorganized clutter, she wondered just where to begin. What would she have done as a budget analyst in a similar situation?

2.2 Getting Started on the Budget

While few agency directors face as daunting a task as that confronting Keppler, annual budget preparation is an important management task in all public and non-profit agencies. Sloppy budgeting can affect the level and quality of service provided by the agency, and can damage the reputation of the director. Agency directors ignore budgeting at their own and their agency's peril.

Annual budget preparation, especially in a harsh fiscal environment, is analogous to walking a tight rope. In developing a budget, the agency director has to try to accomplish the chief executive's programmatic goals, be responsive to the clients of the program, appease powerful interest groups and legislators affected by the program, and stay within the budget constraints imposed by the central budget office (or finance department). While astute directors can use budgeting strategy to protect their budget, usually their best strategy is to develop strong analysis to defend their budget request. Good budgetary analysis doesn't always carry the day, but in the long run it pays dividends by strengthening the credibility of the director and the agency. The objective of the next three lectures is to provide you the tools to develop defensible budgets, and, equally importantly, to understand what drives your agency's costs and performance.

2.2.1 Budget history

Returning to the situation confronted by Keppler, where does a new public manager begin when developing the annual budget? Clearly, there is no sense reinventing the wheel. If key staff members involved in budget preparation are still in the agency, their experience, and their records should be the first stop. Of particular importance is their institutional knowledge of how past budgets have been prepared in the agency, what political problems the agency has faced in defending its budget, and what constraints are likely to face the agency this year. Detailed worksheets used in past budget development provide an excellent starting point for this year's budget, and will help a new director defend both past actions taken by the agency, and any proposed changes she may make.

What if such institutional knowledge and past records are not readily available? One source of information that should always be available is past budgets. What can we learn from past budgets? While budget documents don't usually provide the full detail of budget calculations, they are a historical record of spending by program and line item. As you found in exercise #1 in Lecture 1, budget documents usually provide information on expenditures by object of expenditure (personnel, travel, etc.), program, and organizational unit for several years. In the fiscal year 2014 budget, for example, expenditure data is usually provided on actual spending in FY 2012, approved budget and estimated actual spending in FY 2013 (which is still being executed), and proposed spending in FY 2014.

By utilizing several past budgets, it is possible to develop budget trends, which provides a new director with visibility on previous spending decisions and priorities, and changes in the types of resources that are used. For example, has the agency moved to contract out more services to private or non-profit organizations in recent years? Has the agency invested heavily in computer systems and automation, and reduced personnel costs? Have there been significant differences between the budget approved by the legislature and actual spending levels, and what accounts for these discrepancies. Are there executive budget recommendations, such as increases in travel spending that are consistently cut by the legislature? Has this agency fared better or worse in terms of its budget increases, than the department or total government as a whole?

Budgets often provide more than spending information on an agency that can also be useful in budget preparation.

(1) **Agency mission statement and program structure** and how they are linked to actual appropriations can reveal the true priorities of an agency by indicating where money is allocated. For example, assume the ORB is supposed to guarantee the safety and welfare of nursing home patients, yet very few resources are devoted to hiring nursing home inspection staff. This would provide a good indication that this program is considered less important by the chief executive and/or legislature than other programs.

(2) **Personnel schedules** from past years can provide significant information on the workforce of the agency. Is the workforce getting more or less experienced? Has the agency had trouble filling some types of vacant positions? Has the workforce kept up with the growth in agency workload? Have some types of positions been replaced with outside contracts? Besides helping the director determine required staffing levels and personnel expenditures for this budget, an analysis of past personnel information will help in setting future personnel policy.

(3) **Workload, productivity, and performance** measures on public agencies are increasingly being included in budget documents. **Workload** or output measures capture the demands for the agency's services. This data can be used to identify historical trends, and to develop projections of future workload. Information on workload and personnel or total expenditures can be used to develop **labor productivity ratios** (acres fertilized per employee) or **efficiency measures** (costs per acre fertilized). Changes in productivity measures across time can provide some indication as to whether staff productivity has improved, and whether investments in technology, such as new computer systems, have increased employee productivity. **Effectiveness measures** can capture both the quality and timeliness of the service provided by the agency (% of brush management completed), and the outcomes from the services experienced by clients and the public (citizen/customer satisfaction rating).

Compare this to the performance measures in the FY 2017 San Diego Parks and Recreation budget. How would you classify these types of measures?

Park & Recreation

Key Performance Indicators

Performance Indicator	Actual[1] FY 2015	Target[2] FY 2016	Actual FY 2016	Target FY 2017
1. Percentage of park acreage assessed	N/A	N/A	16%	20%
2. Percentage customer satisfaction with park system	93%	94%	93%	93%[3]
3. Percentage of acres of brush management completed	99%	N/A	112%	95%
4. Percentage of park acres decommissioned and converted to sustainable landscapes	N/A	N/A	1.6%	3.0%
5. Number of acres where habitat restoration occurred	N/A	N/A	25	5
6. Percentage increase in on-line registration participation	N/A	N/A	N/A[2]	1%
7. Percentage customer satisfaction with recreational program activities	93%	93%	94%	94%[3]
8. Number of aquatic users	311,788	320,000	304,125	320,000
9. Number of hours of operation of recreation centers	135,877	154,440	154,101	155,780
10. Number of acres of parks and open spaces per 1,000 population	32.05	32.06	32.06	32.26

1. During Fiscal Year 2016, new department tactical plans and key performance indicators were developed. As such, Fiscal Year 2015 data may be unavailable.
2. New performance indicators for Fiscal Year 2016. Some baseline data is currently under development.
3. The target is based on a five-year average.

Source: City of San Diego, Fiscal Year 2017 Adopted Budget.
https://www.sandiego.gov/sites/default/files/fy2017parkandrecreationdepartmentbudget.pdf

2.2.2 Budget guidelines

The budget guideline or as it is informally called, the "budget call" is essentially a statement of the chief executives priorities, the constraints on agency budget requests, and the instructions which the agencies must follow in preparing the budget. The budget call represents the top-down part of the process, where the chief executive tries to control the budget requests of the agencies.

Priorities: The budget guideline is above all a statement of the chief executive's priorities or objectives for this year's budget. Generally, the chief executive or the budget director will send out a memo or letter to agency heads spelling out what are to be the areas of primary concentration and what are the constraints they face. The budget office becomes a primary means for the chief executive to communicate his or her priorities to the executive agencies. These priorities may come from previous campaign commitments, from long-term objectives of an administration, or from policy analysis in the previous year identifying major areas of need.

Whatever their source, most chief executives try to use the budget process to accomplish a few key policy objectives over the course of the year. In addition, an astute executive will clearly have a good "feel" for which objectives are most feasible in the prevailing political climate, especially in the legislature. Often times, the guidelines will provide some general objectives and priorities without getting too detailed. This will not only provide the agencies more freedom in the budget preparation, but allows the chief executive more maneuvering room to adjust to the changing "political winds".

Below is an excerpt from the budget letter sent by budget directors for the governor and legislature of Texas to agency heads in June of 2012 for the FY 2014–2015 biennial budget. What are their major priorities? What fiscal environment will agencies face?

Agencies face a tough fiscal environment. Most agencies will have to reduce expenditures from their FY 2013 budget and they have to submit plans as to how they will cut 10% from the budget. How might an agency protect its base, and possibly ask for an increase? One mechanism is to appeal to the governor's priorities, which are in this case education, health, and human services. This letter also mentions constraints such as required interest payments, requirements for the Medicaid entitlement program, and required contributions to the state pension system.

Legislative Budget Board
Robert E. Johnson Bldg.
1501 N. Congress Avenue, 5th Floor
Austin, TX 78701
(512) 463-1200

Governor's Office of
Budget, Planning and Policy
1100 San Jacinto, 4th Floor
Austin, TX 78701
(512) 463-1778

MEMORANDUM

June 4, 2012

TO: State Agency Board/Commission Chairs
State Agency Heads/Executive Directors
Appellate Court Justices and Judges
Chancellors, Presidents, and Directors of Institutions and Agencies of Higher Education

Detailed instructions for the submission of legislative appropriations requests for the 2014–15 biennium have been posted on the external websites of the Legislative Budget Board and the Governor's Office. A staggered schedule of submission dates is included as an appendix to the instructions.

As a starting point for budget deliberations, an agency's baseline request for General Revenue Funds and General Revenue-Dedicated Funds may not exceed the sum of amounts expended in fiscal year 2012 and budgeted in fiscal year 2013. Establishment of agency budget baselines through the legislative appropriations request process does not preclude the possibility that state agencies may be asked to reduce their fiscal year 2013 budgets should state fiscal conditions warrant it. Agencies must also submit a supplemental schedule detailing how they would reduce the baseline request by an additional 10 percent (in 5 percent increments) in General Revenue Funds and General Revenue Dedicated Funds.

Exceptions to the baseline request limitation include amounts necessary to:

- maintain funding for the Foundation School Program;
- satisfy debt service requirements for bond authorizations;
- maintain benefits and eligibility in Medicaid entitlement programs, the Children's Health Insurance Program, the foster care program, the adoption subsidies program, and the permanency care assistance program; and
- satisfy employer contribution requirements for state pension systems and employee group benefits (not including payroll contributions made by state agencies and institutions of higher education for group health insurance), though group benefit modifications may be considered.

Funding requests for other purposes that exceed the baseline spending level may not be included in the baseline request but may be submitted as Exceptional Items.

We appreciate the opportunity to work with you and your staff during this budget cycle.

Sincerely,

Ursula Parks
Acting Director
Legislative Budget Board

Jonathan Hurst
Director
Governor's Office of Budget, Planning and Policy

Source: The State of Texas Legislative Budget Board, http://www.lbb.state.tx.us/Instructions/LAR/LAR%20Policy%20Letter.pdf

Constraints: The budget guidelines are one of the principal means the chief executive has to communicate the constraints that the agencies are under in preparing the budget. These constraints may be in the form of **expenditure ceilings**, which dictate the size of agency budgets. Constraints may be in terms of procedures, which ask the agencies to prepare baseline, or reduced service budgets to provide the budget office more information on where cuts can be made. The budget letter above both imposes a ceiling, and asks agencies to prepare budget reduction plans. The constraints faced by the chief executive can include:

(1) **Revenue growth:** Tax increases are politically unpopular, thus, one of the key constraints on expenditure growth is how much revenue will grow without major discretionary tax increases. This is closely related to the concept of tax elasticity, which is defined as the percent change in tax revenue with a one percent change in personal income, holding tax policies, and rates constant. Essentially, the chief executive has to have a revenue forecast prepared for the coming year (and sometimes out years). Assuming that the chief executive is not willing to increase tax rates, forecasted growth in revenues will serve as a binding constraint on the growth in the budget.
(2) **Tax and expenditure limitations (TELs):** The 1970s and 1980s was a time of political turmoil for many state and local governments in the US. A movement emerged in many states to limit the growth in government spending through statutes or constitutional amendments in the form of TELs. These limitations usually involved setting some sort of ceiling on the growth of revenues and expenditures, which limit expansion to the growth rate for population, inflation, personal income or some other indicator. To get around these limitations often required some sort of "super-majority" in the legislature, such as a two-thirds vote, which would be difficult to achieve.
(3) **Uncontrollable expenditures:** The chief executive's ability to shape the budget is constrained by certain uncontrollable expenditures. As the term implies, a significant share of the

budget may already be committed to pay debt service (principal and interest) on loans, cover fringe benefits provided to employees, such as pensions, health insurance, and social security, and to fund entitlement programs. Entitlements are programs, typically passed by statute, that guarantee a certain payment to individuals that meet eligibility requirements. Medicaid, funded by both the federal and state government, is a good example of an entitlement program. Although these expenditures may be difficult to change in the short-run, it is important for the chief executive to keep track of significant changes in them, because along with the forecast of revenues, they will help to determine the amount of the budget, which is available for discretionary action.

(4) **Judicial mandates:** A growing constraint on state and local governments is the actions of the judiciary regarding the level of service provided by the government. These usually come in the form of court orders, which require the government to provide service of a certain quality or be in violation of the law. Areas where the judiciary has played a particularly active role in the US include prisons, mental health facilities, environmental infrastructure (e.g., wastewater treatment), and education finance. For example, the growing problem of prison overcrowding has led to mandates from federal or state courts for state and local governments to relieve the overcrowding since they are subjecting prisoners to "cruel and unusual punishment". This may force the chief executive to propose a prison construction program to comply with the mandate.

2.2.3 Preparation instructions

Accompanying the budget memo or letter from the chief executive is a set of detailed instructions on how each agency should prepare their budget. The number of the instructions will typically vary in direct proportion to the size of the government. For a small local government or non-profit agency, the instructions and guidelines may be contained in a memo from the chief executive, legislature, or non-profit board. For the federal government of the US, instructions are included in Circular A-11 from the Office of Management and Budget, which are over 500 pages in length.[1] Budget instructions commonly include three types of information:

(1) **Budget timetable** that outlines when budget requests from agencies are due, and other key steps in the budget process. The following figure presents the budget process in the City of Seattle for the fiscal year beginning January 1. The budget process in Seattle begins in the February of the preceding year with the central budgeting office (CBO) providing city agencies with budget instructions. In March–April, CBO prepares its revenue projections, and provides departments more detailed budget development instructions. From May to July, agencies prepare their budgets which are submitted along with their capital improvement plan (CIP). During July through September, CBO and the mayor's office review the budget requests, and make final decisions on the budget. The budget is presented to the city council in September, and the budget review process in the council takes place in the fall of the year with final adoption by December 2.

(2) **Forms and procedures** for preparation of the different parts of the budget. There may be forms for requesting additional personnel, promotions among existing personnel, new capital equipment, or new programs. Worksheets may be provided for calculating the major components of the operating budget. If workload and performance information is to be displayed in the budget, forms, and instructions are included for these measures as well. For an example of budget forms and instructions used by the Colorado Office of State Planning and Budgeting see https://sites.google.com/a/state.co.us/ospb-live/image-heavy-page.

(3) **The budget office or finance department often supplies key cost factors to assure consistency in budget calculations**. For example, inflation rates may be provided for

[1]This circular is available on the web at http://www.whitehouse.gov/omb/circulars_a11_current_year_a11_toc/.

Budget Process Diagram

Phase			
PHASE I – Budget Submittal Preparation	FEBRUARY-MARCH CBO provides departments with the general structure, conventions and schedule for the next year's budget	MARCH - APRIL CBO prepares revenue projections for the current year	APRIL CBO issues budget and CIP development instructions to departments
	MAY Departments submit Budget Issue Papers (BIPs) to describe how they will arrive at their budget targets	MAY-JUNE Mayor's Office and CBO review the BIPs and provide feedback to departments	JULY Departments submit budget and CIP proposals to CBO based on Mayoral direction CBO reviews departmental proposals for organizational changes
PHASE II – Proposed Budget Preparation	JULY-AUGUST The Mayor's Office and CBO review department budget and CIP proposals	AUGUST-SEPTEMBER Mayor's Office makes final decisions on the Proposed Budget and CIP Proposed Budget and CIP documents are produced	SEPTEMBER Mayor presents the Proposed Budget and CIP to City Council on the last Monday of the month
PHASE III – Adopted Budget Preparation	SEPTEMBER-OCTOBER Council develops a list of issues for review during October and November CBO and departments prepare revenue and expenditure presentations for Council	OCTOBER-NOVEMBER Council reviews Proposed Budget and CIP in detail Budget and CIP revisions developed, as are Statements of Legislative Intent and Budget Provisos	NOVEMBER-DECEMBER Council adopts operating budget and CIP Note: Budget and CIP must be adopted no later than December 2

Source: The City of Seattle 2016 Adopted Budget, http://www.seattle.gov/financedepartment/16adoptedbudget/documents/budgetprocessdiagram.pdf

different components in the budget, such as supplies, utilities, private contracts, etc. Negotiated increases in personnel salaries and fringe benefits are provided for calculating the personnel budget.

2.3 Current Service Budget and Improvements

The majority of the preparation part of the budget cycle is taken up in the detailed development of budget requests by each agency. The length of time for this process and the formality of the requests depend on the size of the government. For a small government or non-profit agency, budget preparation may be done directly by the director or a staff person in less than a month, and presented directly to the legislature or non-profit board. Large governments may devote up to six months in the budget preparation stage, with multiple stages or review and revisions. Budget preparation usually begins with agency head passes on the budget guidelines as well as his or her own priorities or instructions to the subunits of an agency. Then, this becomes essentially a bottom-up process in which the smallest budget units within an agency submits requests "up the line" until full agency requests are submitted to the budget office. Each level of the agency generally acts as a screen filtering out requests that are not justified or go against established priorities.

The heart of budget preparation involves assessing whether there have been changes in program costs, demand for agency services, or requirements for new or expanded programs. Increasingly, governments are adding a formal stage to their budgeting process, which requires agencies to prepare a baseline or current service budget, and to identify improvements or additions to the budget. Improvements generally get closer scrutiny in the budget process; thus, agencies have an incentive to avoid labeling any part of their budget as improvements.

Baseline/current services budget: A part of the budget preparation required in some governments is for agencies to prepare a baseline, or current services budget. This can be roughly defined as the cost of providing "the same as last year". The key question is the same what?

(1) **Same spending:** The simplest and most constraining form of baseline budget is one where the same level of spending is maintained from the previous year. The agency may be asked to

estimate the effects of this budget on service levels. If there is inflation and no drop in workload for the agency, this baseline budget implies a cut in real resources and either an increase in efficiency or drop in services provided. Referring back to the budget letter from the budget director in Texas, it is telling agencies that same spending will be the norm in next budget.

(2) **Same resources:** Another type of baseline budget would require agencies to determine the spending level required to maintain the same resources as the previous year. Given that prices of goods and services naturally go up over time, this budget would allow adjustment for inflation only. If there is an increase in workload or demand for the agency's services, then again either the agency improves its efficiency or the level of service decreases.

(3) **Same service level:** The term current services budget implies a budget that will fund the same quantity and quality of service as the previous year. If the workload is increasing, this implies an increase in personnel and spending, even with no inflation.

Current service budgets almost always allow the agency to control for inflation (the rate to be used by the agency often preset by the budget office). Much more controversial is how much changes in demand are controlled for. When is an increase in demand viewed as continuation or an "improvement" in the agency's services? Agencies would obviously prefer to include all growth in demand in the baseline budget since it will get less attention from the budget office. The budget office, not surprisingly, tends to take a narrower view of what should be included in the baseline budget.

A recent report by the Center on Budget and Policy Priorities did a report on the use of current service budgets in states (http://www.cbpp.org/files/12-14-06sfp.pdf). They found that 13 states prepare current services budgets but there was variation in how current services was calculated, what is made available to the public, and what level of detail is used in the calculation (Table 2.1).

Example: An example of a state budget which includes information on the current service budget along with the budget request is the State of Connecticut for the 2013–2015 biennial budget

Table 2.1. Features of current services baselines.

Table 1 Features of Current Services Baselines	
	Number of States
Project beyond next budget:	6
Spending projections include:	
Previously approved program changes	13
Inflation used for all programs	12
Population or caseload changes	13
Level of Detail:	
Summary level only	4
Detailed program level	10
Availability:	
Unpublished	3
In agency requests or other non-budget	1
Published in annual budget	10

Source: CBPP Survey
Note: Counts include DC where applicable.

(http://www.ct.gov/opm/cwp/view.asp?a = 2958&Q = 518404&PM = 1). It compares what the agency requested to the current service budget and what was actually recommended by the governor. For this particular agency (Health and Hospitals), the governor is recommending (last column reporting total agency funds of $276.9 million) a substantial cut below the current service budget (second to last column reporting total agency funds of $293.89 million) in FY 2015. The difference between the agency request (third to last column reporting $295.55 million) and the current service budget would be the changes the agency is proposing. In this case, the agencies are proposing a $2 million increase in the budget over the current service budget. The governor on the other hand has recommended a $19 million cut in spending over the agency requested budget.

Improvements: Often the budget process will require separate documentation for any planned improvements in the level of service provided by an agency. In a sense, agencies need to justify why an expansion of program service is justified. To justify these improvements, an agency will typically have to provide more than object of expenditure data. This data may include workload measures,

Agency Programs by Total Funds	FY 2012	FY 2013	FY 2014	Current	FY 2014	FY 2015	Current	FY 2015
(Net of Reimbursements)	Actual	Estimated	Requested	Services	Recommended	Requested	Services	Recommended
Commissioner's Programs	6,819,267	10,368,553	10,466,292	10,461,589	10,423,323	10,537,303	10,532,904	10,451,893
Public Health Initiatives	156,401,151	179,237,987	191,444,962	191,212,517	187,644,985	195,514,989	195,310,516	181,244,028
Regulatory Services	18,068,068	16,553,136	18,557,907	18,779,142	18,443,747	19,058,427	19,296,525	16,772,351
Laboratory Services	10,944,992	13,655,627	13,944,258	13,262,200	13,208,299	14,279,900	13,672,752	13,541,654
Healthcare Quality and Safety	25,951,004	25,772,125	25,295,797	24,334,924	24,273,984	25,938,737	24,930,640	24,860,149
Agency Management Services	9,178,500	10,912,222	11,399,741	11,000,096	11,050,100	11,821,431	11,439,700	11,454,595
Health Statistics and Surveillance	20,244,577	19,594,920	19,220,498	19,244,620	19,243,652	17,268,573	17,307,733	17,305,068
Office of Health Care Access	1,510,466	1,619,289	1,695,549	1,704,553	1,702,831	1,761,990	1,793,668	1,788,921
TOTAL Agency Programs - All Funds Gross	249,118,025	277,713,859	292,025,004	289,999,641	285,990,921	296,181,350	294,284,438	277,418,659
Less Turnover	0	0	-614,849	-632,482	-632,482	-633,294	-665,071	-665,071
Nonfunctional - Change to Accruals	0	0	0	181,663	201,698	0	272,404	147,102
TOTAL Agency Programs - All Funds Net	249,118,025	277,713,859	291,410,155	289,548,822	285,560,137	295,548,056	293,891,771	276,900,690
Summary of Funding								
General Fund Net	80,906,635	99,861,229	113,906,851	112,045,518	108,141,833	117,433,969	115,777,684	108,689,912
Federal and Other Activities	134,316,496	144,474,837	148,960,173	148,960,173	148,960,173	150,347,221	150,347,221	140,643,912
Private Funds	33,894,894	33,377,793	28,543,131	28,543,131	28,458,131	27,766,866	27,766,866	27,566,866
TOTAL Agency Programs - All Funds Net	249,118,025	277,713,859	291,410,155	289,548,822	285,560,137	295,548,056	293,891,771	276,900,690

Source: State of Connecticut for the 2013–2015 biennial budget (http://www.ct.gov/opm/cwp/view.asp?a=2958&Q=518404&PM=1).

or performance indicators, or estimates of the revenue that they can raise from other sources. Agencies often use several types of justifications to support the requirement for expanded service or a new program.

(1) **Rising level of expenditure need:** Agencies will try to show that there is increasing demand for the services that they are providing. This would imply that there is no real improvement in the quality of service provided, just a larger clientele to serve. Anything less than a funding of this increase will imply a cut in service quality. Agencies will try to put this type of funding in the current services budget if possible.
(2) **Legislative/court mandate:** The agency is under pressure from the legislature or the court to improve the service up to some minimum standard. For example, spending increases in corrections and mental health over the last several decades were often justified by court orders to improve facilities.
(3) **Will pay for itself:** Another common approach to selling an improvement is to show that this increased service will actually pay for itself so that it is actually not costing more. For example, there will be an increase in user fee revenues, or productivity gains, which will reduce expenditures in some other department. For example, a public health agency might justify a drug education program by showing that it will reduce expenditures on drug enforcement or treatment.
(4) **Addresses urgent problem:** Agencies will try to couch these increases in terms of issues, which are "hot" at a particular time.

Example: Budgeting improvements in Georgia. Table 2.2 provides an illustration of a form of current service budget used in the state of Georgia in FY 1999. (Georgia has changed its budget format since then.) The second column in the FY 1999 Governor's Recommendations table are estimates for the "adjusted base" for the Department of Natural Resources. The adjusted base budget is calculated by taking the previous year's budget, subtracting non-recurring expenditures, and adding in funds for adjustments, such as salary increases and inflation. However, the line between what is

Table 2.2. Financial summary, state of Georgia budget report department of natural resources, FY 1999 governor's recommendations.

Budget Classes/ Fund Sources	Redirection Level				Enhancements	Totals
	Adjusted Base	Funds to Redirect	Additions	Redirection Totals		
Personal Services	76,803,557	(3,240,637)	1,236,207	74,799,127	673,013	75,472,140
Regular Operating Expenses	14,694,783	(1,183,199)	544,324	14,055,908	31,200	14,087,108
Travel	589,709	(5,748)	10,500	594,461	26,000	620,461
Motor Vehicle Purchases	1,048,943	(17,275)		1,031,668	750,000	1,781,668
Equipment	2,232,175	217,730		2,449,905		2,474,905
Real Estate Rental	2,376,062		25,000	2,401,062	68,640	2,444,702

considered simply an adjustment to the base versus an enhancement is probably an area of conflict between the budget office and agencies.

Georgia's budget process also has some other interesting features. The third through fifth columns in Table 2.2 refer to the "redirection level". The redirection process requires all agencies to reexamine how they do business, and eliminate or downsize activities that are no longer needed. All department heads are required to reallocate at least 5% of their budget from the previous year to fund service expansion or enhancements, particularly in priority areas. The budget office may choose to shift some or all of these funds to another agency. In essence, this process requires agencies to put at least 5% of their past budget into better use than it is now. In addition, agencies can request "enhancements" to the budget, but these are limited to 4.5% of the adjusted base budget. It is likely that the budget office will require justification from agencies as to why the enhancements were not funded with redirected funds.

2.4 Personnel Budget

The majority of the budget for public and non-profit agencies is devoted to funding personnel, because the services they provide are labor intensive. For example, the main service of police departments is patrol and apprehension of potential criminals, which requires trained police officers. While use of more automated communication, surveillance, and security equipment can make police departments more productive, the major resource used by a police department remains police officers. In addition, the hiring of personnel often implies a long-term obligation, since contractually it may be difficult to remove permanent personnel without strong justification. Thus, agencies usually need to provide detailed justification as to why they are requesting additional personnel, or promotions of existing staff.

Calculating a personnel budget involves several basic steps: (1) determine the number of staff by type that are needed to provide the required level of service, (2) determine the salary associated with each of these staff, and (3) calculate other personnel costs, commonly called fringe benefits, associated with this staff. While each of these steps can actually get quite involved, keeping these basic steps in mind helps to keep from getting lost in the details. To illustrate the calculation of a personnel budget, we will start with the case where you are budgeting for an established service with no change in the number of required personnel over the previous year. This will help to highlight Steps 2 and 3, calculating the salaries and fringe benefits. We will then turn to the case where required personnel and personnel budgets have to be developed for a new or expanded program.

2.4.1 Updating personnel budgets

Salary budget: For an established agency, calculating the annual personnel budget involves updating previous personnel budgets. In the simplest case where no personnel leave, no new personnel are added to the agency, and where all personnel receive the same percent increase in salary for cost-of-living adjustment (COLA), updating the salary budget involves simply taking last year's budget and multiplying it by one plus the COLA percent.

Unless the agency is very small, however, updating the salary budget is usually more involved. Calculating the salary budget involves three types of information:

(1) **Personnel schedules** from the previous year's budget. A personnel schedule is a list of staff in the agency by position, grade, and step. The grade of a position reflects the responsibility and salary level of a position. Moving from one grade to another is

Table 2.3. Budgeted positions by organization, FY 2015 budget Onondaga County Sheriff Department, patrol.

Title of Position	Grade	Pay Range	2013 Actual	2014 Requested	2014 Adopted
Lieutenant	06	74,720–78,652	8	8	8
Sergeant	05	65,309–68,747	20	20	20
Patrol Officer	04	44,467–63,297	119	119	119

Source: Onondaga County, New York 2015 Annual Budget, http://www.ongov.net/finance/documents/2015AdoptedBudgetFinal.pdf

Table 2.4. Positions by grade and step, FY 2014 (hypothetical) Onondaga County Sheriff Department, patrol.

Title of Position	Grade	Less than One (1) Year	Step A 1 Year	Step B 2 Years	Step C 3 Years	Step D 4 or more Years	Total
Patrol Officer	04	10	20	20	30	39	119
		Probationary Rate		**Maximum Rate**			
Lieutenant	06	2		6			8
Sergeant	05	6		14			20

usually called a promotion. The step of a position captures the seniority or experience level of a staff. It is common for staff to receive increases in salary for seniority up to some experience level (last step). Table 2.3, provides an example of a personnel schedule from the budget for the Onondaga County (New York) Sheriff Department (patrol program) for FY 2015. (We have included only three of the positions for simplicity.) The budget proposal for FY 2015 did not include any increase in patrol personnel over the previous year. This schedule provides all the information required for updating your personnel schedule except the steps of the various employees. Table 2.4 presents a hypothetical schedule with seniority levels with the personnel classifications that are similar to those the County uses. (The years of seniority for Steps C and D have been modified to simplify the example.) For the deputy sheriffs that serve as officers, only two steps (probationary, or maximum) exist, and there is no set time period where an officer moves from one classification to another. In this example, deputy sheriff personnel in patrol were quite experienced with many of the deputies at the top step.

(2) **Updated personnel schedules** must be constructed, which estimate the grade and step of employees during the budget year using the personnel schedule of the previous year (Table 2.4), and the estimated change in personnel by type during this budget year. One of the key decisions in estimating a personnel budget, as indicated by Fishbein and Vehaun (2009) is how to treat potential **vacancies**. It is common to have some turnover in personnel during the year and for some types of positions the turnover rates may be very high. How this affects the personnel budget depends on the assumptions made.

   (a) **No turnover:** As in Fishbein and Vehaun (2009), if the "government fully funds salaries associated with vacancies, it is building some potential cushion into the budget that may come in hand to make up shortfalls in other areas at year's end." (p. 67).[2] The most conservative version of this is to assume no turnover and have everyone move up a step because of seniority. For the Onondaga County example, this would imply that everyone in Steps A, B, and C would move to the next highest step. Those in Step D wouldn't move to being a Lieutenant because this would be a promotion and these are not automatic. For those lieutenants and sergeants paid at the probationary rate, they may not move to the maximum rate. Let's assume that they do all move up to the maximum rate. The new personnel schedule will look like Table 2.5.

   (b) **Using historical turnover rates:** As Fishbein and Vehaun (2009) indicate, one way to estimate turnover is to use historical turnover to calculate a historical turnover rate (or vacancy rate). This is typically calculated for each year by

[2]John Fishbein and David Vehaun. 2009. "Managing the Personnel Budgeting Process." *Government Finance Review* (August): 67–73.

Table 2.5. Positions by grade and step, FY 2015 (hypothetical) Onondaga County Sheriff Department, patrol.

Title of Position	Grade	Less than One (1) Year	Step A 1 Year	Step B 2 Years	Step C 3 Years	Step D 4 or more Years	Total
Patrol Officer	04	0	10	20	20	69	119
		Probationary Rate		**Maximum Rate**			
Lieutenant	06	0		8			8
Sergeant	05	0		20			20

Table 2.6. Historical turnover rates by grade and step (hypothetical) Onondaga County Sheriff Department, patrol.

Title of Position	Grade	Less Than One (1) Year	Step A 1 Year	Step B 2 Years	Step C 3 Years	Step D 4 or More Years
Patrol Officer	04	10%	8%	8%	7%	10%
		Probationary Rate		**Maximum Rate**		
Lieutenant	05	5%		10%		
Sergeant	06	7%		5%		

dividing the number of people in each step and grade that leave during a year by the total number positions in that step and grade. Typically, you would want to average this over multiple years, such as 5-years. Table 2.6 presents a hypothetical example of turnover rates for patrol personnel. For example, 10% of the patrol officers with less than 1 year of experience have left the job by the end of the year.

If these rates are multiplied by the personnel schedule for FY 2014 (and rounded to the nearest integer), this will give you an idea of how many people are expected to leave before next year (Table 2.7).

To use these estimates to calculate the expected personnel schedule for FY 2015 requires one more assumption — with what level of experience will the new officers be hired. The least expensive alternative is to assume that the Sheriff's department will hire new personnel with no experience in this grade. In other words, all new patrol officers are in the first step, and all sergeants

Table 2.7. Estimated turnover, positions by grade and step (hypothetical) Onondaga County Sheriff Department, patrol.

Title of Position	Grade	Less than One (1) Year	Step A 1 Year	Step B 2 Years	Step C 3 Years	Step D 4 or more Years	Total
Patrol Officer	04	1	2	2	2	4	11
		Probationary Rate		**Maximum Rate**			
Lieutenant	06	0		1			1
Sergeant	05	0		1			1

Table 2.8. Positions by grade and step, FY 2015 (hypothetical) Assuming turnover and everyone at top of the step (All new hires are in lowest step).

Title of Position	Grade	Less than One (1) Year	Step A 1 Year	Step B 2 Years	Step C 3 Years	Step D 4 or more Years	Total
Patrol Officer	04	11	9	18	18	63	119
		Probationary Rate		**Maximum Rate**			
Lieutenant	06	1		7			8
Sergeant	05	1		19			20

and lieutenants are hired as probationary. To calculate the new schedule:

(a) First, subtract the vacancies in Table 2.7 from the positions in FY 2014 (Table 2.4).
(b) Then move all of these positions up one step except for Step D and Maximum Rate.
(c) Finally, using the vacancies listed on Table 2.7 by grade, put these in the least experienced category (Step A) or probationary.

The new personnel schedule is illustrated in Table 2.8. You can compare the difference with the personnel schedule which assumes no turnover (Table 2.5).

(3) **Revised salary schedules** are provided to agencies, typically by the budget or finance department, which reflect inflation and any negotiated increases in salaries. Table 2.9 was the actual salary schedule for FY 2015 negotiated between Onondaga

Table 2.9. Negotiated salaries by grade and step, FY 2015 Onondaga County Sheriff Department, patrol.

Title of Position	Grade	Less than One (1) Year	Step A 1 Year	Step B 2 Years	Step C 3 Years	Step D 4 or more Years
Patrol Officer	04	46,718	54,033	55,801	57,632	66,501
		Probationary Rate		**Maximum Rate**		
Lieutenant	06	80,465		84,700		
Sergeant	05	70,331		75,033		

Table 2.10. Salary budget by grade and step, FY 2015 (no turnover) Onondaga County Sheriff Department, patrol.

Title of Position	Grade	Less than One (1) Year	Step A 1 Year	Step B 2 Years	Step C 3 Years	Step D 4 or more Years
Patrol Officer	04	0	540,330	1,116,020	1,152,640	4,588,569
		Probationary Rate		**Maximum Rate**		
Lieutenant	06	0		677,600		
Sergeant	05	0		1,500,660		
TOTAL BUDGET	9,575,819					

County and the Deputy Sheriff's Benevolent Association (sheriff's union).

(4) **Salary budget:** The salary budget is calculated by multiplying the revised personnel schedule (Tables 2.5 or 2.8) by the salary schedule (Table 2.9) for each grade and step to produce the estimate of the salary budget. Since we have estimated personnel schedules with and without turnover, we can do the same for the estimate of the salary budget. Comparing Tables 2.10 and 2.11 there is a \$142,166 difference, which is less than 2% of the salary budget. It appears in this example, we probably don't need to worry too much about turnover in calculating the personnel budget. Fishbein and Vehaun (2009) would probably recommend using Table 2.10.

Table 2.11. Salary budget by grade and step, FY 2015 (with turnover) Onondaga county sheriff department, patrol.

Title of Position	Grade	Less than One (1) Year	Step A 1 Year	Step B 2 Years	Step C 3 Years	Step D 4 or more Years
Patrol Officer	04	513,898	486,297	1,004,418	1,037,376	4,189,563
		Probationary Rate		**Maximum Rate**		
Lieutenant	06	80,465		592,900		
Sergeant	05	70,331		1,425,627		
TOTAL BUDGET	9,400,875					

Fringe benefits: Wages and salaries usually represent 60–70% of the personnel budget. A number of other employee related expenses are budgeted by an agency. Some of these fringe benefits are legally required (e.g., social security, worker's compensation), while others are optional (e.g., pensions, life insurance, etc.) For larger governments, the budget or finance office typically handles all fringe benefit calculations, leaving agencies to calculate the salary budget only. Agencies might be expected to multiply the salary budget by some fixed percent, often between 20 and 40%, to calculate fringe benefits. For smaller agencies or non-profits, the director or finance staff may need to calculate the detailed fringe benefits by type as part of the budget process. The following is a brief discussion of typical fringe benefits;

(1) **Social security (OASDI)/Medicare:** The old-age, survivors, and disability insurance (OASDI), or more commonly called Social Security is a national program that provides monthly payments to retired and disabled workers. Both employers and employees contribute to this program with an equal percent of 6.2%. Almost all private, government and non-profit employees are covered.[3] Medicare is a national health care insurance

[3]Exceptions include federal civilian employees hired before 1984, certain employees of state and local governments who are covered under a retirement system (e.g., fire and police in some local governments), and employees of religious

program that covers all employees under the Social Security system. Hospital Insurance (Medicare) is provided to all eligible workers, and contributions of 1.45 of gross wages are contributed by both the employer and employee.

(2) **Workers' compensation:** The following is an excerpt from the "Employer's Handbook" published by the New York State Worker's Compensation Board, http://www.wcb.state.ny.us/content/main/Employers/EmployerHandbook.pdf. "The New York Workers' Compensation Law was enacted in 1914 to protect both injured workers and their employers. Under this landmark legislation, workers who suffered injuries or illnesses on the job received timely medical treatment and wage replacement assistance, while employers were protected from being sued by those injured workers." (p. 3)

Workers' compensation systems are run by each individual state, and how they are financed can be different. Some states require that employer's contribute a percent of their payroll, and withhold a certain percent of an employee's check for workers' compensation. New York requires that employers either purchase an insurance policy, or set up an approved self-insurance fund.

(3) **Unemployment insurance:** The unemployment insurance (UI) program was created in 1935 to provide temporary wage replacement for unemployed workers. The federal government sets some guidelines and finances state administration of the program, but benefits are generally funded through employer taxes at the state level. Tax rates vary across states with the generosity of coverage. Within a state, tax rates typically vary across employers based on the level of claims that employees have made in the past. The more claims per employee in the organization, the higher the tax rate the employer will need to

---

organizations, who elect not to join the system. For a good summary of the provisions of the Social Security and Medicare programs, the Social Security Administration puts out the *Annual Statistical Supplement* every year. Payroll taxes apply only up to a maximum earnings level, which is adjusted automatically each year.

make. Nationally, the average tax rate for new employers was 2.5% in 2008.[4]

(4) **Pensions:** Most governments and many non-profit agencies provide pension benefits to their full-time employees. Pensions are generally of two types: (1) defined benefit plans, where the employer guarantees the employee a certain benefit under certain conditions, and (2) defined contribution plans, where the employer contributes a set percent of the employee's salary to an independent investment pool. The first type of pension systems places more risk on the employer, and there will be more variation in the employer contribution on an annual basis. Most private employers are now using defined contribution plans, but many governments still used defined benefit plans. Pension contributions for employers are typically a certain percent of the salary budget.

(5) **Health insurance:** A major benefit provided usually to fulltime employees is access to health insurance or a health maintenance organization. The costs of these plans are typically split between the employer and employee. This has become an increasingly expensive fringe benefit for employers, and more attention is being focused on how to hold down health insurance costs. Many governments also provide health insurance benefits to retirees. Health insurance contributions by an employer can be structured in a number of ways, so as an employer you would need to look carefully at the health insurance plan.

2.4.2 Budgeting personnel for new or expanded service

When the workload of an agency changes significantly either up or down, or the agency adds a new service, a more fundamental analysis of the personnel budget should be done if possible. Requests for expanded staff usually undergo careful scrutiny from the budget office. Weak justifications or mistakes in the calculations are likely

[4]Tax Policy Center. Tax Facts. "State Unemployment Rates, 2008." Available at: http://www.taxpolicycenter.org/taxfacts/displayafact.cfm?Docid=541.

to be detected, and will hurt the credibility of the proposal and the agency. At the heart of estimating a new personnel budget is understanding the link between the agency's staff and the services provided by the agency. Some of the more common types of staffing arrangements include:

1. Personnel provide coverage for a geographic area for potential problems that may arise, such as a fire or criminal activity.
2. Staff provides direct services to clients, which is common in social service, education, and recreation agencies.
3. Staff operates or maintains physical infrastructure, with staffing commonly tied to the size of the physical plant (e.g., transportation and public utilities).
4. Personnel monitor contracts with private firms, or regulate the actions of public or private agencies.
5. Staff provides support services, such as legal, financial, and personnel services, to other public agencies in the government.

The first case involves tying personnel to geographic size and the required time of coverage. This will be illustrated below using the example of the Onondaga County Sheriff's Department. Cases 2–4 are similar in that most staff can be tied to some measure of output, such as clients served, tons of garbage collected, or contracts audited. Many non-profit agencies would fall into this category, and a non-profit example will be used to highlight key steps in building a personnel budget. The last category, support staff, is not easily tied to an agency's services. In the next lecture, methods for connecting support personnel to agency output will be discussed.

Example: Adding Sheriff patrols: To illustrate the preparation of a personnel budget for a public safety agency, assume that the Onondaga County Sheriff's Department wanted to add three more patrols, because of expanding population. Patrols are for 24 hours per day, 365 days per year. Assume that the union contract requires two officers per patrol car; officers work 8 hours per day, 5 days per week, and receive 3 weeks of vacation and 1 week of sick leave per year. The department planned to staff the cars with two officers with 2 years of experience (Step B). The budget office required the department to set aside an additional $30 for fringe benefits. Estimating the personnel budget in this case involves four steps:

(1) Calculate the **number of personnel hours or shifts** (8 hours) required to continually staff three patrols.

$$\begin{aligned}&3 \text{ shifts per patrol}\\&\quad\times 3 \text{ patrols per day} \times 2 \text{ officers per car} \times 365 \text{ days}\\&= 6{,}570 \text{ shifts per year} \times 8 \text{ hours}\\&= 52{,}560 \text{ patrol hours per year.}\end{aligned}$$

(2) Determine the number of **hours or shifts one patrol officer can provide**.

$$\begin{aligned}&52 \text{ weeks per year} \times 5 \text{ days per week}\\&\quad= 260 \text{ potential work shifts.}\\&4 \text{ weeks per year} \times 5 \text{ days per week}\\&\quad= 20 \text{ vacation/sick leave days per year.}\\&260 \text{ days} - 20 \text{ non-work days} = 240 \text{ labor days} \times 8 \text{ hours}\\&\quad= 1{,}920 \text{ hours per year.}\end{aligned}$$

(3) Calculate the **required number of full-time officers**. Generally, you want to round up if you are required to hire full-time personnel, and the service level is mandatory.

$$\begin{aligned}&6570 \text{ shifts divided by } 240 \text{ labor days} = 27.375 \text{ officers}\\&\quad= 28 \text{ officers.}\end{aligned}$$

(This is the same as 52,560 hours divided by 1,920 hours).

(4) Estimate the **salary budget and fringe benefit costs (use Table 2.9 for salary)**.

Salary costs: 28 officers × $55,801	=	$1,562,428
Benefit costs: $1,562,428 × 30%	=	$468,728
Total costs:		$2,031,256.

Example: Meals-on-wheels: Assume you are the director of a non-profit organization that delivers meals to elderly persons in their homes. The state reimburses you a flat rate per person. You provide three meals a day per person, 7 days per week, 365 days per year. Your staff includes two types of personnel; cooks and drivers, who each work full-time, 5 days a week, on average and have 10 days off per year (paid) for vacation. They get 25% salary bonus if they are willing to work on weekends. Cooks get paid $17 per hour and drivers $14 per hour. Your organization contributes $100 per employee per month in health insurance, 5% of their salary to a pension plan, as well as paying the regular rates for Social Security and Hospital Insurance, OASDI (7.65%). Last year, they contributed 5% of payroll in Workers' Compensation and Unemployment Insurance. These fringe benefit percentages would generally apply to the total payroll (with overtime). In general, cooks can prepare three meals per day for a maximum of 50 clients per day and drivers can deliver three meals per day for a maximum of 35 clients per day. What are the personnel costs of providing service to 200 persons every day?

When the agency staff is linked directly to basic service level of the agency, estimating the personnel budget involves these steps:

(1) Project the **workload or the demand** for the agency services. In this case, 200 elderly individuals are to be served in their home three meals per day for 365 days.
(2) Estimate the **labor productivity ratio**, or output per labor hour or shift. This estimate is usually based on past experience and may build in any expected labor productivity improvements. Maximum productivity ratios of 50 clients per cook and 35 clients per driver are given. If the average productivity rate is much lower than the maximum, then a more cautious budget estimate would use the average.
(3) Calculate the **total required labor staff persons per shift** (same as days in this case) by simply dividing the projected need by the expected productivity of agency personnel and rounding up for fulltime personnel.

Cooks: 200 clients per day divided by 50 clients per cook per day
= 4 cooks per day
= 4 cooks × 365 days = 1,460 annual cook shifts
= 1,460 shifts × 8 hours = 11,680 annual cook hours.

Drivers: 200 clients per day divided by 35 clients per driver per day
= 5.71 (round to 6) drivers per day
= 6 drivers × 365 days = 2,190 annual driver shifts
= 2,190 shifts × 8 hours = 17,520 annual driver hours.

It is best to be conservative in your staffing estimates to assure you have adequate budget.

(4) Calculate extra pay shifts (for weekend days):

Cooks: 52 weeks × 2 days/week × 4 cooks
= 416 extra pay shifts.
416 shifts × 8 hours = 3,328 hours per year.

Drivers: 52 weeks × 2 days/week × 6 drivers
= 624 extra pay shifts.
624 shifts × 8 hours = 4,992 hours per year.

(5) Determine the number of **hours or shifts one staff member can provide per year**.

365 days minus (52 week × 2 days off per week) = 261 paid work shifts.
261 days × 8 hours per day = 2,088 paid labor hours per year.
261 days − vacation days = 251 shifts per year worked by each staff person.
251 days × 8 hours per day = 2,008 hours per year worked.

(6) Estimate the number of **agency personnel required** to meet the demand for agency services. This involves dividing total labor hours or shifts by an estimate of the number of hours or shifts of work available per employee.

Cooks: 1,460 cook days per year divided by 251 shifts per cook year $= 5.82$ cooks $\rightarrow$ round up to 6 cooks.

Drivers: 2190 driver days per year divided by 251 shifts per driver year $= 8.725$ drivers $\rightarrow$ round up to 9 drivers.

(7) Calculate annual salary:

Cooks: 2,088 paid days × \$17 per hour = \$35,496 per year.
Drivers: 2,088 paid days × \$14 per hour = \$29,232 per year.

(8) Estimate the **salary budget and fringe benefit costs**.

Base salary:	6 cooks × \$35,496	=	\$212,976
	9 drivers × \$29,232	=	\$263,088
	Subtotal	=	**\$476,064**.
Extra pay:	3,328 hours × \$17 × 25%	=	\$14,144
	4,492 hours × \$14 × 25%	=	\$17,472
	Subtotal	=	**\$31,616**
Total salary budget			**\$507,680**.
Benefit costs:			
	Health: 15 staff × \$1,200	=	**\$18,000**
	Pension: 5% × \$507,680	=	\$25,384
	Social Security: 7.65% × \$507,680	=	\$38,838
	WC and UI: 5% × \$507,680	=	\$25,384
	Subtotal	=	**\$107,606**
Total costs			**\$615,286**.

You will be doing these calculations generally in a spreadsheet. The spreadsheet tables with these calculations are at the end of these notes.

Staffing factor: As you can tell from the above examples, the total number of personnel you need to hire is typically more than those working at any one time due to vacation time (and holidays), and operating hours that are longer than the typical employee shift (usually 8 hours). A simple tool for determining the additional staff that need to be added is called a staffing factor, which is just the ratio of the total hours (or work days) needed to provide one additional staff on duty divided by the hours one employee can provide per year. For the sheriff example, to add on more officer on duty all the time will require 8,760 hours per year. One officer can provide 1,920 hours so the staffing factor is 8,760/1,920 = 4.56. In other words, to add one more officer on duty all the time will require hiring 4.56 officers (five fulltime officers). Even for cases where the hours of operation match one employee's shift (5 days per week, 8 hours per day), the staffing factor will be more than one. In the Meals on Wheels case where the employee receives 2 weeks of vacation, then the staffing factor would be 1.45 (365 days/251 days).

2.5 Non-personnel Operating Budget

A significant part of an agency's operating budget may be composed of other expenditures besides personnel. In the case of some services that require expensive capital equipment or facilities, the non-personnel expenditures may comprise over half the budget. Despite their importance, most of these expenditures seldom receive the level of attention devoted to the personnel budget. One exception is travel expenditure, which may be scrutinized closely even though it is usually a very small part of the budget. The potential bad publicity that may arise from an ill-conceived business trip to Las Vegas, for example, overshadows the small size of the travel budget.

Methods for estimating non-personnel can range from simple adjustments for inflation to elaborate systems that link expenditures to the activities using these resources. Lecture 3 will focus on one method, cost accounting, for producing more accurate and defensible estimates of non-personnel costs. Three of the commonly used techniques for estimating non-personnel operating costs include:

(1) An **incremental** method is the simplest approach to estimating the budget. Using an incremental approach last year's budget is used as the base and is increased by some set percentage, usually some measure of inflation. Certainly, this is a good starting place for budget estimates. However, it is difficult using this method to defend changes in your budget or to predict the impact on

expenditures if there is a significant increase or decrease in service levels. An incremental method may make sense for resources that don't vary significantly with service levels. This may also be a cost effective approach for budgeting small miscellaneous expenditures, where detailed analysis is not justified.

(2) **Standard cost method:** Another common technique is for an agency to determine average cost per employee for specific resources. For example, facility space may be estimated on a square footage per employee basis. Assuming a constant rental rate per square foot, it is possible to estimate the facilities budget multiplying the number of employees by the square footage allocation and the rental rate per square foot. While not directly linking costs to output, this approach at least ties budget requests to staffing levels. If staffing reflects changes in demand, and the resource is tied closely to the number of personnel, then the use of a standard cost method may be reasonably accurate.

One problem with such an approach is that it doesn't allow for the possibility for factor substitution in the production of a government service. In other words, this approach assumes that there is no change in how the service is provided over time. For example, if introduction of new computers into an agency is expected to significantly increase the productivity of employees, then we would expect that the money spent on computers would increase relative to that spent on employees. By assuming some fixed computer expenditure per employee, you will "under budget" for computers and "over budget" for personnel using this technique.

(3) **Unit cost estimates:** Unit costs are based on the concept of variable costs, which are costs that vary directly with the activity performed by the agency. For example, it is likely that travel to review nursing home patients will vary directly with the number of nursing homes and patients to be reviewed (as well the average travel distance). Constructing unit costs generally involves three steps: (1) projecting the demand for the agency services (e.g., nursing home patients to visit per year), (2) estimating the number of units of resources consumed per

unit of output (e.g., miles per nursing home patient review), and (3) determining the average cost per unit of input used (e.g., dollars per mile traveled). Calculating the budget involves simply multiplying these three items together. To illustrate this, assume that demand for nursing home patient reviews in FY 2010 is projected to be 9,913 patient reviews. If the mileage per patient remains 33, and the rate per mile is \$0.25 (Table 2.13), then the estimate of the travel budget is:

$$9{,}913 \text{ reviews} \times 33 \text{ miles per review} \times \$0.25 \text{ per mile} = \$81{,}782.$$

2.5.1 Example: Okiana nursing home patient review

Returning to the example at the beginning of the lecture of the ORB, Table 2.12 provides an illustration of an object-of-expenditure budget for the Nursing Home Patient Review Unit.

Staff at this unit reviews the quality and necessity of care for each nursing home resident in the state receiving financial support

Table 2.12. State of Okiana. Object of expenditure budget. Nursing home patient review unit.

	2008 Actual	2009 Appropriation	2009 Est. Actual	2010 Budget Request
Personnel	\$846,800	\$962,339	\$962,339	
Contract Services	\$25,124.99	\$27,834.30	\$28,947.67	
Rent	\$86,400.00	\$99,200.00	\$104,000.00	
Equipment Maintenance	\$6,178.28	\$6,844.50	\$6,844.50	
Telephone	\$14,467.50	\$15,957.10	\$15,586.60	
Supplies/Xerox	\$60,180.98	\$71,948.18	\$75,111.56	
Travel	\$57,206.25	\$78,000.00	\$80,437.50	
Electricity	\$10,687.50	\$15,437.50	\$14,950.00	
TOTAL	\$1,107,045.43	\$1,277,560.10	\$1,288,216.35	

through Medicaid. The reviews are to be carried out in person by a team of physicians, nurses, and social workers implying significant travel. There is also significant documentation involved with each review. Non-personnel expenditures represent approximately 25% of the budget. Other operating expenditure categories in this budget, such as supplies, equipment, travel, utilities, telephone, facilities rental, and contracted services, are common categories found in many budgets.

Exercise: Before proceeding, pull out a sheet of paper and indicate for each object of expenditure in Table 2.12, which of the three methods is the most appropriate. For those items you have marked as unit costs, identify an appropriate measure of inputs per unit of output, and a cost rate per unit of output.

Attached in Table 2.13 is a detailed breakdown of non-personnel expenditures and factors used to calculate the budget. It is surprising given the logic of the factors used in the table, how seldom this type of unit cost breakdown is actually used. The following is a brief discussion of these cost factors:

(1) **Contract services:** It is common for public agencies to hire outside firms to provide services. These can be law firms or consulting firms providing legal, management, technical or financial advice. Since an hourly fee is often charged for these services, it is useful to breakdown the budget into expected hours of service and average cost per hour. If the agency used several different types of these services, then it would be useful to provide this type of breakdown for each type. Ideally, these consulting hours could be linked directly to the amount of service provided by the agency, but this will often be difficult. In this example, the contract services have been for legal fees, which are tied to the number of patient reviews using an average rate (contract hours per review).
(2) **Rent:** Public agencies may or may not be charged rent for the facilities they use depending on accounting practices. If they are, then the rent is typically per square foot of space utilized. Facilities can be an example of a standard costs, since they

Table 2.13. State of Okiana. Detailed breakdown of expenditures by cost factor. Nursing home patient review unit.

Object of Expenditure	2008 Actual	2009 Appropriation	2009 Est. Actual	2010 Budget Request
Nursing Home Patient Reviews	9,153	9,750	9,750	
Personnel Budget	$846,799.94	$962,338.52	$962,338.52	
Total Staff	18	20	20	
Direct Service Staff	14	14	14	
Visits per Direct Service Staff	654	696	696	
Contract Services	$25,125	$27,834	$28,948	
Total Hours	458	488	507	
Hours per Patient Review	0.050	0.050	0.052	
Avg. Rate ($/hr.)	$54.90	$57.10	$57.10	
Rent	$86,400	$99,200	$104,000	
Square Feet (40/person)	720	800	800	
Rate ($/Sq. Ft.)	$120.00	$124.00	$130.00	
Equipment Maint.	$6,178	$6,845	$6,845	
Maint. Hours	275	293	293	
Maint. Hours per Review	0.030	0.030	0.030	
Avg. Rate ($/Hr.)	$22.50	$23.40	$23.40	
Telephone	$14,468	$15,957	$15,587	
Number of Phones (1/person)	18	20	20	
Rate ($/phone)	$41.00	$42.23	$42.23	
Number of L.D. Calls	4,577	4,875	4,680	
L.D. Calls per Review	0.500	0.500	0.480	
Avg. Rate ($/L.D. call)	$3.00	$3.10	$3.15	
Supplies	$45,765.00	$48,750.00	$48,750.00	
Xerox	$14,415.98	$23,198.18	$26,361.56	
Number of Copies	137,295	214,500	243,750	
Copies per Inspection	15.0	22.0	25.0	
Avg Rate ($/copy)	$0.1050	$0.1082	$0.1082	
Travel	$57,206.25	$78,000.00	$80,437.50	
Mileage	228,825	312,000	321,750	
Avg. Rate ($/mile)	$0.2500	$0.2500	$0.2500	
Total Mileage/Patient Review*	25	32	33	
Electricity	$10,688	$15,438	$14,950	
Kilowatt Hours (KWH)	85,500	95,000	92,000	
KWH per Employee	4,750	4,750	4,600	
Avg. Rate ($/KH)	$0.1250	$0.1625	$0.1625	

are usually directly related to the number of personnel. Using historical information on space and personnel, it is possible to estimate average square footage per staff member. In this unit, they have determined that additional personnel require 40 sq.ft. on average. In calculating the budget you take the number of personnel required, multiply this by 40 sq.ft. and you have the required facility space. Facility costs are calculated by multiplying this square footage total times the rental rate per square foot. This method oversimplifies the process given that the director of this unit will get more facility space than a junior clerk for example, but is reasonably accurate if most personnel have a similar requirement for space.

(3) **Equipment maintenance:** A common expense for a public agency is maintenance of its photocopier, computer, fax, and other equipment. Often the agency will have a "service contract" with a local vendor to maintain the equipment. This can be a flat fee and/or an hourly charge depending on the amount of maintenance required. In this case, the unit has a maintenance agreement on its photocopy equipment, which charges by the hour. It is useful in this case to keep track of the number of hours of maintenance and estimate maintenance hours per patient review. This will help you in both estimating future budgets and determining when it is time to replace the equipment (when the maintenance expenditures get too high).

(4) **Telephone:** There is usually a flat monthly charge for local service and a per minute charge for long-distance calls. The number of phones required usually depends on the number of people in the agency, thus this part of the phone bill is best treated as a standard cost. If long distance calls are related directly to the number of patient reviews, then a unit cost method can be used. You can calculate the average number of calls per review, and average cost per call.

(5) **Office supplies/photocopying:** Almost all agencies use some type of office supplies (e.g., paper, pens, paper clips, folders, etc.) While these items seem trivial compared to personnel expenditures, they can add up. This is particularly true for photocopy

supplies! It is useful to try and keep track of photocopy use in your agency and estimate the cost per page to supply the machine. Ideally, the use of the photocopy should be linked to the level of service provided by the agency, in this case the number of copies per patient review. This helps you anticipate future costs and the level of service changes. Office supply costs are an example of a category, which is often estimated with incremental methods — last year's budget times some percent change (usually for inflation).

(6) **Travel:** One area in a public agency's budget besides personnel that commonly gets a lot of attention is travel and usage of publicly supplied motor vehicles. Bad publicity from excess or unjustified travel is the major reason for the level of interest in this area, rather than their importance to the budget. The basic cost factor for automobile usage is mileage. Often travel reimbursements to employees are based on a flat per mile rate. In addition, the expenditures associated with using state-owned vehicles should also be tied to mileage. The next, and often more difficult, step is to link mileage to the level of agency service. In Table 2.13, an average rate of miles per patient review has been calculated based on historical data.

(7) **Electricity:** Utility expenditures, such as electricity, water, sewer, and garbage are another common object of expenditure. Utility expenditures in a service agency, such as electricity, are often directly related to the number of people in the staff. For example, we might expect for electricity that use of heat, light and computers goes up proportionately to the size of the staff, thus an estimate could be made of kilowatt-hours per person. This rate times the number of staff, and the average cost per unit of energy will produce an estimate of the electricity budget.

Lecture 2

Personnel Budget Example for Meals on Wheels
Key Information

Operational information:

Workload	200 Individuals per day
Operational days per year	365 days per year

Personnel information:	**Cooks**	**Drivers**
Length of shift (hours)	8	8
Work days per week	5	5
Weeks per year	52	52
Vacation days per year	10	10
Hourly wage	$17	$14
Fringe benefits:		
Pension contribution	5%	5%
Social security (OASDI)	7.65%	7.65%
Unemployment insurance and workers comp	5%	5%
Health insurance (contribution per employee)	$100	$100
Bonus pay on weekends (percent of base salary)	25%	25%
Productivity rate average (individuals served per employee)	50	35

Lecture 2
Personnel Budget Example for Meals on Wheels
Existing Productivity Rates

Cooks:	**Cooks**	**Drivers**	**Total**
(1) Demand (individuals served per day)	200	200	
(2) Divided by productivity rate (individuals served per employee)	50	35.0	
(3) Equals staff per day	4.00	5.71	
Rounded up	4	6	10
(4) Times operational days equals annual labor time required			
Annual days (shifts) required	1,460	2,190	
Annual hours required	11,680	17,520	
(5) Calculate extra pay shifts (2 weekend days x 52 weeks x required staff)	416	624	
Extra pay hours (8 hours per day)	3,328	4,992	
(6) Annual labor time per employee			
Paid days per year (365 days minus 104 days off)	261	261	
Paid hours per year	2,088	2,088	
Minus vacation days	10	10	
Equals annual work days per employee	251	251	
Actual work hours per employee	2,008	2,008	
(7) Required staff (required labor time divided by labor time per employee)	5.82	8.73	
Rounded up to	6	9	15
(8) Calculate equivalent annual salary:			
(Paid hours times hourly wage)	$35,496	$29,232	
(9) Calculate the Salary Budget:			
Base salary budget (staff times salary)	$212,976	$263,088	$476,064
Bonus Pay	$14,144	$17,472	$31,616
Total Salary Budget	$227,120	$280,560	$507,680
Fringe benefits:			
Health insurance (# of employees x $100 x 12 months)	$7,200	$10,800	$18,000
Pension (5% x total salary budget)	$11,356	$14,028	$25,384
Social Security (7.65% x total salary budget)	$17,375	$21,463	$38,838
UI and WC (3% x total salary budget)	$11,356	$14,028	$25,384
Total Fringe Benefits	$47,287	$60,319	$107,606
(percent of salary budget)	21%	21%	21%
TOTAL PERSONNEL BUDGET	$274,407	$340,879	$615,286

Lecture 3

The Use of Cost Accounting to Improve Budgeting

3.1 Introduction

You were introduced in the last lecture to the basics of preparing a line-item budget. We covered in depth how to calculate the appropriate personnel budget to meet the demand for agency services. However, for non-personnel objects of expenditure, budgeting methods are generally less precise. You could simply multiply last year's budget by a flat inflation rate (incremental method), but then you would run the risk of underestimating what you need, especially if demand for the agency's services have gone up. All non-personnel spending could be tied to full-time personnel in the agency (standard costs), but it would be difficult to reflect productivity improvements in the budget. All non-personnel spending could be tied directly to agency output (unit costs), but this assumes that all spending varies directly with service levels of the agency.

In this lecture, we are going to review a set of tools that can be valuable in budget preparation, especially for non-personnel costs. For most public managers, cost accounting, and cost analysis may appear to be the domain of accountants and financial analysts. What relevance does cost analysis have to the typical director of a public or non-profit agency? We will argue in this lecture that cost accounting should be a basic part of building a budget.

The one constant for public and non-profit managers is change. The external environments facing many public agencies and non-profits are not stable. Economic, fiscal, and political changes can have significant effects on the revenue available to an agency, and the demand for agency services. Pressures to improve productivity and compete with the private sector are becoming the norm rather than the exception. Cost accounting and cost analysis are fundamental tools available to public managers to get control of their budget and to adapt their budget and operation to a changing environment.

The first step in preparing your budget should be to understand what it costs to operate your organization. Without this understanding, you run the risk of not asking for enough resources, especially if the environment that your agency is operating in is changing. The focus of this lecture is to help you categorize your budget into cost factors, that is, develop a cost accounting system. While elaborate cost accounting systems may exist in some agencies, the focus of this lecture will be on creating simple systems that can be implemented with some basic agency data and a spreadsheet. In the next lecture, we will use the results of cost accounting to do cost analysis.

3.2 A Brief Introduction to Financial Accounting

Financial management in government and not-for-profit organizations requires a common language, so that all parts of the financial control function can be compared. That language is the governmental accounting system. Accounting is sometimes called "the language of business," but it is equally important for public and not-for-profit organizations. It is the set of definitions and rules which guide the collection, categorization, and reporting of financial data. Without a common accounting system and language, it would be difficult, if not impossible, to compare the operations of one organization with that of another.

The design of the accounting system depends on the objectives of the financial statements that are being produced. Not surprisingly, a major objective of government accounting is financial control. The accounting system is the principal tool used to assure that money was spent as it was legally mandated. In addition, the accounting system provides information on potential financial problems, such as cash shortfalls and underfunded pension systems. In other words, the accounting system is the means by which agencies themselves and other actors control spending. Much of this financial information is used by outside or government auditors to carry out financial audits of a government agency. These audits focus on legal compliance and control.

3.2.1 Elements of financial data

An accounting system is a collection of financial information, which helps to represent the financial position of the organization. What type of information is commonly collected in government accounting?

3.2.1.1 *Assets*

Assets represent property and legal rights owned by an organization. What are some of the assets of a government? Clearly, some of the most important include:

— cash on hand or short-term investments,
— accounts or revenues receivable, which represent money owed to the government,
— inventory of material and supplies,
— the value of buildings and equipment owned by the government, net of depreciation.

The importance of assets for government accounting is that they indicate the value of the property that government owns and has a responsibility to maintain.

3.2.1.2 *Liabilities*

Liabilities represent legal commitments owed by an organization. What are some of the liabilities of a government? Some common liabilities include:

— accounts payable represent money owed to suppliers,
— wages payable represent money owed to employees,

— deferred revenues represents future revenues for which payment has been received before goods or services are provided,
— bonds payable indicate the principal payments owed to lenders by a government, most of which are typically due in more than one year (long-term debt).

Because liabilities represent future commitments by a government, it is very important to keep accurate records on such commitments. This will be very important in deciding how to manage cash flows and it is far more difficult to adjust payments related to pension and debt.

3.2.1.3 *Net assets/fund balances*

Net assets or fund balances refer to the difference between total assets and total liabilities. In business accounting, the differences between assets and liabilities is usually referred to as equity. A fundamental principal of accounting is that Assets = Liabilities + Fund Balances. So that any increase in assets must be offset by an equal increase in liabilities and/or fund balance. Some portion of fund balances might be reserved for specific uses, referred to as restricted balances and other portions maybe unrestricted.

3.2.1.4 *Revenues and expenses/expenditures*

Revenues represent increases in net assets (or fund balance), while expenses (or expenditures) represent reductions to net assets (or fund balance). Not surprisingly, these categories look very similar to the classification of revenues and expenditures we went over earlier in this course. The accounting system is the principal place where such information is collected.

Revenues: Additions to net assets (or fund balance)

— Property tax
— Sales tax
— User fees
— Intergovernmental revenue (e.g., federal aid)
— Fines
— Investment income

Expenses/Expenditures: Reductions from net assets (or fund balance)

— Personal services
— Contractual services
— Supplies/materials
— Utilities
— Interest
— Depreciation

3.2.2 Measurement focus/basis of accounting

The purpose of an accounting system is called the measurement focus, and the issue of when transactions are recorded in the accounting system is the basis of accounting. The measurement focus for business accounting is measuring equity or measuring profit. This is much different from the measurement focus of government accounting, which is monitoring spending. This difference in measurement focus changes the "basis of accounting" or when transactions are recorded. For example, do you record expenditure for supplies when the money is legally committed, when the supplies are received, when cash is paid or when the supplies are actually used? The answer to this question depends on the basis of accounting, which in turn depends on the measurement focus.

3.2.2.1 *Accrual accounting*

The focus of business accounting is on the maintenance of the equity of the firm. Since equity is simply total assets minus total liabilities, under accrual accounting it is important to keep track of all assets and liabilities. This implies that even the value of long-term assets, such as buildings and equipment, must be recorded and long-term liabilities, such as debt, pension obligations, etc., should be reported when the government incurs the legal commitment to pay them.

In addition, since the accounting system is being used for internal planning purposes, it is important that the financial information help to analyze the profit and efficiency of the firm. For this reason, revenues are recorded when they are earned (the organization is legally entitled to them) and expenses are recorded when the resources are used.

So consider how acquisition and use of supplies are treated in accrual accounting. When the business incurs a commitment to pay for supplies a liability is recognized, usually in an account payable. Usually, this commitment to pay coincides with when the supplies are received and so, the increase in liability would be offset by an increase in assets, namely the new supplies that are on-hand. When cash is actually used to pay for the supplies, a decrease in an asset, namely cash, is recognized and this is offset by a decrease in a liability, accounts payable. When the supplies are used, a decrease in assets is recorded as well as a decrease in equity (net assets). So the expense for supplies is only recorded when the supplies are actually used.

3.2.2.2 *Modified-accrual accounting*

The basic objective of government accounting is spending accountability — that is ensuring that agencies do not spend more than the amount they are authorized to spend in the annual or biannual budget and that expenditures do not exceed the revenues. Thus, the focus of government accounting is on those assets and liabilities, which tend to be short-term in nature — that is, those bills that have to paid soon (i.e., within the current budget period) and assets that can be quickly converted (i.e., in the current budget period) to cash to pay the bills. This implies that a modified accrual accounting system focuses on current resources, that is, assets that are expected to be converted to cash or used up in the current fiscal year and liabilities that need to be paid in the current fiscal year. Although long-term assets and liabilities, such as debt are tracked, they are not part of the primary financial information reported in the fund financial statements.

The emphasis on spending accountability also changes how revenues and expenditures are recorded. As a hedge against non-payment, revenues are recorded only when they are measurable and available. This implies that many taxes are recorded only when the cash is received or will be received shortly. It also implies that debts that are not expected to be collected in the short-term are not recorded as revenue. Expenditures are recorded not when resources are used, but when a legal commitment to pay arises. So in the case of supplies, an expenditure is recorded when the firm incurs the obligation to pay for the supplies, not when the supplies are actually used.

In other words, modified accrual accounting is more conservative in its recording of revenues and expenditures, which is consistent with the governmental interest in assuring a balanced budget.

3.2.2.3 *Cash accounting*

A third type of accounting system, which is used in many smaller governments and not-for-profit agencies (as well as most personal accounting systems!), is called cash accounting. As the name implies, this involves simply recording the cash transactions of government. For example, the only asset is cash and there are no liabilities in a cash system. Revenues and expenditures are recorded when the cash is received or spent.

This type of system has been heavily criticized for governments because it is too myopic in focus. It does not provide any information on long-term commitments of the government. This may lead to serious financial problems in the future if the government has been systematically shifting expenditure burdens on to future generations. A good example is public employee pension systems, in which currently employees are earning benefits that will have to be paid in future years. However, cash accounting is appropriate as a supplement to the other forms of accounting, since it provides valuable information in cash management.

3.2.3 Fund accounting

Another crucial difference between the public and private sector accounting is in the use of different funds in the public sector. Funds are separate fiscal and accounting entities developed to record separate transactions associated with certain government functions. Private business firms, because they are interested in equity maintenance and profit of the whole firm, include all financial information in one fund. Governments on the other hand, because of their interest in accountability, tend to use a number of separate funds. By breaking up government financial information into funds, it is easier to keep track of different types of government activities. In keeping with their stewardship responsibilities, many not-for-profits use separate funds for their internal accounting. However, they do not report these separate funds in their financial statements. Under the new accounting rules, governments may continue to use fund accounting but are also required to prepare government-wide financial statements that combine the separate funds and use accrual accounting methods.

Generally, for governments there are three different types of funds; governmental funds, proprietary funds, and fiduciary funds, as shown in Figure 3.1, we discuss each fund below.

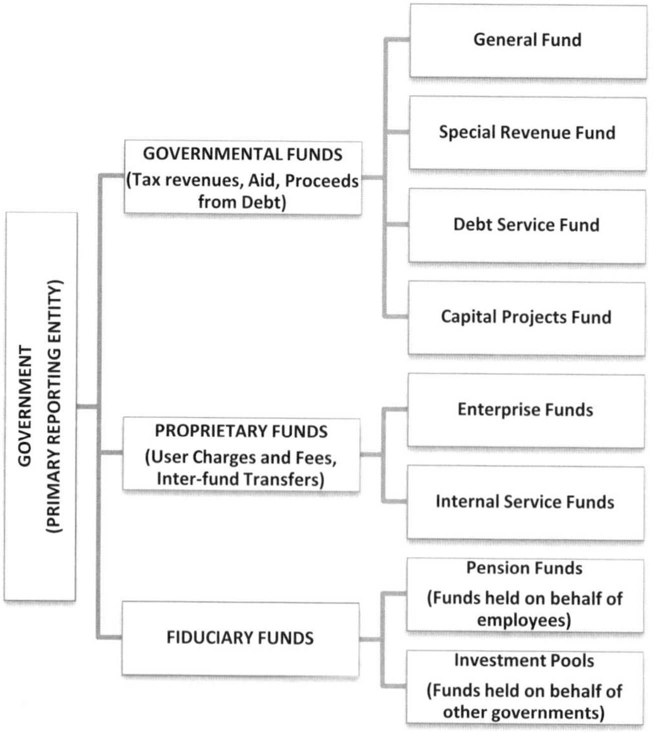

Figure 3.1. Fund structure in government.

3.2.3.1 *Governmental funds*

These are the funds used to account for general governmental operations, which are not like a business firm. For example for a local government, most of the financial information for the fire, police, parks, and recreation departments would be recorded in governmental funds. These funds use the modified accrual basis of accounting.

(a) **General fund:** The largest single fund in most governments is the "general fund". As the name implies, this fund used to account for all revenues, expenditures, assets, and liabilities not required to be reported somewhere else. Most general revenue sources go directly into the general fund and most of the current operations of government departments are recorded in this fund. In addition, there are typically many transfers between other governmental funds and the general fund.
(b) **Special revenue fund:** This is a fund used to account for special revenue sources, which are earmarked for use for specific purposes. An example might be designation of gasoline tax for the "highway trust fund" for the maintenance of state highways.
(c) **Capital project fund:** This is used to account for resources being accumulated for the construction of general government capital projects. For example, cash being saved or borrowed for the construction of government buildings, city streets, etc. would generally be recorded under this fund. In the case of cash that is being saved, revenues to the capital project fund is usually offset by transfers out of, that is, reductions in fund balance in the general fund. In the case of cash that is borrowed, revenue to the capital project fund comes as a transfer from the debt service fund, and is thus, offset by an increase in a liability, for example, bonds payable, in the "debt services" fund.
(d) **Debt service fund:** This is used to account for resources being accumulated to pay for the principal and interest on long-term "general-obligation" debt. The revenues from these payments will generally come from the general fund.
(e) **Special assessment funds:** These are used to account for financing of public improvements, which are to be paid by the

users. An example might be a special assessment of the property tax used to finance sidewalk repair in a neighborhood. This fund will record not only revenues but also the construction costs and debts incurred for construction of this sidewalk.

3.2.3.2 *Proprietary funds*

These funds used to account for government activities that are intended to be self-supporting like a business firm. These activities are supposed to receive their revenue primarily from the sale of their services to customers, either external or internal to the government. Because they operate in a similar manner to for-profit firms, these funds use the accrual basis of accounting.

(a) **Enterprise funds:** These are used to account for agencies of the government, which produce a self-financing service for external customers. Examples might include a city water/sewer system, garbage collection, or public electric utilities. Because this is intended to emulate a private firm, these funds are generally self-contained, including all debt, and capital construction transactions.
(b) **Internal service fund:** This is a parallel type of fund used to record transactions for a government agency, which provides services to other government agencies. Examples might be a motor pool/repair department, computer support, or a print shop. Other government agencies are supposed to be charged the full cost of the service.

3.2.3.3 *Fiduciary funds*

Generally, these are funds used to record either short-term (agency) or long-term (trust) assets held for someone else. These assets do not belong to the government, *per se*, and are not available for government operations. For example, public employee pensions system resources would be accounted for in a trust fund since they will be used to finance the future retirement of public employees. Similarly, if a government temporarily holds tax revenue it has collected on behalf of another government, these resources would be accounted for in an agency fund. The major activity of these funds is recording the value of the assets and liabilities of this trust fund. Fiduciary funds use the accrual basis of accounting.

Below is the fund structure for city of Pembroke Pines, FL *http://www.ppines.com/finance/citybudget-link.html*, which includes basis of accounting (modified accrual or accrual) and measurement focus (current financial resources or economic resources) for FY 2010–2011.

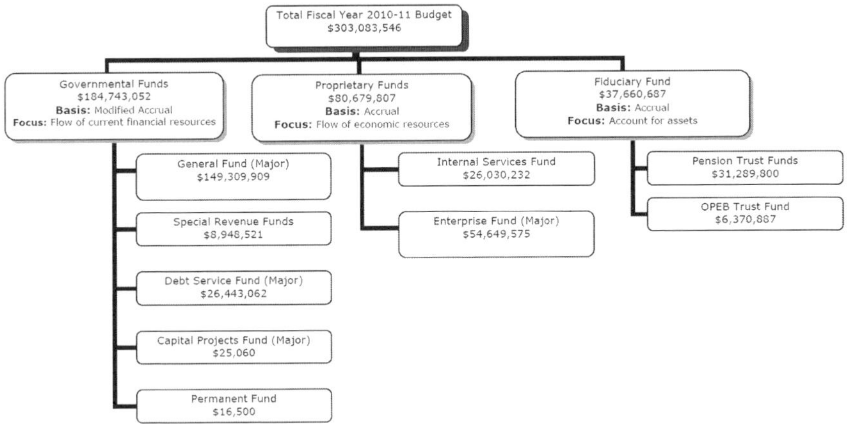

3.3 Cost Accounting

Cost accounting involves the careful classification of financial information from an agency's budget or financial reports into cost categories. Classification may be based on careful analysis of the cost structure of an agency or educated guesses about how spending on a particular resource is related to the major services provided by an agency. The accuracy of the cost analysis is determined primarily by the care with which the cost accounting system is built. However, perfection can be the enemy of the good in cost accounting if the lack of time and resources to do an excellent job are used as excuses not to begin at all. It is better to start by building a simple cost accounting system, and then incrementally improving the accounting system over time as new information is collected.

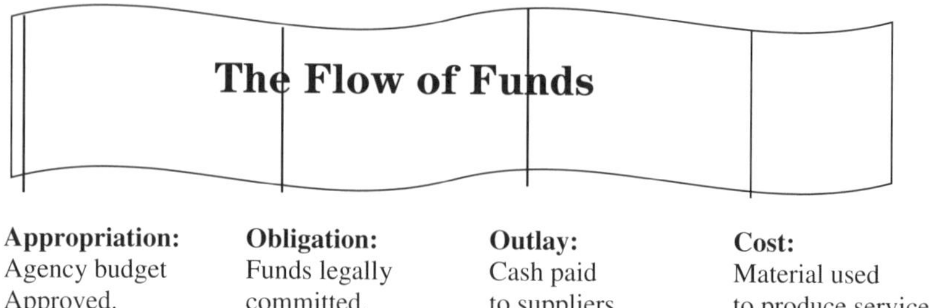

Figure 3.2. Spending definitions and the flow of funds.

3.3.1 Flow of funds

For most of us, the concepts of expenditure, spending, expenses, costs, and outlays all seem like the same concept — when we write the check to pay for something we have purchased. While all of these terms are closely related, in government financial management they have precise definitions. As illustrated in Figure 3.2, they differ by where they fall in the budget process.

3.3.1.1 *Appropriation*

Appropriations represent the spending level approved in the budget. It provides a maximum the agency can spend over the course of a fiscal year for certain functions and/or objects of expenditure. For example, assume that the public works department receives an appropriation of $10,000 for purchase of gravel.

Use: This is the concept used in the budget documents. You have already seen appropriations in the budget documents you have read.

3.3.1.2 *Obligations*

Obligations or encumbrances refer to when the order is placed by the agency for resources. For example, when the public works department orders 100 tons of gravel ($10,000), this money is encumbered or obligated. In modified accrual accounting, an expenditure is recognized and recorded when an obligation is incurred.

Use: Typically used in both budget control during the course of the year and in "modified accrual" accounting to record expenditures.

3.3.1.3 *Outlay*

When the bill is actually paid in cash, it is called an outlay. A "check book" budget records cash outlays and receipts, and is valuable for identifying the "cash flow" of the agency.

Use: This is used in monitoring of an organizations cash flow, as part of a cash management system.

3.3.1.4 *Cost*

Costs are recorded when the resource are actually used or consumed. If 50 tons of the gravel are used in this fiscal year, then the value of this, let us say $5,000, would be recorded as the cost of gravel for this year. In a business (accrual) accounting system, the term expense refers to the costs incurred during a fiscal year.

Use: The focus of this lecture is converting a budget into a cost accounting system. We will discuss how this information will be used in Lecture 4.

While the budget you work with may record anticipated obligations or cash outlays, ultimately the concept of most interest to you in managing your agency is the cost of the resources actually used to produce your agency's services. For operating resources, which are consumed during the course of the year, differences between obligations, outlays, and costs are usually small. Capital assets, on the other hand, may be used over a number of years. Costs refer to the consumption or depreciation of the asset, not to the initial obligation of funds or outlays to pay for the asset. Cost accounting further decomposes costs into several categories, which are important for cost analysis, and which are quite different than the categories typically used in the budget.

3.3.2 Direct versus indirect costs

If possible, we would like to connect all costs incurred by an agency directly to a service provided by the agency. If the agency provides more than one type of service, then we need to be able to divide costs between these different services. As pointed out by Pariser and Brooks, an important distinction in a cost accounting system is between direct costs and indirect costs.[1] To understand the distinction, you first need to understand the idea of a mission or service center.

3.3.2.1 *Mission centers and service centers*

The first step in developing a cost accounting system is determining the major missions of your agency. Mission centers are usually associated with direct services provided to the public, such as garbage collection, and collection of recyclable materials. For some agencies, the main services they provide are to other agencies in the government. For example, a central information and technology services agency may provide a number of services to other government agencies. We generally call these organizations, internal service centers. Almost all organizations have what can be called overhead functions, which typically include the chief executive and her staff. Common overhead functions include finance, personnel, legal services, and strategic planning.

3.3.2.2 *Direct costs*

Any costs that can be accurately assigned directly to mission centers are called direct costs. As noted in Pariser and Brooks, "Direct costs can be easily traced to a particular service."[2] What this means is that provision of the service clearly causes an identifiable reduction or use of a particular resource, such as staff time, supplies, etc. Ideally, all costs would be turned into direct costs, but realistically, overhead functions will exist in all organizations. Direct costs typically include the salaries and fringe benefits of direct service providers, the supplies, equipment and facilities they use, and transportation associated with service provision.

---

[1] David B. Pariser and Richard C. Brooks. 2003. "Determining the Full Cost of Residential Solid Waste Services" in Aman Khan and W. Bartley Hildreth (eds.) Case Studies in Public Budgeting and Financial Management, pp. 519–542. New York: Marcel Dekker, Inc.

[2] *Ibid.*, p. 521.

3.3.2.3 *Indirect costs*

Any costs that cannot be assigned directly to a mission center are called indirect costs. However, there are some important differences between types of indirect costs. As indicated above, overhead is a term usually applied to cost categories, such as central administration, that are difficult to connect directly to a particular service. For a general-purpose government, such as a city, overhead can be at several levels including the mayor's office, the finance department, and director of a city department. In general, the farther down the administrative hierarchy the overhead costs are, the easier it should be to connect them to agency services. The costs associated with internal service centers (i.e., printing services) can potentially be tied directly to services provided if the cost accounting system is designed to identify and record when an internal service center provides services to a particular mission center in a particular agency. One of the goals of a cost accounting system is to turn as many indirect costs into direct costs as possible.

3.3.3 Developing a cost accounting system

Cost accounting systems do not develop overnight. They are usually built in incremental fashion. You start initially with the obvious direct costs, and make simple assumptions about how to assign indirect costs to mission centers. As more information is collected on how resources are used to produce services in the agency, you will be able to move more costs to the direct category. For example, if the central legal staff of the agency charges by the hour for their services, we can collect information on how many hours of legal services are used on average to produce different services. Building a cost accounting system can be broken down into a few basic steps.

3.3.3.1 *Determine mission centers*

The first step in organizing cost information is deciding the basic services provided by the agency. On one level, this seems straightforward. Determine the major services provided to the public — these are your mission centers. However, where services are not homogeneous deciding on what represents mission centers is more difficult. For example, if you work for a non-profit that provides home health care services, how do you decide which services to treat separately and which to lump together? In some cases, this is determined by the revenue sources. If home health care visits are reimbursed by a government agency, that agency may define the different classes of service (e.g., Medicaid recipients versus Medicare recipients). Generally, you want to pick mission centers that are related to the types of decisions, you need make as a manager. In the example of a solid waste department, there might be interest in moving the operation into an "enterprise fund," which would be self-supporting based on fees and grants. Since different fees and grants may be charged for garbage refuse collection, disposal, and recycling, it makes sense to make these the mission centers. Given the time and effort required to organize cost information by mission center, thinking carefully about the appropriate mission centers is very important. It is expensive to correct a poor choice of mission centers.

3.3.3.2 *Determine direct costs*

The next step is to identify direct costs. The agency budget may already breakdown some costs by programs or missions. Using the personnel schedule accompanying the budget, it is usually possible to identify, which personnel are directly providing services to the public. Looking at the detailed worksheets used to calculate the budget, equipment, and supplies used for particular services may be specified. You can ask agency personnel themselves, which items in the budget can be tied directly to particular services. For costs charged to the agency from internal service centers, budget personnel in the service center may have records on service usage by mission center.

3.3.3.3 *Allocate indirect costs*

Once direct costs are determined, the remainder of costs incurred by the agency are by definition indirect costs. If we are going to produce total unit costs by mission center, then indirect costs will have to be allocated to mission centers. One of the key functions of a cost accounting system is the allocation of these indirect costs. In some cases, the allocation methods will be determined by the funding provider. Particularly for non-profit agencies, or local government agencies providing social or health services, many of the services will be reimbursed by a higher-level government. The central government agency providing the funds may provide detailed specifications on indirect cost allocation.

Several indirect cost allocation methods exist, which vary significantly in their sophistication and accuracy. Even the most sophisticated cost accounting system has to make some basic assumptions about how to allocate overhead costs among mission centers. The simplest approach is to develop a series of cost allocation factors, which represent educated guesses about division of indirect costs by mission center. Pariser and Brooks talk about three simple allocation strategies, which any agency can implement.[3]

a. Budget share method: The indirect costs are allocated by the center's share of the direct costs.

   Allocation ratio (%)
   = Center's direct costs/(total costs − indirect costs).
   Center's allocation ($)
   = Allocation ratio × total indirect costs.

b. Personnel share method: The indirect costs are allocated by the center's share of total personnel.

   Allocation ratio (%)
   = Center personnel/total personnel.
   Center allocation ($)
   = Allocation ratio × total indirect costs.

[3] *Ibid.*

c. **Direct method:** The direct method combines both the budget share and personnel share methods by examining for each indirect cost categories what might be the appropriate allocation factor. For some indirect costs (e.g., general administrative costs), the budget share method could be used. For other indirect costs (e.g., payroll and human resources), the personnel share method might be appropriate. For other indirect costs, other allocation factors might capture better the underlying use of the resource. Other examples of cost allocation factors include:
   - Units of service (e.g., clients) could be used as an allocation factor for office supplies, legal fees, and liability insurance, if these items are related to the level of service provided.
   - Data processing budget could be allocated by the relative number of computers within a mission center.
   - Phone/communications budget could be allocated by the relative number of phones within a mission center.
   - Costs of facilities rental and maintenance could be allocated by square footage.

Once a cost allocation factor is determined, we simply calculate the percentage of that factor associated with a particular mission center. This allocation percent is then multiplied by the total budget for the indirect cost category to determine the indirect costs associated with a particular mission center. For example, assume that a road department resurfaces both paved and gravel roads. To allocate the cost of the maintenance facility, we need an estimate of the percent of the facility used for equipment and supplies for paved roads, versus gravel roads. If we estimate 60% of the facility is for paved roads and the total cost of the facility is \$5 million per year, then the facility cost for paved roads is simply 60% × \$5 million = \$3 million. The remaining 40% or \$2 million would be allocated to gravel roads.

3.3.3.4 *Example: Cost analysis at Helping Hands*

To help illustrate the concepts, we will present an example of a hypothetical non-profit agency. The non-profit organization, Helping

Hands, specializes in training for low-income adults to help them acquire the skills needed to find better jobs. In particular, they provide two courses: (1) a basic literacy class to help adults improve their reading comprehension and (2) a training class that describes how to find and retain jobs. Helping Hands hires full time instructors to teach these classes and the organization rents an old school for the classes. In the past, Helping Hands received a reimbursement for the full cost of the program from the state department of social services (DSS). Due to a decline in state revenue, DSS has set a ceiling on the per student reimbursement rate of $325 for the adult literacy class and $500 for the job skills class. You are the newly appointed director of Helping Hands, and you are worried that these reimbursements will not cover costs. You need to estimate the unit costs for each type of class and develop a strategy for cutting costs if necessary. Using the following actual spending information from last year, classify which costs are likely to be direct and which are indirect.

(1) The first step in the process is to **identify the different mission centers**. Remember that mission centers typically reflect the services your agency is providing the public. In this case, the mission centers are fairly obvious since Helping Hands provides two distinct types of classes — literacy education and job skills.
(2) The second step is to identify **direct costs**, those that can be attributed directly to each mission center. Past budgets and personnel tables often provide good information to assist with this classification. In this case, the expenditure table breaks out salaries for literacy trainers from trainers of job skills classes and separates training material expenditures for these two types of classes. No other expenditures have been divided within the actual spending report, but with some additional information, we might be able to attribute some other types of costs directly to each mission center:

    - *Facility lease*: The facility lease is for the whole facility, but if we can identify the square footage used by literacy classes compared to training classes, we might be able to turn a portion of the lease into direct costs. However, if there is excess capacity in the facility, and the lease is for the whole facility, the excess capacity will probably need to be classified as indirect cost.

- *Phone, computers, and internet service*: If the expenditures for these items is on a per item basis (e.g., lease per computer, monthly charge per phone, and internet access), you should be able to determine the allocation of these expenditures to individual employees and mission centers. For example, if all employees have a phone, computer, and internet connection, then the expenditures associated with trainers can be classified as direct costs.
- *Printing costs and lease of the copying machine*: If records are kept on copying and printing costs by type of class, then these expenditures can also be turned into direct costs. While this information may not be available the first year, one of the refinements to the cost accounting system in the future can be to develop record keeping practices to turn as many indirect costs into direct costs as possible.

(3) For indirect costs, the next step is to **develop allocation factors**. The accuracy of the allocation of indirect costs to mission centers will depend on the care with which the cost allocation factors are selected. For the first year, the cost allocation may be partially an educated guess about the distribution of indirect costs. In later years, the allocation can be improved by interviewing staff or keeping records on the use of resources by mission. For example, the director, assistant director, and secretary can be interviewed about what percent of their time is spent on one type of class versus another, and how this changes when students and trainers are added. Some of the logical allocation factors for this type of organization include:

- *Number of students*: For any resources that are linked to the number of students served, the percent of total students by type of class is a good allocation factors. Among the items

Table 3.1. Helping Hands — actual expenditures for fiscal year 2014.

Description	**Actual Spending**	**Description**	**Actual Spending**
1. Salaries and Fringe Benefits:		4. Miscellaneous:	
		Office supplies	$5,500
Director	$70,000	Lease of copy machine	$4,110
Assistant director	$50,000	Phones and internet service	$9,000
Secretary $30,000		Printing and postage	$7,700
Literacy trainers	$300,000	Computer lease	$15,000
Job skills trainers	$420,000	Utilities (electricity)	$15,500
Subtotal	$870,000	Insurance	$6,500
		Miscellaneous	$3,750
2. Training material:		Subtotal	$67,060
Literacy class	$67,500		
Job skills trainers	$52,500	TOTAL	$1,177,060
Subtotal	$120,000		
3. Facility Lease	$120,000		

listed on Table 3.1, the indirect costs that might be allocated by the share of students include:

— printing and postage,
— lease of the copy machine,
— insurance, if it is primarily liability insurance.

It is also possible that the salaries of the administrative staff could be allocated based on students, if they spend most of their time on student affairs. Insurance is a category that can include a number of different types of insurance, such as fire/theft, liability, and health insurance. Ideally, each would be listed separately and allocated by the appropriate factor. For example, fire/theft insurance is usually related to the facility and could be allocated by facility use, while liability insurance may be related to the number of students served. "Contract services" is another composite category that can include a number of types of contracts, such as legal services, financial services, custodial services, etc.

- *Number of trainers*: Since trainers represent the direct personnel hired by the organization, any indirect costs associated with staff support could be allocated by the relative share of direct staff in each mission. This is similar to the personnel share method. If we assume that most of the time for the administrative staff is associated with managing personnel, we could allocate all costs associated with central administration by the relative share of trainers in each mission center.
  - salaries of director, assistant director, secretary,
  - administrative staff computers, phones, and internet service,
  - office supplies.
- *Facility usage*: Most costs associated with the physical facility can be allocated by the percent of the facility used by each mission center. In this case, the square feet used in literacy classes can be compared to the space used for job skills classes. Costs allocated using this factor could include:
  - facility lease,
  - utilities (electricity, gas, water).

Developing allocation factors is an iterative process. You first identify reasonable allocation factors for each cost type, and then try to collect data for these factors. Undoubtedly, alternative factors will have to be developed when data limitations become clear. Assume you have the assistant director of Helping Hands put together a table with basic operating information (Table 3.2).

Under each of the potential allocation factors, the percent in each mission center is indicated. These percentages will be multiplied by the total cost in each indirect cost category to develop estimates of indirect costs by mission center. For example, the total administrative salaries are \$150,000 (includes Director, Assistant Director, and Secretary — see Table 3.1). If they are allocated between the mission centers using the share of trainers in each center, then the estimated costs by mission center are:

- Literacy: 41.7% × \$150,000 = \$62,500.
- Job skills: 58.3% × \$150,000 = \$87,500.

Table 3.2. Helping Hands — basic operating information for FY 2014.

Category	Director's Office	Literacy Classes	Job Skills Classes
Students		1,500	1,050
		58.8%	41.1765%
Staff	3	5	7
		41.7%	58.3%
Classrooms used		5	7
		41.7%	58.3%
Square feet per classroom	700	600	
Square feet used	1,000	3,500	4,200
		45.5%	54.5%
Vacant space (Capacity = 10,000 sq.ft.)	1,300		

For a small organization, such as this non-profit, using simple allocation factors for indirect costs is probably adequate to provide reasonably accurate results. For a large organization with a number of levels of management and support services, use of simple allocation factors may lead to large distortions in cost allocation. A more detailed cost accounting method, such as activity based costing (ABC), may provide significantly more accurate cost estimates.

3.3.4 Classifying costs by how they vary

An important part of cost analysis is determining how costs change with the level of service provided by an agency. Do the costs vary in direct proportion with output? Do they represent one-time startup costs? Do costs tend to vary in lumps as output changes? In many respects, the heart of a cost accounting system is dividing costs into the following categories. These differences are illustrated in Figure 3.3.

1. Variable costs: Costs that vary directly with the level of service provided are called variable costs. As illustrated in Figure 3.3, costs go up at a fixed rate as output goes up. For example, the supplies used to provide hot meals to homebound elders are

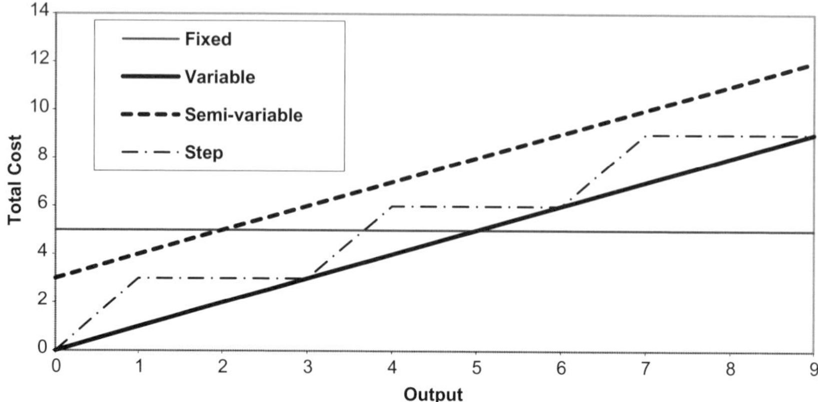

Figure 3.3. Comparison of cost types.

likely to vary in direct proportion to the meals provided. Other examples of variable costs may include gasoline and other travel expenses, utilities used in direct service provision, maintenance of equipment, and wages of part-time personnel directly providing services (e.g., nurses). The key step in identifying and employing variable costs is estimating the rate of resource use in dollar terms per unit of output (e.g., food costs per meal).

Variable costs are closely related to the concept of marginal costs. Marginal costs refer to the increased costs incurred to produce an additional unit of output. Marginal costs will include all variable costs; however, any cost that varies in some fashion with output could be classified as a marginal cost.

2. Fixed costs: Costs that remain fixed no matter how much service is provided are classified as fixed costs, as represented by the horizontal line in Figure 3.3. In the long run, there are generally no fixed costs, since the use of almost every resource can be altered if necessary. For a manager making decisions about a budget this year, some categories of costs may be out of her control to change. For example, if the agency signed a 3-year lease of a facility, then the agency is committed to pay this lease regardless of service demand. As long as the facility is large enough to handle all anticipated levels of agency output, then this facility

cost is fixed for the 3-year period of the lease. After 3 years, the agency will be able to renegotiate the lease or change facilities. Other resources that might be classified as fixed include; salaries and office expenses of administrators and support staff, and fire insurance and utilities for a fixed facility.

Fixed costs are closely related to the concept of sunk costs, which refer to costs that have already been incurred at a previous time, and thus they cannot be changed. Sunk costs often refer to fixed start-up costs, but this does not have to be the case. For example, if the director of the Cleveland Symphony Orchestra hires a marketing consultant to provide advice on effective advertising and marketing campaigns, once incurred this expense is a sunk cost. Whether the orchestra actually uses this advice in future marketing campaigns will not change the fact that the resources have already been expended.

3. Semi-variable costs: Semi-variable costs refer to costs that have a fixed and variable component. For example, the lease contract for copying equipment might include a fixed annual charge, and a charge per page. If the number of pages of copying can be tied to agency output, then this portion can be expressed as a variable cost. As illustrated in Figure 3.3, a semi-variable cost crosses the Y-axis above zero indicating that there is a fixed component. It then goes up at a constant rate indicating a variable component. Besides lease rates on equipment, other examples of semi-variable costs might include utility charges, local phone service, and legal expenses.
4. Step costs: When costs vary with output in discrete jumps or steps, they are referred as step costs. The most common type of step cost is full-time personnel providing direct services. An example would be a full-time garbage collector is paid $30,000 per year and can typically collect 100 tons of garbage a year. Step costs are usually expressed as dollars per step, $30,000 per 100 tons. Step costs are fixed costs on a step, but vary once you move to a new step. As long as the number of tons remains under 100, the cost for a collector is $30,000 regardless of the number of tons. If the number of tons exceeds 100, an additional employee

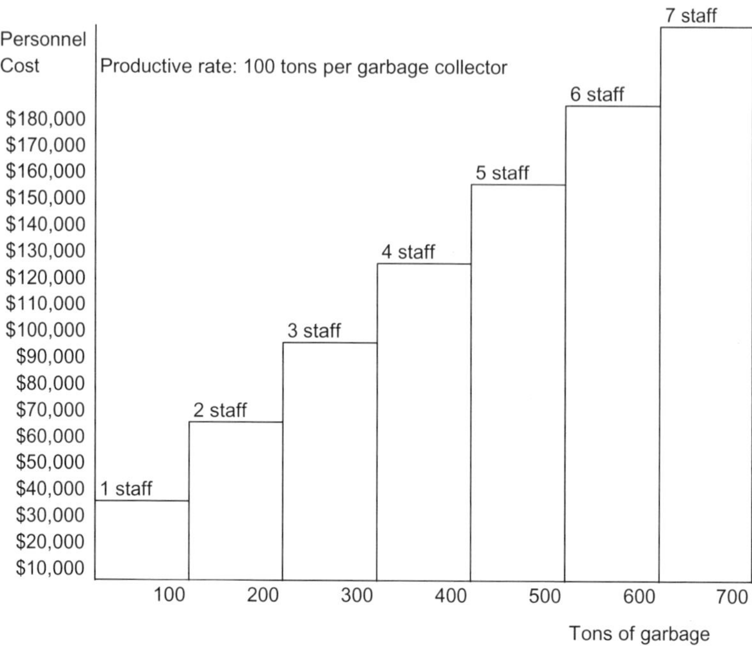

Figure 3.4. Illustration of step costs for garbage collectors.

will have to be added. Figure 3.4 illustrates this example of step costs. Any costs that are tied directly to full-time personnel, such as facilities, utilities, phones, uniforms, etc., may be best classified as a step cost.

Classifying costs into fixed, variable, semi-variable, and step costs, is a learning process. The more you understand about how resources are utilized in the production of your agency's services, the easier it is to classify types of costs into these categories. Important steps in the classification process includes the following.

3.3.4.1 *Defining the units of output or activities provided by the agency*

The output or service levels of a public or non-profit agency may be less easily defined and measured than in the private sector. It is best to start with the principal goals of the agency and identify quantitative measures of these goals that can be measured accurately, and are acceptable to agency personnel. You should have at least one output measure for each mission center. For a social service agency output might be expressed as the number of clients served, or more precisely the time spent serving clients (e.g., client hours). For public works departments, output can often be expressed as units of maintenance provided, for example, road miles paved. Output measures for public safety agencies may be more difficult to identify, but important activities can often be measured. Examples might include the number of crimes investigated, hours of patrol provided, fire alarms responded to. The output or activity measures identified should reflect the use to which cost analysis will be employed. If cost analysis will be used to set user fees, then the output should measure the services to be charged for, such as tons of garbage. If cost analysis will principally be used to improve internal efficiency, then internal activity measures, such as number of cases reviewed, may be more appropriate.

3.3.4.2 *Collecting cost data*

The heart of a cost accounting system is the collection of cost information. While the introduction of integrated accounting software packages with cost accounting modules facilitates the collection of cost information, most cost data are available from operating and capital budgets, combined with some simplifying assumptions. In addition, it is typically necessary to involve the employees in your organization directly in developing the cost categories and developing data collection systems, since they are often the most knowledgeable about how resources are used.

(a) *Operating costs*: Actual spending data from the previous year in a line-item operating budget generally provides a good approximation for operating costs. While there can be some differences between committed operating expenditures (expenditures in modified accrual accounting) and the resources used during the year (costs or expenses in accrual accounting), these differences are usually small. It is important to separate true operating costs from items in an operating budget, such as debt service or equipment lease payments, that are related to capital costs.

(b) *Capital costs*: Measuring capital costs are more difficult, because by definition they span multiple years. Ideally, the capital costs would reflect the actual amount of the capital asset that was used during the year, commonly called depreciation. If estimates of depreciation do not exist for an asset, reasonable assumptions can often be made about an asset's useful life, and salvage value at the end of its life. If we assume, for example, that a fire station has a life of 40 years and a salvage value of 20%, then annual depreciation would be equal to 2% ((1 – 0.20)/40 years) times the purchase price of the asset. For leased equipment, the lease rate may be a reasonable approximation for capital costs. If the capital asset is financed with a loan, then the debt service payments (principal and interest) may be a reasonable measure of capital costs, especially if the cost accounting system is used to set user fees.

3.3.4.3 *Classify inputs*

Classify inputs in the line-item budget into variable, fixed, semi-variable, and step cost categories. The first attempt at classification will often be based on your own knowledge of agency operations and educated guesses. The initial classifications can be refined with interviews of agency staff, and use of historical spending data.

3.3.4.4 *Develop cost rates*

Develop cost rates for all types of costs except fixed costs.

(a) *Variable costs*: Rates for variable costs can be calculated by simply taking the spending on this resource from the previous year divided by the units of output or activity actually provided. The rate expressed as dollars per unit of output can be multiplied by projected workload to estimate the required budget.

$$\text{Variable cost rate} = \text{Variable spending/units of output.}$$

(b) *Step costs*: It is first important to identify the length of the step. How much output can be provided by one unit of the input? The output–input ratio is commonly called a productivity rate. For example, how many students can be served by one teacher without a serious reduction in the quality of teaching? The cost or price per unit of input, such as teacher's salary, represents the cost for each step.

$$\text{Productivity rate} \\ = \text{Total output/number of direct service providers.}$$

(c) *Semi-variable costs*: The rates for semi-variable costs are usually set by outside contractors. Begin by looking at the contracts or bills provided to the agency, and try to identify if there is a fixed and variable component. The variable component will usually be expressed as dollars per unit of input, for example, $0.05 per page of copying. If you can estimate the number of copies typically required per unit of output, then a variable cost rate can be calculated.

$$\text{Semi-variable cost rate} = \text{Variable part of cost/output.}$$

3.3.4.5 *Example: Cost analysis at Helping Hands*

Once the costs have been divided into direct and indirect costs, the next step in developing a cost accounting system is to determine how costs vary with output. An important part of this is developing cost and productivity rates. During the first year, the administrative staff of Helping Hands will not have time to do a detailed review of costs. But using some basic finance and operating information, reasonable initial estimates can be made.

Defining units of output

In the case of a non-profit providing educational service, the most intuitive output measures are the numbers of students attending a particular class. Simple counts of students do not, of course, tell us anything about the quality of the classes, or how much students learned. More refined measures might include the number of students passing a basic literacy examination and the number of students obtaining a job that matches their skill level. Eventually, both student counts and quality measures could be included in the cost analysis.

Collecting cost data

The expenditure information provided in Table 3.1 provides a good place to start in developing cost rates. For facilities, we can assume that the facility lease is approximately equal to annual facility cost. It is important in looking at leases, service contracts, and utility bills to determine if the contract establishes a semi-variable cost by requiring a fixed payment, and then additional payments tied to input usage. Looking at existing contracts, the assistant director identifies the following leases and charges that are relevant for cost analysis:

— phone: $25 per month per phone for local service,
— internet connection: $25 per month per connection,
— lease of copy machine: $200 per month + $0.03 per page copied,
— lease of computer: $1,000 per year per computer.

Classify inputs

Using expenditure records and discussions with agency staff, determine how each input type varies with output. Look at Table 3.1, and place each input into a category.

(a) *Variable costs*: Supplies used for class, printing and postage if related to the number of students served.
(b) *Step costs*: Since the trainers are fulltime, they will be step costs. Any costs directly associated with personnel, such as phones, computers, internet connections, utilities, and health insurance could also be step costs.
(c) *Semi-variable costs*: Remember, these costs have both a fixed and variable portion. After looking through the lease contracts and utility bills, you determine that the copy machine is a semi-variable cost. All the other leases either are step costs, because

they are tied to the number of people, or are associated with a fixed cost, such as administrative personnel in the agency.

(d) *Fixed costs*: In the long run, almost all costs vary to some degree. Initially, some costs may be classified as fixed, because of a lack of information on how the costs vary. As the agency gains more experience with cost accounting, additional information may be collected on how costs vary. Using Table 3.1, it is reasonable to treat the following costs as fixed for this year:

   (1) Administrative staff will remain relatively stable over most enrollment levels.
   (2) The factors tied to this staff, computers, telephones, and internet access will also be treated as fixed.
   (3) Office supplies and miscellaneous costs may be treated as fixed initially until better information is acquired.
   (4) The facility lease could be treated as either a fixed cost or step costs. Given that Helping Hands has to pay a fixed lease, regardless of how much they use the facility and there is excess capacity, this suggests that the lease is a fixed cost.
   (5) Utilities could be treated as fixed this year since they are linked to facilities. In the future, you should try to get more detail on types of utility costs and how they might be linked to the number of classes provided (or the number classrooms used).

Develop cost rates

For fixed costs, there is no need for cost rates; costs do not change with volume. For the other types of costs, we need to develop rates that connect the cost of the resource with the volume of service provided.

(a) *Variable costs*: The key assumption behind variable costs is that costs vary in proportion with output. In other words, there is a linear relationship between costs and output that can be expressed in a simple cost ratio, cost per unit of output. To calculate the rates, either we can use contractual information that defines this relationship exactly or we can calculate a rate from historical data. We have identified classroom material, and printing as variable costs. For classroom materials, we have expenditure data by type of class allowing us to calculate direct costs. The rates for classroom material would be:

— Literacy class: $67,500/1,500 students = $45 per student.
— Job skills class: $52,500/1,050 students = $50 per student.

For printing and postage, we do not have separate information for the two different types of classes. Until we have more details on printing use by class type, it is technically an indirect cost. If we allocate these costs by the share of students in each class, this is equivalent to assuming that the cost rate is the same for each class.

— Printing rate: $7,700/2,550 students = $3.02 per student.

Whether we classify printing as a direct cost or indirect cost is not an important decision. What is important is identifying it as a variable cost. It is not a bad idea to keep printing in the indirect cost category as a reminder that we need to collect more specific information on printing costs by type of class.

(b) *Step costs*: The key rate for step costs is the productivity rate since it defines the length of the step. The productivity rate combined with the cost per unit of input, such as annual salary, provides the cost associated with each step. As we discussed in Lecture 2, productivity rates are important for calculating personnel budgets. Average rates can be found using historical information on total output and direct personnel. For the literacy class, we would calculate the productivity as the number of classes taught per instructor per year.

Literacy classes: Calculate the average students per trainer:

1,500 students/5 instructors = 300 students per instructor.

Job training classes: Calculate the average students per trainer:

1,050 students/7 instructors = 150 students per instructor.

Even though the step is expressed as the number of students that one trainer can serve each year, it can be broken down into average class sizes multiplied by the number of classes a trainer teaches. It is common in teacher union contracts, for example, to negotiate over both class sizes and the number of classes per year a teacher is responsible for. It may be possible to look for benchmark productivity rates from other similar programs to determine whether trainers can adequately handle more students. For example, let us assume that state benchmark is 375 students per trainer for literacy classes and 180 for job skills classes. Productivity rates are listed in Table 3.3. The salary and fringe benefits for each trainer is $60,000 on average, which represents the costs associated with each step.

For other step costs linked directly to personnel, the relevant rates are the number of inputs per person. For example, each trainer has a phone, computer, and internet connection in their classroom.

(c) *Semi-variable costs*: The only cost identified as a semi-variable cost is the lease of the copy machine. The terms of the lease are: $200 per month + $0.03 per page copied. The $200 per month ($2,400 per year) is treated as a fixed cost. If we can link the number of copies to the number of students served, then the second part of the lease would be a variable cost.

Table 3.3. Helping Hands — key operating rates for FY 2014.

Category	Director's Office	Literacy Classes	Job Skills Classes
Productivity rates:			
Average students per trainer		300	150
Maximum students per trainer		375	175
Other rates:			
Computers per employee	1	1	1
Phones per employee	1	1	1
Internet lines per employee	1	1	1
Photocopies per year	57,000		
Photocopies per student	22.35		

Table 3.4. Helping Hands — key cost rates for FY 2014.

Category	**Director's Office**	**Literacy Classes**	**Job Skills Classes**
Reimbursement rate from the state		$325	$500
Cost rates:			
Material cost/student		$45.0	$50.0
Salaries per trainer		$60,000	$60,000
Lease of copy machine			
Per year	$2,400		
Per copy	$0.03		
Per student	$0.67		
Annual lease per computer	$1,000	$1,000	$1,000
Internet service provider per connection	$300	$300	$300
Local phone service per phone	$300	$300	$300
Printing costs/student	$3.02	$3.02	$3.02

Using basic operating information, we can estimate the variable cost rate;

57,000 copies/2,550 students = 22.35 copies per student.
22.35 copies × $.03 per copy = $0.67 per student.

Cost rates are summarized in Table 3.4. Given that the cost accounting system will probably be constructed using a spreadsheet, tables with basic operating information (Tables 3.2 and 3.3) and a table with a summary of rates can be linked directly to the unit cost tables to increase the flexibility of the budget process. Projections of future costs and sensitivity analysis can be performed by changing the information in these tables.

3.3.5 Improvements to cost accounting system

In summary, the central function of a cost accounting system is the collection and categorization of cost information. A cost accounting system will draw most of its information from other financial documents, particularly budgets and financial reports. Financial information is combined with basic operating information from the agency to produce productivity rates and cost rates that connect costs to the output or activities of the agencies. The classification may be based initially on educated guesses and simplifying assumptions. In future years, the accuracy of the system can be improved in several ways.

- We can try turning most indirect costs into direct costs. Using the Helping Hands example, we could collect information on the allocation of administrative staff time by type of class. We could ask the printer to itemize printing costs by type of material printed, or add a meter to the copy machine to track copies by account.
- Costs, such as insurance, can be broken down into types of insurance and then information collected on what affects variation in these costs.
- For fixed costs, we can try to link them to the output or activities of the agency. It is likely that office supplies, utilities, and miscellaneous expenditures will change to some degree as output changes. Facility costs will certainly change if there is a significant increase or decrease in students served by the agency. The agency could look at alternative facilities and lease arrangements.

While certainly improvements can be made to the accuracy of the cost accounting system, the benefits of these improvements need to be balanced against their costs. For example, asking staff to keep track of time spent on particular projects can be costly in staff time and morale. Professional staff may resent close tracking of their activities. Establishing new data collection systems for printing, copying, phone usage, etc. may be more expensive than the improvements in accuracy are worth. For small agencies, including most non-profits, elaborate cost accounting system is probably not warranted. The objective of this lecture is to show that basic systems using spreadsheets are feasible with existing information and some basic assumptions.

3.3.6 Estimating unit costs

The most direct application of cost analysis is to estimate total costs for each mission center and tie all costs except fixed costs to the output of the agency. Careful cost analysis should simplify and improve the accuracy of the budget process. Simply estimate the service demand for each mission centers and determine if any of the cost or productivity rates have changed. Plug this new information, into your cost accounting system, and if this system is set up in a flexible fashion, your budget estimates will be generated automatically. The more care that is taken in the development of the cost rates, the easier it will be to defend the budget, since you will have much better visibility on where the money is going. Also, as we will illustrate later, this is foundation from which you can carry out various types of sensitivity analysis.

One of the most common uses of cost information is to generate estimates of total costs per unit of output for each mission center, commonly called unit costs. Unit costs can be used to set user fees for public enterprises, or may be necessary in requests for reimbursement.

3.3.7 Example: Cost analysis at Helping Hands

Using the Helping Hands example, the agency is going to be reimbursed per student served. The unit cost will help to identify whether the agency will cover its costs for one or both mission centers. Thus, unit costs are a good place to start in identifying where cost reductions may need to take place. The unit cost table for Helping Hands is presented in Table 3.5. Some of the calculations behind the table include the following (note small differences in calculations due to rounding of percentages):

Direct costs:

Training material:

Literacy classes: 1,500 students × \$45 = \$67,500.

Job skills classes: 1,050 students × \$50 = \$52,500.

Table 3.5. Helping Hands — estimated unit costs for FY 2014.

Category	Cost Type	Allocation Factor	Literacy Classes	Job Skills Classes	Total Costs
Students per year			1,500	1,050	2,550
Required trainers			5	7	12
Direct Costs:					
Training material	Variable		$67,500	$52,500	$120,000
Salaries of trainers	Step		$300,000	$420,000	$720,000
Phones and internet service	Step		$3,000	$4,200	$7,200
Computer lease	Step		$5,000	$7,000	$12,000
Total direct costs			$375,500	$483,700	$859,200
Direct per student			*$250.3*	*$460.7*	*$336.9*
Indirect Costs:					
Administrative staff					
Salaries	Fixed	Trainers	$62,500	$87,500	$150,000
Phones/internet service	Fixed	Trainers	$750	$1,050	$1,800
Computer lease	Fixed	Trainers	$1,250	$1,750	$3,000

(Continued)

Table 3.5. (*Continued*)

Category	**Cost Type**	**Allocation Factor**	**Literacy Classes**	**Job Skills Classes**	**Total Costs**
Facilities-related					
Facility lease	Fixed	Square feet	$54,545	$65,455	$120,000
Utilities	Fixed	Square feet	$6,458	$9,042	$15,500
Other overhead					
Lease of copy machine	Semi-variable	Students	$2,418	$1,692	$4,110
Printing and postage	Variable	Students	$4,529	$3,171	$7,700
Office supplies	Fixed	Trainers	$2,292	$3,208	$5,500
Insurance	Fixed	Students	$ 3,824	$2,676	$6,500
Miscellaneous	Fixed	Students	$2,206	$1,544	$3,750
Total indirect costs			$140,772	$177,088	$317,860
Indirect per student			*$93.8*	*$168.7*	*$124.7*
TOTAL COST			$516,2/2	$660,788	$1,177,060
TOTAL COST PER STUDENT			*$344.2*	*$629.3*	*$461.6*
REIMBURSEMENT RATE			$325.0	$500.0	$397.1
TOTAL REVENUE			$487,500	$525,000	$1,012,500
SURPLUS/(DEFICM)			**(28,772)**	**(135,788)**	**(164,560)**
DEFICIT PER STUDENT			*(19.18)*	*(129.32)*	*(64.53)*
PERCENT OF SPENDING			−5.6%	−20.5%	−14.0%

Salaries of trainers:

Literacy classes: 1,500 students/300 students per trainer = 5 trainers.

5 trainers × \$60,000 per trainer = \$300,000.

Job skills classes: 1,050 students/150 students per trainer = 7 trainers.

7 trainers × \$60,000 = \$420,000.

Phones and internet service:

Literacy classes: 5 trainers × \$600 per trainer = \$3,000.

Job skills classes: 7 trainers × \$600 = \$4,200.

Computer lease:

Literacy classes: 5 trainers × \$1,000 per trainer = \$5,000.

Job skills classes: 7 trainers × \$1,000 = \$7,000.

Indirect costs:

Administrative salaries (allocated by number of staff):

Literacy classes: \$150,000 × 41.7% of staff = \$62,500.

Job skills classes: \$150,000 × 58.3% of staff = \$87,500.

Phones/internet service

Literacy classes: \$1,800 × 41.7% of staff = \$750.

Job skills classes: \$1,800 × 58.3% of staff = \$1,050.

Computer lease:

Literacy classes: \$3,000 × 41.7% of staff = \$1,250.

Job skills classes: \$3,000 × 58.3% of staff = \$1,750.

Facility lease (allocated by square feet):

Literacy classes: \$120,000 × 45.5% of square feet = \$54,545.

Job skills classes: \$120,000 × 54.5% of square feet = \$65,455.

Utilities:

Literacy classes: \$4,110 × 45.5% of staff = \$2,418.

Job skills classes: \$4,110 × 54.5% of staff = \$1,692.

Lease of copying machine (allocated by students):

Total lease cost = \$2,400 (fixed) + \$0.67 × 2,550 students = \$4,110.

Allocation by students:

Literacy classes: \$4,110 × 58.8% of students = \$2,418.

Job skills classes: \$4,110 × 41.2% of students = \$1,692.

Printing and postage (allocated by students):

Literacy classes: \$7,700 × 58.8% of students = \$4,529.

Job skills classes: \$7,700 × 41.2% of students = \$3,171.

Office supplies (allocated by number staff):

Literacy classes: \$5,500 × 41.7% of staff = \$2,292.

Job skills classes: \$5,500 × 58.3% of staff = \$3,208.

Insurance (allocated by students):

Literacy classes: \$6,500 × 58.8% of students = \$3,824.

Job skills classes: \$6,500 × 41.2% of students = \$2,676.

Misc (allocated by students):

Literacy classes: \$3,750 × 58.8% of students = \$2,206.

Job skills classes: \$3,750 × 41.2% of students = \$1,544.

Summary:

Direct costs per student:

Literacy classes: \$375,500/1,500 = \$255.3.

Job skills classes: \$491,183/1,050 = \$460.7.

Indirect costs per student:

Literacy classes: \$140,772/1,500 = \$93.8.

Job skills classes: \$177,088/1,050 = \$168.7.

Total costs per student:

Literacy classes: \$344.2.

Job skills classes: \$629.3.

The unit cost table can be reorganized in the form of the budget so that the budget document could be linked directly to the cost accounting system. Given that the form of the budget may be set by a budget office under the guidance of the chief executive or legislative body to accomplish certain objectives, the agency will usually have to recast the information in Table 3.5 into this form. One of the advantages of cost analysis is that the presentation of information can be in both line-item and program (mission centers) form.

The director of Helping Hands can use the information in Table 3.5 to check on whether the agency will be able to cover costs with the new reimbursement rates of \$325 per literacy student and \$500 per job skills students. It is clear that the director is facing a budget crisis. The cost per literacy student is $20 too high, and for job skills, the cost-reimbursement gap is 20.5% of spending ($129 per student)! Some serious measures will have to be taken to reduce per student costs.

Before the director proceeds with a cost-cutting program, it is useful to do some sensitivity on the indirect cost allocation factors, to see how sensitive the results are to different assumptions. Table 3.6

Table 3.6. Helping Hands — estimated unit costs for FY 2014 — different allocation factors.

Category	Literacy Classes	Job Skills Classes
Allocation by trainers		
Total indirect costs	$132,442	$185,418
Indirect costs per student	$88.3	$176.6
Total cost	$507,942	$669,118
Total cost per student	***$338.6***	***$637.3***
Deficit per student	–$13.6	–$137.3
Allocation by square feet		
Total indirect costs	$144,482	$173,378
Indirect costs per student	$96.3	$165.1
Total cost	$519,982	$657,078
Total cost per student	***$346.7***	***$625.8***
Deficit per student	–$21.7	–$125.8
Allocation by students		
Total indirect costs	$186,976	$130,884
Indirect costs per student	$124.7	$124.7
Total cost	$562,476	$614,584
Total cost per student	***$375.0***	***$585.3***
Deficit per student	–$50.0	–$85.3
Allocation by direct costs		
Total indirect costs	$138,916	$178,944
Indirect costs per student	$92.6	$170.4
Total cost	$514,416	$662,644
Total cost per student	***$342.9***	***$631.1***
Deficit per student	–$17.9	–$131.1

illustrates what the per unit cost by mission center with different cost allocation factors.

3.3.8 In-class exercise: Heartland county road department

You have taken over as the director of the Heartland county road department in the midst of turmoil. The previous director was forced to resign after a serious budget deficit in the previous year. The budget deficit was precipitated by a drop in the state reimbursement rate for maintenance of county roads. Previously, the state had been willing to reimburse up to $6,000 per mile for gravel roads, and $9,000 per mile for paved roads. After a report by the state auditor indicated gross inefficiencies in many county road departments, the state department of transportation decided to cut rates to force counties to become more efficient. The previous director ran a pretty "loose ship", and did not have good visibility on what it actually cost to maintain roads. He and the county executive were caught completely off guard when the road department had a deficit of over 25%.

The county executive hired you precisely because of your background in finance and budgeting, and she expects you to clean up this mess, and eliminate deficits while maintaining the level of service. After digging through piles of disorganized papers, you are able to put together some basic operating information on the department for last year, which you summarized in the attached table. Using this information, you have laid out a series of tasks that you need to complete before you can get a handle on the road department budget.

(a) You need to first identify the mission centers for this department, and the logical output measures.
(b) You then need to determine, which costs you can link directly to a mission center and which are indirect.
(c) The next step is to determine how each cost category varies with output by identifying fixed, variable, step, and semi-variable costs.

(d) Using this information, calculate appropriate cost rates and develop a unit cost table with each mission center. How large is the deficit compared to the state reimbursement rate?
(e) Assume staff can work up to the maximum productivity rate — by how much does this reduce the deficit?
(f) Do a flexible budget for Heartland county road department, assuming that output varies by 20% above and below last year's output level. What happens to unit costs and the deficits? (You can assume that the indirect fixed costs for each mission center remain the same as in part d).
(g) What would happen to the amount of miles of gravel roads maintained if there was a 20% cut in the budget for gravel roads. (You can assume that the indirect fixed costs for gravel roads remain the same as in part d).
(h) Determine what would happen to per unit and total deficits if the county dropped maintenance of paved roads. (You can assume that the state department of transportation will take it over.) Does this reduce the deficit per unit and in total?
(i) If a private contractor agreed to take over paving roads for $7,000 per mile, should the department accept this contract?

Heartland Road Department Cost Analysis

Mission: To maintain the county's 500 miles of roads which are both paved and gravel. Construction of new roads is carried out by the state.

Revenues: The state department of transportation will reimburse the county at a fixed rate per mile.

Personnel: All personnel are fulltime and work 225 days/year on average. All maintenance personnel receive the same salary and fringe benefits, which total $50,000 per maintenance employee in FY 2013.

Workload in 2014: The County Legislature has proposed that the department should maintain 120 miles of gravel roads and 85 miles of paved roads in 2014.

The following is a summary of the activity and cost information that was put together for FY 2013. For simplicity, no inflation was assumed in the initial cost analysis for FY 2014.

Heartland Road Department
FY 2013 Actual Cost Data

Director	$85,000	
Secretary	$45,000	
Maintenance facility (depreciation)	$400,000	
Other information:	***Gravel road***	***Paved road***
Supplies expenditures	$125,000	$140,000
Miles repaired	100	70
Personnel (FTE)	3	4
Equipment lease (FY 2013):		
Fixed charge/month	$3,500	$5,000
Variable rate/mile	$450	$850
State reimbursement/mile	$5,750	$7,250
Benchmark miles per person per day	0.17	0.10
Benchmark miles per person per year	38.25	22.5

Lecture 4

Getting Control of Your Budget: The Use of Cost Analysis in Budgeting

4.1 Introduction

In the last lecture, we saw how a budget can be converted into a cost accounting system that produces estimates of the full cost per unit of output for the mission centers of the agency. In this lecture, we will show how the cost accounting system can be used to do various types of analyses that can be valuable in budgeting and financial management decisions, what is commonly called cost analysis. The tools of cost analysis are valuable for:

- Developing budgeting systems that are easily adaptable to changing service demands. A detailed analysis of your agency's costs can also help a manager to defend their budget in front of the budget office or legislative body;
- Determining the effects of possible productivity improvements or cost reductions on the budget;
- Estimating required user fees to breakeven, and designing a user fee structure that matches the cost structure of the agency;
- Evaluating the addition or deletion of a service provided by the agency;

- Deciding whether to carry out certain functions (e.g., computer maintenance) internally, or whether to contract these out to other organizations.

4.2 Cost Analysis

Ultimately, cost accounting systems are built for management purposes, to help you as a manager in preparing your budget and managing your agency. There are a number of different applications of information provided by a cost accounting system, which fall under the heading of cost analysis. In this lecture, we will cover a few of these and illustrate them with the Helping Hands example.

4.2.1 Estimating unit costs

As we covered in Lecture 3, one output of a cost accounting system is a unit cost table that captures the full cost per unit of output for each mission center. As we saw for the Helping Hand example (see Table 3.5 in Lecture 3), the organization would not be able to cover its costs with the new reimbursement rates. The deficit is particularly large for the job skills classes.

4.2.2 Flexible budgets

Most budgets are for fixed or static service levels. You estimate the most likely service level and then prepare your budget based on this. This is acceptable where service levels are generally fixed or if variable and step costs are only a small share of total costs. However, if there is significant variation in the demand for the agency's services and variable costs are important, then a "static budget" provides you with no visibility on the effect of varying service levels on the budget. Static budgets are also not very conducive to analyzing why actual budgets differ from what was budgeted. If the agency is experiencing volatile service demand, static budgets can be particularly problematic.

The use of flexible budgets is a way to address these weaknesses. A flexible budget estimates what the agency budget would be at different service levels. This is based on the division of costs into those that are fixed and those that vary with output. A key requirement for flexible budgeting is that you can measure the level of service activity. You generally will want to prepare a flexible budget for each mission center and then aggregate them for the whole agency.

Flexible budgets are a direct application of cost analysis. For each mission center, a range of service levels are selected that encompass the range of possible service demand levels. If historical information exists on service demand, then it is possible to use various forecasting tools to determine both the trend in service demand (if there is any), and the average variation around the trend. Once the range of output is determined for each mission center, different budgets are calculated using the classification of costs, and productivity and cost rates in the cost accounting system.

- *Variable costs*: Calculating variable costs involves simply multiplying output by the variable cost rate (cost per unit of output).
- *Semi-variable costs*: Remember that semi-variable costs involve both a fixed portion and a variable portion. Treat the variable portion in a similar fashion to variable costs.
- *Step costs*: Step costs are fixed along a range of output, called a step. The length of the step is determined by a productivity rate. To calculate the number of resources needed take each level of output, divide by the productivity rate, and round up. If the resulting number is only slightly above a whole number, then a decision can be made whether a small productivity improvement is possible.
- *Fixed costs*: By definition fixed costs do not vary with the level of service output. Thus, use the same levels of fixed costs originally allocated to each mission center.

NOTE: *It may seem strange not to allow the fixed costs to be reallocated since the units of output and staff change. It is certainly possible to allow for reallocation of these costs but since the overall cost to the organization has not changed, reallocating fixed costs* *across mission centers will have no impact on the bottom line cost for the operation. It also can obscure what the change in output has done to those costs that do vary. If fixed costs are truly fixed, then they do not change with changes in output.*

Example: Helping Hands

We are going to illustrate the concept of a flexible budget for Helping Hands example. Assume that the non-profit board wants to know what happens to overall costs and unit costs if there is a 20% reduction in the demand for both types of classes. If your answer is that there will be a 20% reduction in costs, then you (and the board) may be very disappointed when this does not occur. The simple reason is that fixed costs do not go down with decrease in demand. The first step is to calculate what happens to output (students) and number of staff if demand is cut by 20%. If we assume that the class sizes will stay the same, then:

Students:
  Literacy classes: 1,500 students × 0.8 = 1,200
  Job skills classes: 1,050 students × 0.8 = 840

Required trainers:
  Literacy classes: 1,200 students/300 students per trainer
    = 4 trainers
  Job skills classes: 840 students/150 students per trainer
    = 5.6 trainers Round up to 6 trainers

Actual students per trainer:
  Literacy classes: 1,200 students/4 trainers
    = 300 students per trainer
  Job skills classes: 840 students/6 trainers
    = 140 students per trainer

**The productivity rate for job skills classes has dropped from 150 students per trainer the previous year to 140. One way to keep the productivity rate the same is to hire five fulltime instructors and one part-time (0.6 FTE) trainer.

Direct costs:

Training material:
Literacy classes: 1,200 students × \$45 = \$54,000
Job skills classes: 840 students × \$50 = \$42,000

Salaries of trainers:
Literacy classes: 4 trainers × \$60,000 per trainer = \$240,000
Job skills classes: 6 trainers × \$60,000 = \$360,000

Phones and internet service:
Literacy classes: 4 trainers × \$600 per trainer = \$2,400
Job skills classes: 6 trainers × \$600 = \$3,600

Computer Lease:
Literacy classes: 4 trainers × \$1,000 per trainer = \$4,000
Job skills classes: 5 trainers × \$1,000 = \$5,000

Indirect costs: Only changes in costs are to the lease of copy machine and printing and postage.

Lease of copying machine (allocated by students):
Total lease cost = \$2,400 (fixed) + \$0.67 × 2,040 students
= \$3,768
Allocation by students:
Literacy classes: \$3,768 × 58.8% of students = \$2,418
Job skills classes: \$3,768 × 41.2% of students = \$1,692
Printing and postage (allocated by students):
Literacy classes: \$6,160 × 58.8% of students = \$3,624
Job skills classes: \$6,160 × 41.2% of students = \$2,536

Summary:

Total Cost: \$1,027,978

(1) Total reduction from 20% cut in demand:

Total: \$1,027,978 – \$1,177,060 = –149,082
% reduction: –12.7% (–\$149,082/\$1,177,060)
Change in cost per student:
\$503.9 – \$461.6 = \$42.3 (9.2% increase)

(2) Overall Deficit: –$217,978

Change in deficit: $217,978 – $164,560 = $53,418
% change in deficit: 32% ($53,418/$164,560)
Change in deficit per student:
$106.9 – $64.5 = $42.4 (65.7% increase)

(3) Direct costs per student:

Literacy classes: $300,400/1,200 = $250.3
Change: $250.3 – $250.3 = 0
Job skills classes: $411,600/840 = $490.0
Change: $490.0 – $460.7 = $29.3 (29.3/460.7 = 6.4% increase)
Overall: $349
Change: $349 – $336.9 = $12.1 (12.1/336.9 = 3.6%)

(4) Indirect costs per student:

Literacy classes: $139,665/1,200 = $116.4
Change: $116.4 – $93.8 = $22.5 (24.0% increase)
Job skills classes: $177,088/840 = $209.9
Change: $209.9 – $168.7 = $41.2 (24.5% increase)
Overall: 154.9
Change: $154.9 – $124.7 = $30.2 (24.3%)

See Table 4.1 for the full results. Based on this evaluation, you have some sobering news to report to the board.

- The costs only dropped 12.7% after a 20% cut in demand. **The reason is the substantial number of fixed costs.**
- We can see that the cost per student have gone up significantly ($42.3 per student, 9.2%), especially for the job skills classes ($70.6 per student, 11.2%). There has been some growth in direct costs per student driven entirely by higher per student costs for job skills classes (because of a drop in the productivity rate). The largest increase in per student costs is in indirect costs ($30.2, 24.3%), since the fixed costs are being spread across fewer students.
- The total deficit actually went up by $53,418 (32%) even with a reduction in demand! This certainly is counter-intuitive and is driven by both the fixed costs and the fact that the productivity rate for job skills trainers dropped to 140 students per year.

Table 4.1. Helping Hands — estimated unit costs for FY 2014 flexible budget — 20% decrease in demand.

Category	Cost Type	Allocation Factor	Literacy Classes	Job Skills Classes	Total Costs
Students per year			1,200	840	2,040
% change compared to 2010			−20%	−20%	−20%
Productivity rates:					
Maximum students per trainer			375.0	175.0	
Actual students per trainer			300.0	140.0	
Required trainers			4	6	10
Square feet used			2,800	3,600	7,400
Maximum capacity (sq. ft.)					10,000
Direct costs:					
Training material	Variable		$54,000	$42,000	$96,000
Salaries of trainers	Step		$240,000	$360,000	$600,000
Phones and internet service	Step		$2,400	$3,600	$6,000
Computer lease	Step		$4,000	$6,000	$10,000
Total direct costs			$300,400	$411,600	$712,000
Direct per student			$250.3	$490.0	$349.0
Indirect costs:					
Administrative staff					
Salaries	Fixed	Trainers	$62,500	$87,500	$150,000
Phones/internet service	Fixed	Trainers	$750	$1,050	$1,800
Computer lease	Fixed	Trainers	$1,250	$1,750	$3,000
Facilities-related					
Facility lease	Fixed	Square feet	$54,545	$65,455	$120,000
Utilities	Fixed	Square feet	$6,458	$9,042	$15,500

(Continued)

Table 4.1. (*Continued*)

Category	**Cost Type**	**Allocation Factor**	**Literacy Classes**	**Job Skills Classes**	**Total Costs**
Other overhead					
Lease of copy machine	Semi-variable	Students	\$2,216	\$1,552	\$3,768
Printing and postage	Variable	Students	\$3,624	\$2,536	\$6,160
Office supplies	Fixed	Trainers	\$2,292	\$3,208	\$5,500
Insurance	Fixed	Students	\$3,824	\$2,676	\$6,500
Miscellaneous	Fixed	Students	\$2,206	\$1,544	\$3,750
Total indirect costs			\$139,665	\$176,313	\$315,978
Indirect per student			\$116.4	\$209.9	\$154.9
TOTAL COST			\$440,065	\$587,913	\$1,027,978
TOTAL COST PER STUDENT			\$366.7	\$699.9	\$503.9
% CHANGE IN TOTAL COST			−14.8%	−11.0%	−12.7%
% CHANGE IN UNIT COST			6.5%	11.2%	9.2%
REIMBURSEMENT RATE			\$325.0	\$500.0	
TOTAL REVENUE			\$390,000	\$420,000	\$810,000
SURPLUS/DEFICIT			−\$50,065	−\$167,913	−\$217,978
DEFICIT PER STUDENT			−\$41.7	−\$199.9	−\$106.9
PERCENT OF SPENDING			−11.4%	−28.6%	−21.2%

This provides a good illustration of the benefits of using cost analysis in budgeting. Without this tool, it would have been easy in this case to conclude that the way to reduce the deficit is to cut demand. When there are significant fixed costs, reducing demand may not be the way out of a deficit. What would happen to the deficit if demand went up by 20% (Table 4.2)?

Table 4.2. Helping Hands — estimated unit costs for FY 2014 flexible budget — 20% increase in demand.

Category	Cost Type	Allocation Factor	Literacy Classes	Job Skills Classes	Total Costs
Students per year			1,800	1,260	3,060
% change compared to 2010			20%	20%	20%
Productivity rates:					
Maximum students per trainer			375.0	175.0	
Actual students per trainer			300.0	140.0	
Required trainers			6	9	15
Square feet used			4,200	5,400	10,600
Maximum capacity (sq. ft.)					10,000
Direct costs:					
Training material	Variable		$81,000	$63,000	$144,000
Salaries of trainers	Step		$360,000	$540,000	$900,000
Phones and internet service	Step		$3,600	$5,400	$9,000
Computer lease	Step		$6,000	$9,000	$15,000
Total direct costs			$450,600	$617,400	$1,068,000
Direct per student			$250.3	$490.0	$349.0
Indirect costs:					
Administrative staff					
Salaries	Fixed	Trainers	$62,500	$87,500	$150,000
Phones/internet service	Fixed	Trainers	$750	$1,050	$1,800
Computer lease	Fixed	Trainers	$1,250	$1,750	$3,000
Facilities-related					
Facility lease	Fixed	Square feet	$54,545	$65,455	$120,000
Utilities	Fixed	Square feet	$6,458	$9,042	$15,500

(*Continued*)

Table 4.2. (*Continued*)

Category	Cost Type	Allocation Factor	Literacy Classes	Job Skills Classes	Total Costs
Other overhead					
Lease of copy machine	Semi-variable	Students	$2,619	$1,833	$4,452
Printing and postage	Variable	Students	$5,435	$3,805	$9,240
Office supplies	Fixed	Trainers	$2,292	$3,208	$5,500
Insurance	Fixed	Students	$3,824	$2,676	$6,500
Miscellaneous	Fixed	Students	$2,206	$1,544	$3,750
Total indirect costs			$141,879	$177,863	$319,742
Indirect per student			$78.8	$141.2	$104.5
TOTAL COST			$592,479	$795,263	$1,387,742
TOTAL COST PER STUDENT			$329.2	$631.2	$453.5
% CHANGE IN TOTAL COST			14.8%	20.4%	17.9%
% CHANGE IN UNIT COST			−4.4%	0.3%	−1.8%
REIMBURSEMENT RATE			$325.0	$500.0	
TOTAL REVENUE			$585,000	$630,000	$1,215,000
SURPLUS/DEFICIT			−$7,479	−$165,263	−$172,742
DEFICIT PER STUDENT			−$4.2	−$131.2	−$56.5
PERCENT OF SPENDING			−1.3%	−20.8%	−12.4%

Looking at Table 4.2, costs have gone up by $210,682 (17.9%) but the cost per student has dropped slightly (1.8%). Surprisingly, the total deficit has gone up as well by $8,182 (5%). Why has not the deficit dropped when demand increased? The likely explanation is that the productivity rate for job skills has dropped from 150 students per trainer to 140. ***This should give you an idea of just how important the labor productivity rate is to the cost***

of public services. We will examine this more closely in the next section.

4.3 Strategies for Reducing the Deficit

The flexible budgets and full cost estimates developed previously provide a valuable set of tools for managing an agency. Particularly in times of fiscal crisis, it is imperative to find ways to reduce costs and improve the productivity of the agency. Some strategies you could evaluate with cost analysis include:

- **Improve labor productivity:** As we saw in the last section, this could have a large impact on the required staff and other resources linked to staff. We will examine this approach using the Helping Hands example.
- **Expand service levels:** We have already looked at this as part of examining flexible budgets. We will examine this more formally using the Helping Hands example.
- **Drop one of the services:** While for a government dropping a service may not be possible, a non-profit can decide whether it wants to stop providing certain services. We will examine below the effects of dropping job skills for the Helping Hands example.
- **Privatize services:** The alternative to dropping a service for a government is privatizing it. The analysis is very similar to that done for dropping a service.
- **Reduce costs:** Cost reduction is often the surest strategy for bringing down unit costs, but it can involve painful sacrifices. Cost reduction usually requires a careful review of each cost category to determine if cost savings are possible. If a long enough lead-time exists, most fixed costs are open to review as well. Can we move to a smaller or less expensive facility? Can we renegotiate with suppliers for reduced rates from bulk purchases, use of less expensive materials, etc.? Can we "outsource" some of the services we are providing internally? Can we work with other non-profit agencies to negotiate lower rates? While drastic reductions in cost rates or fixed costs are unlikely, especially this year, a series of small changes can add up.

4.3.1 Increasing productivity

In addition to negotiating lower cost rates, the most pro-active strategy of the agency is to work on improving productivity; that is, reducing resources used per unit of output. Productivity improvements are generally related to increasing the productivity of labor. One of the principal benefits from technological innovation is the potential increase in labor productivity. But productivity improvement can occur in almost all categories of inputs. Using the Helping Hands example, we could reduce the required photocopying or printing per student, or encourage several trainers to share one computer or phone. It is important, however, that these productivity improvements do not lead to a significant reduction in the quality of service. For example, a trainer could certainly have 40 students in a class, but it is highly likely that the resulting educational experience for students will have been diminished. One of the principal uses of benchmarking is to collect information on productivity rates in other organizations. Table 4.3 shows the effects on unit costs if benchmark productivity rates are used (see also Table 3.3 in Lecture 3).

We can see that increasing productivity to industry benchmarks has made a significant difference. The deficit has dropped by three-quarters to $41,360. The deficit now is only 3.9% of total spending down from 14% of total spending. The trainers have been reduced from 12 to 10. The agency is now making money on the literacy skills function ($32,828) and the losses on job training classes have been cut in half. While assuming that your staff can reach benchmark productivity rates in the first year would be very risky, it does suggest that productivity improvement should be a major part of your budget balancing strategy. It is likely that trainers will resist significant increases in class size and class load (classes per year) using the argument that this will hurt the quality of the instruction they provide. Thus, it will be important to work with them to identify ways to improve productivity without hurting quality. One common strategy is to purchase equipment to improve the productivity of labor. In this case, computer-aided instruction in the classroom might allow the trainer to work with larger classes. However, this also implies

Table 4.3. Helping Hands — estimated unit costs for FY 2014 using benchmark productivity rate.

Category	Cost Type	Allocation Factor	Literacy Classes	Job Skills Classes	Total Costs
Students per year			1,500	1,050	2,550
% change compared to 2010			0%	0%	0%
Productivity rates:					
Maximum students per trainer			375.0	175.0	
Actual students per trainer			375.0	175.0	
Required trainers			4	6	10
Square feet used			2,800	3,600	7,400
Maximum capacity (sq. ft.)					10,000
Direct costs:					
Training material	Variable		$67,500	$52,500	$120,000
Salaries of trainers	Step		$240,000	$360,000	$600,000
Phones and internet service	Step		$2,400	$3,600	$6,000
Computer lease	Step		$4,000	$6,000	$10,000
Total direct costs			$313,900	$422,100	$736,000
Direct per student			$209.3	$402.0	$288.6
Indirect costs:					
Administrative staff					
Salaries	Fixed	Trainers	$62,500	$87,500	$150,000
Phones/internet service	Fixed	Trainers	$750	$1,050	$1,800
Computer lease	Fixed	Trainers	$1,250	$1,750	$3,000
Facilities-related					
Facility lease	Fixed	Square feet	$54,545	$65,455	$120,000
Utilities	Fixed	Square feet	$6,458	$9,042	$15,500

(*Continued*)

Table 4.3. (*Continued*)

Category	Cost Type	Allocation Factor	Literacy Classes	Job Skills Classes	Total Costs
Other overhead					
Lease of copy machine	Semi-variable	Students	$2,418	$1,692	$4,110
Printing and postage	Variable	Students	$4,529	$3,171	$7,700
Office supplies	Fixed	Trainers	$2,292	$3,208	$5,500
Insurance	Fixed	Students	$3,824	$2,676	$6,500
Miscellaneous	Fixed	Students	$2,206	$1,544	$3,750
Total indirect costs			$140,772	$177,088	$317,860
Indirect per student			$93.8	$168.7	$124.7
TOTAL COST			$454,672	$599,188	$1,053,860
TOTAL COST PER STUDENT			$303.1	$570.7	$413.3
% CHANGE IN TOTAL COST			−11.9%	−9.3%	−10.5%
% CHANGE IN UNIT COST			−11.9%	−9.3%	−10.5%
REIMBURSEMENT RATE			$325.0	$500.0	
TOTAL REVENUE			$487,500	$525,000	$1,012,500
SURPLUS/DEFICIT			$32,828	−$74,188	−$41,360
DEFICIT PER STUDENT			$21.9	−$70.7	−$16.2
PERCENT OF SPENDING			7.2%	−12.4%	−3.9%

additional cost for computers and software. The tools of cost analysis would allow you to evaluate whether this is an appropriate strategy.

4.3.2 Increase output

As we discussed in the section on flexible budgets, one strategy for reducing deficits can be to **grow your way out of the deficit**. This seems counterintuitive since expanding a money-losing service sounds like it will increase rather than decrease the deficits. However, under the right conditions, this may be an effective strategy. There are several key conditions to evaluate before undertaking this strategy:

- First, is there adequate demand for this increased service? While this is less likely to be the case for governments, for non-profit organizations, it is possible that they are working in an area of pent-up demand. It would be important to do a marketing study to determine if there is adequate demand before undertaking a significant expansion of service.
- Second, it is important to examine what might happen to "fixed costs" with a significant expansion in service. As discussed previously, it is likely that some of these costs are not really fixed. For example, if demand for literacy classes and job training classes increase significantly at some point the capacity of the facility may be exceeded. This should be checked. It is also possible that utilities, office supplies, and insurance will increase.
- The increase in service should be matched with the labor productivity rate. In other words, you want to add output until you are at the end of a step. For example, if one literacy trainer can work with 300 students, then you should add demand in increments of 300. As we saw in Table 4.2, increased output that reduces the actual productivity rate could actually increase the deficit.
- Most importantly, compare the non-fixed costs per unit of output to the reimbursement rate per unit of output. ***If the non-fixed cost per unit is lower than the reimbursement rate, then it is possible (but not necessarily realistic) to increase demand sufficiently to breakeven. However, if the reimbursement rate is lower than the non-fixed costs per unit, then expanding demand will actually increase the deficit.*** Using the Helping Hands example and Table 3.5:

  Non-fixed costs per student
  = (Direct costs + variable indirect costs
  + the variable part of the semi-variable costs)/students

Literacy: Cost: (\$375,500 + 4,529 + \$1006)/1,500
= \$254 per student
Reimbursement rate: \$325 per student
Job skills: Cost: (\$483,700 + 3,171 + \$714)/1,050
= \$464.4 per student
Reimbursement rate: \$500 per student

For both literacy classes and the job skills classes, the non-fixed cost per student is less than the reimbursement rate. This implies that expanding demand might be a strategy the agency should consider for eliminating the deficit.

To illustrate with the Helping Hands case, assume that you feel that a 10% increase in labor productivity is realistic (330 students per literacy trainer, 165 students per job training instructor). Since literacy classes are more apt to break even than job training, one strategy is to increase the literacy students served and reduce the job training students served. Table 4.4 provides one example, where literacy students are expanded by 76% while the job skills students are cut by 5.7%. The result is an operation that has a very slight surplus. However, based on estimates of square footage needed per trainer, this operation would slightly exceed the capacity of the building you are leasing. It is close enough so you can probably make some small adjustments to scheduling of classes to provide adequate space. But this does suggest that this demand will have reached facility capacity; any more expansion will require more space.

4.3.3 Drop one of the services

A relatively extreme approach an agency can take to reduce costs is to stop providing a particular service. For most government agencies this is not a choice, but for non-profit organizations that provide a range of services, dropping a service may be possible. Looking at Table 4.2, this would appear a feasible alternative for Helping Hands since the cost per student for literacy classes is very close to the reimbursement rate, but the cost per student for job skills classes significantly exceeds its reimbursement rate even at maximum

Table 4.4. Helping Hands — estimated unit costs for FY 2014 — 10% increase in productivity rate and increase in demand.

Category	Cost Type	Allocation Factor	Literacy Classes	Job Skills Classes	Total Costs
Students per year			2,640	989	3,629
% change compared to 2010			76%	−5.72%	42%
Productivity rates:					
Maximum students per trainer			330.0	165.0	
Actual students per trainer			330.0	164.8	
Required trainers			8	6	14
Square feet used			5,600	3,600	10,200
Maximum capacity (sq. ft.)					10,000
Direct costs:					
Training material	Variable		$118,800	$49,450	$168,250
Salaries of trainers	Step		$480,000	$360,000	$840,000
Phones and internet service	Step		$4,800	$3,600	$8,400
Computer lease	Step		$8,000	$6,000	$14,000
Total direct costs			$611,600	$419,050	$1,030,650
Direct per student			$231.7	$423.7	$284.0
Indirect costs:					
Administrative staff					
Salaries	Fixed	Trainers	$62,500	$87,500	$150,000
Phones/internet service	Fixed	Trainers	$750	$1,050	$1,800
Computer lease	Fixed	Trainers	$1,250	$1,750	$3,000
Facilities-related					
Facility lease	Fixed	Square feet	$54,545	$65,455	$120,000
Utilities	Fixed	Square feet	$6,458	$9,042	$15,500

(*Continued*)

Table 4.4. (*Continued*)

Category	Cost Type	Allocation Factor	Literacy Classes	Job Skills Classes	Total Costs
Other overhead					
Lease of copy machine	Semi-variable	Students	\$3,516	\$1,317	\$4,834
Printing and postage	Variable	Students	\$7,972	\$2,986	\$10,958
Office supplies	Fixed	Trainers	\$2,292	\$3,208	\$5,500
Insurance	Fixed	Students	\$3,824	\$2,676	\$6,500
Miscellaneous	Fixed	Students	\$2,206	\$1,544	\$3,750
Total indirect costs			\$145,313	\$176,529	\$321,842
Indirect per student			\$55.0	\$178.5	\$88.7
TOTAL COST			\$756,913	\$595,579	\$1,352,492
TOTAL COST PER STUDENT			\$286.7	\$602.2	\$372.7
% CHANGE IN TOTAL COST			46.6%	−9.9%	14.9%
% CHANGE IN UNIT COST			−16.7%	−4.3%	−19.3%
REIMBURSEMENT RATE			\$325.0	\$500.0	
TOTAL REVENUE			\$858,000	\$494,500	\$1,352,500
SURPLUS/DEFICIT			\$101,087	−\$101,079	\$8
DEFICIT PER STUDENT			\$38.3	−\$102.2	\$0.0
PERCENT OF SPENDING			13.4%	−17.0%	0.0%

productivity. Unless you are able to convince the state to increase the reimbursement rate, or major cost savings can be made in providing job training classes, Helping Hands will lose money on these classes. A logical conclusion from looking at this table is that the job skills classes should not be provided anymore. However, making a decisions based on the information in Table 4.2 would be inappropriate, because no distinctions are made between types of costs.

- *Average costs*: Average costs are defined as the total cost per unit of output, which is just the unit cost. Average costs are relevant in setting user fees that will cover costs, and in examining how costs change when the scale of the operation in terms of output changes.
- *Marginal costs*: Marginal costs are defined as the change in total cost with a one-unit increase in output. If there are significant fixed costs, then marginal costs will be lower than average costs, because they do not include fixed costs. Marginal costs include variable costs, the variable portion of semi-variable costs, and any change in the step costs because of the output change.
- *Avoidable costs*: Avoidable costs measure the change in total costs when some discrete change is made in the operation. This can include a reduction in output, dropping of a service, or the contracting out of support services. In general, fixed costs cannot be removed or reduced, at least in the short-run.

To determine the impact of dropping the services by an agency, we need to calculate the avoidable costs from this change. These are the costs that can be eliminated by dropping the service-variable costs and step costs. For semi-variable costs, the variable component can be eliminated but the fixed component of the semi-variable cost can be eliminated only if there is no contractual commitment to pay these costs even with no service. The avoidable costs by dropping the job skills mission include:

- training material costs and printing costs for job skills classes,
- the costs of trainers, and the other costs associated with them (utilities, phones, computers, and internet connections),
- printing and postage associated with these students,
- the variable component of the copier lease associated with these students.

Table 4.5 presents the unit costs for the literacy classes when the job skills mission has been dropped. When the job training classes are dropped, the deficit actually goes up compared to including them! While costs have decreased 27%, revenues have been cut in half. This certainly suggests that it does not make sense to cut job training costs

Table 4.5. Helping Hands — estimated unit costs for FY 2014 drop the job skill classes.

Category	Cost Type	Literacy Classes
Students per year		**1,500**
% change compared to 2010		0%
Productivity rates:		
Maximum students per trainer		300.0
Actual students per trainer		300.0
Required trainers		5
Square feet used		4,500
Maximum capcity (sq. ft.)		10,000
Direct costs:		
Training material	Variable	$67,500
Salaries of trainers	Step	$300,000
Phones and internet service	Step	$3,000
Computer lease	Step	$5,000
Total direct costs		$375,500
Direct per student		$250.3
Indirect costs:		
Administrative staff		
Salaries	Fixed	$150,000
Phones/internet service	Fixed	$1,800
Computer lease	Fixed	$3,000
Facilities-related		
Facility lease	Fixed	$120,000
Utilities	Fixed	$15,500
Other overhead		
Lease of copy machine	Semi-variable	$3,406
Printing and postage	Variable	$4,529
Office supplies	Fixed	$5,500
Insurance	Fixed	$6,500
Miscellaneous	Fixed	$3,750
Total indirect costs		$313,985
Indirect per student		$209.3
TOTAL COST		$689,485
TOTAL COST PER STUDENT		$459.7

(*Continued*)

Table 4.5. (*Continued*)

Category	**Cost Type**	**Literacy Classes**
% CHANGE IN TOTAL COST		4.3%
% CHANGE IN UNIT COST		−27.0%
REIMBURSEMENT RATE		$325.0
TOTAL REVENUE		$487,500
SURPLUS/DEFICIT		−$201,985
DEFICIT PER STUDENT		−$134.7
PERCENT OF SPENDING		−29.3%

unless substantial reductions can be made in "fixed costs" or other changes are made to the operation.

Table 4.6 shows what would be the deficits if job skills classes were dropped, productivity was increased by 10% and demand for literacy classes increased by 76%. While this significantly cut the deficit, it is still higher than if job skills classes are still taught (and the same productivity and output changes were made for literacy classes).

4.3.4 Privatizing one of the services

The cost analysis of the impacts of dropping a service is similar to the analysis of whether privatizing a service makes sense. The analysis of privatization involves the following steps:

- First calculate the "avoidable costs" (or differential costs) per unit if the service is dropped. If you think that some of the overhead costs can be reduced, then the savings from these reductions should be calculated. Included in the avoidable cost is the cost to monitor the contract to assure that the contract has been complied with. The contract will typically discuss the fee, level of service required, and the quality of the service. Any increase in these costs will reduce the total amount of avoidable costs.
- Get bids from vendors on the fee per unit they will require to provide this service.

Table 4.6. Helping Hands — estimated unit costs for FY 2014 — drop the job skill classes 10% productivity increase and increase in demand.

Category	**Cost Type**	**Literacy Classes**
Students per year		**2,640**
% change compared to 2010		76%
Productivity rates:		
Maximum students per trainer		330.0
Actual students per trainer		330.0
Required trainers		8
Square feet used		6,600
Maximum capacity (sq. ft.)		10,000
Direct costs:		
Training material	Variable	$118,800
Salaries of trainers	Step	$480,000
Phones and internet service	Step	$4,800
Computer lease	Step	$8,000
Total direct costs		$611,600
Direct per student		$231.7
Indirect costs:		
Administrative staff		
Salaries	Fixed	$150,000
Phones/internet service	Fixed	$1,800
Computer lease	Fixed	$3,000
Facilities-related		
Facility lease	Fixed	$120,000
Utilities	Fixed	$15,500
Other overhead		
Lease of copy machine	Semi-variable	$4,170
Printing and postage	Variable	$7,972
Office supplies	Fixed	$5,500
Insurance	Fixed	$6,500
Miscellaneous	Fixed	$3,750
Total indirect costs		$318,192
Indirect per student		$120.5
TOTAL COST		$929,792
TOTAL COST PER STUDENT		$352.2

(*Continued*)

Table 4.6. (*Continued*)

Category	Cost Type	Literacy Classes
% CHANGE IN TOTAL COST		40.7%
% CHANGE IN UNIT COST		−44.0%
REIMBURSEMENT RATE		$325.0
TOTAL REVENUE		$858,000
SURPLUS/DEFICIT		−$71,792
DEFICIT PER STUDENT		−$27.2
PERCENT OF SPENDING		−7.7%

- Compare the avoidable cost to the fee per unit.
- If the fee is less than the avoidable cost, then the government should consider contracting out the service. If the reverse is the case, then contracting out will not save money.

Using the Helping Hands example, let's say that non-profit is thinking of contracting out the job skills classes to another non-profit that specializes in these classes and can provide them less expensively. The other non-profit has agreed to provide classes for 1,050 students at a cost of $400 per student. Is it worth it for Helping Hands to contract out job skills classes?

Avoidable costs: Let's say that Helping Hands feels they can eliminate all of their direct costs, printing and postage, and the variable part of the copier lease associated with the job skills classes. In addition, let's say they feel that they can cut utilities, office supplies and miscellaneous by 30%. Assume that the assistant director will do the monitoring of the contract so there is no additional monitoring cost. Using Table 3.5:

$$\begin{aligned}\text{Avoidable costs} &= \$483{,}700 + \$3{,}171 + (\$.67 \times 1{,}050) \\ &\quad + 30\% \times (\$15{,}500 + \$5{,}500 + \$3{,}750) \\ &= \$83{,}700 + \$3{,}171 + \$704 + \$7{,}425 = \$495{,}000\end{aligned}$$

$$\text{Avoidable costs per student} = \$495{,}000/\$1{,}050 = \$471.43$$

The fee is substantially less than the avoidable cost. It would be important before making a decision to evaluate whether there are other costs associated with contracting out this service (e.g., contract monitoring cost) and whether any of the indirect costs can really be reduced.

Lecture 5

Budget Review and Approval

5.1 Budgeting Hardnox

Hardnox Correctional Facility is a maximum-security prison in a Midwestern state in the US. Built in 1910 to house 325 inmates, Hardnox now houses 510 inmates who have been convicted and sentenced for committing serious crimes such as armed robbery, murder, and rape. Inmates housed at Hardnox have sentences that range from five years to life in prison.

Even though Hardnox has exceeded its rated capacity of 325 inmates for several years, the staffing ratio has tended to remain constant at one correctional officer to eight inmates. Nevertheless, the warden, Clem Beasley, is pressing for a substantial increase in correctional officers. In his judgment, more officers are needed because overcrowding in the prison has exacerbated gang violence. There has also been an increase in assaults on correctional officers. Beasley also believes that these factors are having an adverse effect on staff morale and is causing an increase in the turnover rate. He is asking for a 10% increase in correctional officers in next year's budget.

Susan Quill recently earned her Master of Public Administration degree. As a graduate student, Susan had an interest in environmental policy. While she "had a head for numbers," Susan thought that she would begin her professional career either working in a government agency dealing with some aspect of the environment or a non-profit interest group like Greenpeace. She never thought that she would become a *Budget Analyst* in state government — certainly not in the area of criminal justice. Susan has been on the job for less than a month and she will soon have to make recommendations concerning the budget for Hardnox Correctional Facility. Before starting her job, Susan knew nothing about the Department of Corrections that was responsible for the maximum-security prison. All she knew was what she occasionally read in the newspapers. She knew that defendants who were convicted of the most serious crimes were sent to the Hardnox Maximum-Security Prison to serve their sentence — and the sentences were usually long ones. How should she go about reviewing Warden Beasley's request?

5.2 Budget Office Review

Let's back up a bit. Warden Beasley, as a senior manager in the Department of Corrections, is responsible for preparing a budget for Hardnox. Naturally, Beasley has had discussions with the head of the Department of Corrections, Ms. Daphne Jaws, who offered her perspectives about the broad policy goals of the Department and relevant political and fiscal issues that may be important to the governor. It is quite likely that some of Warden Beasley's initial budget requests were changed at the departmental level. Once the budget for Hardnox is completed and informal negotiations are completed between Beasley and Jaws, it will be included in the department's budget along with other departmental programs and facilities. The entire budget of the Department of Corrections is then submitted to the central budget office where it is reviewed on behalf of the chief executive.

5.2.1 Roles of the budget office

Susan Quill is a budget analyst in the budget office. The budget office is an executive agency that serves the chief executive whether that person is the president, governor, or mayor. The role of the central budget office at the federal level and state level has changed and expanded over the years. When the bureau of the budget (BOB) was set up in the federal government in 1920, it served primarily a control function. It reviewed agency expenditures for legal compliance and attempted to control the allocation and expenditure of funds. Agency personnel served primarily an accounting and auditing role. Since then the role of the budget division has expanded in line with the growth in the functions which federal agencies are involved. Typically, the budget office serves a number of roles.

Budget review: The budget office brings together all the agency requests into a unified budget. But the role of the budget office goes beyond just assembling the budget. It acts as the final screening process on agency requests. Since total requests are generally greater than the expenditure levels set by the chief executive, the budget office typically attempts to reduce agency requests with minimal impact on service levels.

This is a major point of contention between the agency and budget office. Agencies feel that they are the experts in their program areas and that the budget analyst does not understand the justification for their budget request. Budget analysts view agency managers as advocates for their programs who will always feel that there is a need for more. The budget office is the one place in the executive branch that gets a view of the whole budget. Traditionally, budget analysts have viewed their perspective as that of "neutral competence."

> "Fiscal sense and fiscal coordination are certainly values. The budgeting organization is designed to give representation in institutional interaction and decision making to this set of values. In one way, there is no point in denying, the budget function is preponderantly negative. It is on the whole rather strongly against program and expenditure expansion. This approach is desirable, because the programmatic agencies and most of the potent pressure groups are so expansive that there will be little danger that the

undeniable values they represent will be overlooked or smothered by budgeteers."[1]

Liaison between agency and chief executive: The budget analyst has a rare position as a liaison between the chief executive and the agency. The analyst is an important source of information to the chief executive on the operation of the agency programs and agency concerns. In addition, analysts are the "frontline" in terms of passing on the budget call to the agency, i.e., instructing the agency on the chief executive's priorities.

Implement management practices: Beginning with President Nixon, the federal BOB was changed to the office of management and budget (OMB). Along with the title came new responsibilities to implement management reforms and improve management practices. This is true also of state budgeting offices. The budget office, not surprisingly, is often the initiator of budget reforms and other management reforms.

Maintain financial management system: Basically, this involves setting up the accounting and financial reporting system in the state. Although these duties may be shared with other agencies (GAO) at the federal level, budget offices have an important role in guiding the financial management system.

Program auditing/evaluation: Closely associated with the financial management function is the control of agency expenditures. This is the traditional control function of the budget office and involves budget execution controls and financial audits of agency expenditures. In addition, in line with the management and planning functions, the budget office may take the lead on management and performance audits as well.

Control of agency legislative proposals/regulations: The budget office is often the place to monitor the legislative proposals of agencies.

[1]Paul Appleby. 1980. "The Role of the Budget Division." In A. Schick (ed.), *Perspectives on Budgeting*. Washington, DC: American Society for Public Administration, pp. 134–135.

Because the budget office is in close touch with the chief executives priorities, it acts as a check on agency submissions to make sure they are consistent with these objectives.

The key staff person in a budget office is the budget examiner (sometimes called the budget analyst). This is a good entry-level position for new graduates of public affair programs since it gives the person a "baptism by fire" into the internal workings of a government agency. The budget analyst is usually assigned one or several agencies to review. He or she is responsible for learning the basic functions and objectives of the agency and monitoring their operation. This is Susan Quill's job. How should she approach her responsibilities?

5.2.2 Budget review process

Susan Quill will most likely approach her budget review task by having informal discussions with Daphne Jaw's budget person and Warden Beasley. These discussions may focus on staffing levels, programmatic changes that are taking place at Hardnox and non-personnel issues that may affect the budget of Hardnox. Her analysis will become increasingly detailed and formalized, culminating with the final formal review in front of the budget director. In general, the examiner's steps in budget review will proceed in the following way[2]:

Rough screening: When the analyst first gets the agency request, he or she has to initially screen it to provide the budget director with the total amount of the agency request, and to identify areas requiring further information. These are often those areas where there have been a significant expansion in the program or where there are basic "gaps" in the information provided by the agency. This allows the analyst to identify quickly the areas where she should focus their attention in reviewing this budget.

Susan Quill should review the budget request to determine if there is anything that "leaps out" at her that may explain the need for a 10% increase in personnel. Perhaps Warden Beasley

[2]Based on John Mikesell. 1995. Fiscal Administration, Fourth Edition, New York: Wadsworth, pp. 154–164.

has provided some explanation in his narrative justification that accompanies the budget request.

One possibility is a change in the inmate population. For example, more recent inmates may have been convicted of particularly violent crimes. Another possibility is that the number of repeat offenders is increasing. These factors may call for an adjustment in the officer/inmate ratio.

Detailed analysis: This is the heart of the review process where the analyst digs into the "nitty gritty" of the agency request. The analyst is essentially examining the justification of most of the major items in the agency budget. Are the expected increases in workload or costs justified based on past experience? Why has a program consistently had poorer performance than anticipated–will an increased appropriation necessarily help improve this performance? Does the agency provide convincing justification for increases in its program? Have past funding increases led to the performance improvements that were promised?

Susan Quill may not be able to answer all of these questions. But she should scrutinize the budget detail carefully. For example, she may want to look at any changes that may have been made in the way correctional officers do their jobs. This may explain why Warden Beasley is requesting a change in the staffing ratio. Perhaps there is a change in the "industry" standard. That is, she may want to know whether changes in Hardnox are unique or reflect changes that are occurring in other maximum-security prisons. To do this, she may need to gather data from correctional facilities in other states. She may also need to visit Hardnox and observe the facility and its activities directly.

Informal budget hearings: Once the analysts have prepared the first round of their review of their agency, there is usually scheduled a series of informal hearings between the analyst (and possibly his or her supervisors) and various persons in the agency. The hearing may start with informal meetings between the analysts in the offices of various agency personnel. These initial hearings may be mainly informational with each party trying to get a sense of the priorities and constraints on the other. Eventually they will work up to the top agency personnel meeting with the analyst and his supervisors. Although informational, these meetings are clearly adversarial proceedings with the agency trying to plead its case before the budget office.

This stage may be difficult for a budget analyst like Susan Quill. After all, she is a new government employee whereas Warden Beasley and other Department of Corrections staff are likely to be seasoned veterans of many budget cycles. Ms. Quill's challenge is to stay focused on these budget review procedures that have been well established for this phase of the budget cycle. In particular, there are common questions that she may raise that will lead toward the resolution of the inevitable tension that exists between the agency personnel, who invariably want more budget support, and the budget office, that must protect the fiscal policy of the chief executive. Ms. Quill might, for example, try to ascertain if there is some "minimum asking price" that the agency head will accept for a particular program. She may ask how agency personnel might explain budget increases or justify poor performance of a program. She may inquire why the agency feels a need for a particular capital outlay this year. In general, these informal meetings are eventually where the recommendations of the budget analyst are finalized.

Formal budget hearings: Once the analyst has thoroughly reviewed the budget and met informally with agency personnel, he or she prepares the final recommendations on the agency budget. They then have to "sell" this recommendation to their supervisors and ultimately the budget director. A key part in selling their request is to "boil it down" to the essential details and the key questions which must be addressed to the agency. Ms. Quill, in other words, will make recommendations to her superior in the budget office about the proposed level of funding for Hardnox including the approval or rejection of any new initiatives that were requested by Warden Beasley. As a rule of thumb, a recommendation to increase funding substantially is more difficult to justify than a recommendation for a modest or no increase.

The budget director then holds a formal hearing with the agency head to review the agency request. These hearings go over the remaining differences between the department and the budget office. While the head of the agency and the budget director are on the same team — they both work for the chief executive, they may sometimes have different perspectives.

Finalizing the budget: The budget director usually presents a draft of the proposed budget to the chief executive. The draft outlines the big issues on which the budget director wants the chief executive to focus. For example, what is the "bottom-line" increase in the budget? What happened to the chief executive's pet projects? Where are the significant areas of difference from last year's budget? What are the likely controversial issues when the budget is sent to the legislature?

Agencies have one last chance at this stage to appeal the decisions of the budget office. Agencies probably use it only as an action of last resort and only on issues that are of such importance that it is worth using up their "political chips" with the chief executive. For example, the head of the Department of Corrections may, despite Susan Quill's recommendation, continue to support Warden Beasley's contention that Hardnox is understaffed. If the head of the Department of Corrections feels very strongly that this is a major budget issue from the departmental perspective, this decision may be appealed directly to the governor. The governor, in turn, will most likely consider the understaffing issue in light of the commitment to criminal justice, the reputation of the department and the relationship between the head of the Department of Corrections and the governor.

Once the chief executive has given final approval to the budget, the preparation of the final executive budget to be sent to the legislature is carried out. There are usually several parts to the budget document:

— budget message,
— the financial plan or summary,
— detailed agency budgets,
— special analyses on economic assumptions, revenue estimates,
— intergovernmental aid, historical trends, etc.

Part of Susan Quill's job is done — the part that focuses on budget review. Her next task is to take part in the collective effort to get the budget passed by the legislature. She will need to be an advocate of the chief executive's spending priorities even if, during the review process, she may have been skeptical of some of the spending priorities of the Department of Corrections.

5.3 Legislative Budget Process

Legislative appropriations are the next phase of the typical budget process. Unfortunately, it is difficult to summarize this phase since there is no general pattern that can adequately explain how legislatures deal with the budget that fits national governments in the world, or even state and local governments in the US. At the national level, it is safe to say that the Congress of the US has more influence on the budget of the US than most, if not all, legislative bodies in the world including parliamentary democracies such as the United Kingdom and Canada.

The role of legislative bodies in the budget process in the US has fluctuated over the years. There is continued tension between the legislative and executive branches over the role that each should play in the process. In the US, the legislative branch played the dominant role in the process until the early 1900s. The agencies would develop budget requests that would be presented directly to the legislative body. The legislative body reviewed and passed these requests, with the chief executive having generally only veto power over the final appropriation bills. This meant that, at the federal level, the president had little power to use the budget to shape policy or to exert fiscal discipline.

The early 1900s in the US witnessed a series of administrative reforms during the Progressive Era. The budget process became a major focus of attention. The legislative budget process was criticized for creating fragmentation, waste, and inefficiency. In addition, because of the generally poor accounting practices, it was difficult for the legislature to monitor and control agency implementation of the budget. At the federal level, the result of these reforms was the Budgeting and Accounting Act of 1921, which established the BOB.

This marked the beginning of what was to be known as the executive budget because the chief executive initiated agency budget requests and assembled them into a budget document. This gave the chief executive significantly expanded power, with the legislative body relegated to budget review and oversight functions. This has resulted in continued tension, particularly at the federal and state levels, between these two branches of government. Legislatures have attempted to maintain influence on policy formulation. Although this executive budget does not necessarily describe all state governments (the state of Texas being a notable exception), it is clearly the dominant form of the budget process in states in this country.

On the other hand, local government budgeting is much more diverse. In large cities and counties, the executive budget form tends to dominate. However, in smaller municipalities and counties, the legislative body often takes a much more active role in budget preparation as well as review. Although we focus on the executive budget model in this chapter, some local governments have budget processes that are dominated by the local legislative body.

5.3.1 Typical state legislative budget process

Because of the diversity of experiences in each individual state, it is not possible to make strong generalizations about the nature of the budget process in state legislatures. However, it is possible to make some basic generalizations.

History of the legislatures' role: As with the federal budget process, the role of legislatures in state budgeting has waxed and waned over the years. Following the installation of executive budgeting in most states early in the 20th century, the role of the legislatures generally diminished. Governors who initiate the process now generally dominate the process. They have sizeable staffs and are able to set the budgetary agendas in the legislature. Legislatures at best can make marginal changes in the governor's proposal.

Legislative initiative was further dampened by the power of most governors to use line item vetoes to surgically remove those parts of the appropriation acts that they did not like.

Since the 1960s, there has been a growing trend for state legislature's to try to reassert their independence in the budgeting process. Legislatures started to build up their staff positions to be able to develop their own sources of information and analysis. In some states, the legislatures have developed large, professional fiscal staffs that are similar to the CBO in their influence on the budget. The bi-annual legislative session was replaced in favor of annual sessions in many states. The legislative sessions were extended and the job of the legislator was changed from part time to full time. Since the 1970s, legislatures have generally taken a much more aggressive position in reviewing and modifying the governor's budget.

Legislative budget process[3]: When the executive budget proposal is submitted by the Governor to the legislature, it is divided into pieces that are to be evaluated separately by different committees. The fiscal committees often are able to get a head start on the budget by getting copies of the agency requests and preliminary drafts of the governor's budget. They may also be allowed to sit in on the final hearings between the agency and budget office

As might be expected, there are significant differences among states in the organization of fiscal committees; however, most states fall into three categories:

(1) Separate appropriations and tax committees in each house of the legislature. This type of committee structure is very similar to the US Congress prior to 1974. The house initiates spending and taxing legislation. Once passed, this legislation is then passed to the Senate. Final legislation will often require a conference committee or some other form of dispute resolution.

[3]For excellent summaries of the budget processes in a number of states, see Edward Clynch and Thomas Lauth, *Governors, Legislatures, and Budgets: Diversity Across the American States*. Westport, CT, 2006. These essays emphasize in particular how the process varies in states with an executive budget and those where the legislature predominates.

(2) Combined revenue and appropriations committees in each house. Tax and appropriation legislation are considered jointly in the same committee. These committees often have large and professional staff. This committee is responsible for producing a balanced budget.
(3) Joint House-Senate appropriations and tax committees. Due to the importance of the budget and technical staff requirements, some states have opted for large centralized joint committees with large professional staffs.

The staffs of the fiscal committees carry out most of the analysis on the budget. Unlike Congress, they typically consider the whole budget, i.e., expenditures, revenues, and debt. In some states such as California, the legislative fiscal staffs may produce essentially a legislative budget in terms of detail and analysis.

Once the fiscal committees have passed the appropriation and revenue bills, they are sent along with supporting documentation for approval by the full houses. There is significant variation in what form the final budget takes but in close to half the states, it is in one "omnibus appropriation bill."

Even though legislatures have reclaimed a significant amount of authority in the budget process, the governor still wields a potent weapon, the line item veto. Key questions are what have these vetoes been used for in the states and have they helped to reduce spending? The general consensus of researchers is that these vetoes have been used primarily as a partisan tool to affect policy decisions, not expenditure levels. The findings suggest that these vetoes have not had a significant effect on expenditure levels in each state.

The budgeting process does not necessarily end with the signing of the appropriation bills by the governor. Due to changing economic and political circumstances, it is often necessary to pass at a later date supplemental appropriations to make up shortfalls in the budget. In the state of Georgia, for example, there is actually a formalized process of mid-course correction. The mid-year appropriation process is a chance in the middle of the fiscal year to evaluate expected revenue levels and expenditure needs. Since there has been a tendency to forecast conservatively on revenues, there has generally been a surplus to be allocated among the agencies. The legislature in particular has taken a special interest in this surplus as a way of meeting constituency needs, i.e., to fill the "pork barrel." Much of this surplus is used to fund one-time capital projects in a legislator's district.

Let's return to the budget for the Hardnox Correctional Facility briefly. Recall that the budget for Hardnox is part of the budget of the Department of Corrections. The legislative committees responsible for overseeing the budget for the department may hold hearings on the department's budget. Legislators will vary in their views concerning the department and its budgetary needs. Some may believe that it is important to be "tough on crime" and it is, therefore, important to support the proposed budget for Hardnox. Legislators from the opposing political party from the governor may use the hearing as a way to criticize the governor's policy priorities. These legislators may question the assumptions behind the budget numbers. For example, they may propose programs that are designed to lower inmate levels in the state prisons. Here is where Susan Quill may come in since she may be asked to supply the information to the inquisitive legislators who may be dubious of the governor's budget. Quill's job at this point is to support the chief executive's budget regardless of any previous reservations that she had during the budget review phase of the process. Now her job is to help "sell" the governor's budget to the legislature.

After hearings are completed, the committee will make a recommendation to the full chamber. In bi-cameral legislatures, this process will occur in both houses of the legislature. If the two chambers differ in their budget decisions, the differences will have to be reconciled before the appropriations become law.

5.3.2 Local budget process

While most states and the federal government use an executive budget process where the chief executive submits the budget to the legislature, this is not necessarily the case for local governments. The type of budget process used by local governments is related directly to the form of government. In large cities and counties, there is usually an elected county executive or mayor.[4] The chief executive usually has a budget office working for him or her and submits a budget to the legislative body. The legislative body, often called the county legislature or the city council, will be a unicameral body. In larger jurisdictions, the legislature will hold hearings about the chief executive's budget before it votes on the entire budget. Since local governments in the US rely on local property taxes as a major source of revenue, the legislature will also enact the property tax rate when it passes the budget (see Lecture 11 for a complete description of the property tax).

For smaller local governments such as towns, villages, and small counties the chief administrative officer (e.g., city manager) may be appointed or there may be no chief executive. In these forms of government, the legislature often takes a much more active role in budget preparation.

[4]For a more detailed description of county government budgeting processes, see Sydney Duncombe, William Duncombe, and Richard Kinney, "Factors Influencing the Politics and Process of County Government Budgeting," *State and Local Government Review*, 24 (Winter 1992): 19–27.

Lecture 6

Federal Budgeting Process

The stability of the Congressional budget process that had been in place since the 1920s began to unravel in the mid-1960s. The process focused on passage of a series of appropriation bills, and the stability of the process had been based on the power of the appropriations committees. The chairman of these committees had considerable political power which allowed them to force elements of each house to compromise to assure passage of the appropriation bills. The chairman of these committees viewed their role as that of guardian, which fit their fiscally conservative philosophy and was in correspondence with their constituent interests. In addition, because of the micro-orientation of the budget, i.e., the focus on separate appropriation bills rather than a government-wide budget, the committee chairman were able to dole out enough benefits to members to allow them to accept compromises. Conflict certainly existed but it was kept "behind closed doors".

The growth in the macroeconomic and redistributive roles of the federal government led to the disintegration of the old process. The new interest in Keynesian economics encouraged the use of the budget as a major tool in economic stabilization. Fiscal policy could not be left as a residual of the process, but needed to be planned in advance, i.e., the interest in fiscal policy led to a more macro-orientation for the budget. The President, in particular, took the lead in reorienting the budget toward his macroeconomic objectives.

In addition, the influx of the "Great Society" social programs under President Lyndon Johnson weakened the power of the appropriations committees. Legislative authorization committees seized the initiative by using annual authorizations and various backdoor spending methods. These included: entitlement programs, contract authority, and borrowing authority.[1] Increasingly, large portions of the budget were being removed from the direct authority of the appropriations committees as illustrated in Figure 6.1.

The growth of entitlements has had significant implications on the budget process. Entitlements are generally outside the normal process since they are not under the jurisdiction of the appropriations committees. Changes to entitlements can only come about through

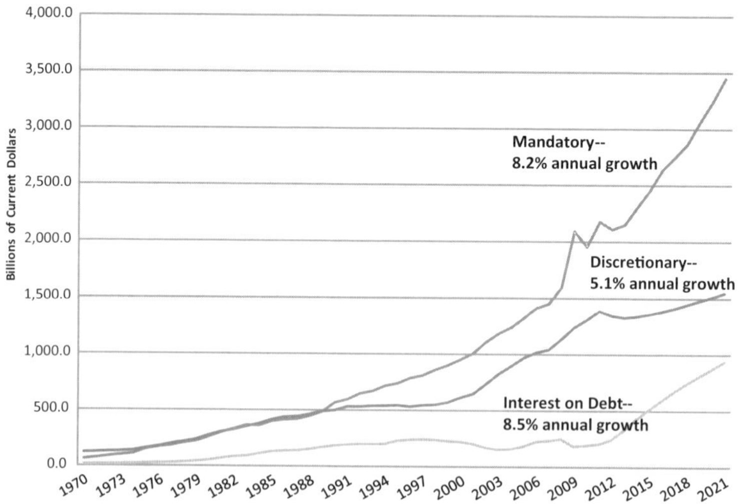

Figure 6.1. Outlays of FY 2012 federal budget — historical and adjusted baseline.

Source: Budget of the United States government, Fiscal year 2012, summary tables and historical tables.

[1]Kim, S. (1968). "The Politics of Congressional Budgetary Process: backdoor spending." *Western Political Quarterly*, 21, 606–623. Lee, R.D., R.W. Johnson, and P.G. Joyce (2013). Public Budgeting Systems, 9th edition, ch. 10. Burlington, MA: Jones & Bartlett Learning.

changes in the authorizing legislation that is either under the jurisdiction of authorizing committees or the finance committees. While the 1996 Welfare Reform legislation demonstrated that it is possible to change entitlements, it is fair to say that such changes are more controversial. This has led to increased conflict within the different committees of Congress.

Also, the increasing use of entitlements has made the budget much more vulnerable to economic changes. Changes in the inflation rate, unemployment, and economic growth can all significantly affect the cost of entitlements. Needless to say, the growth of entitlements has weakened the bottom-up or incremental part of the budget process, since the discretionary budget is not the major game in town.

The rapid growth in entitlements, spending for the Vietnam War, a slow economy, and the decentralized nature of Congressional budgeting all led to growing deficits in the early 1970s. While mild by today's standards, deficits reached $23 billion in 1972, which was 2% of GDP. In response, President Nixon started to impound (refuse to spend) money appropriated by Congress. Congressional leaders (Democrats) were furious and appointed in 1973 a "Joint Study Committee on Budget Control" to propose reforms on the Congressional budget process. The result was the "Congressional Budget and Impoundment Control Act of 1974."

6.1 Congressional Budget and Impoundment Control Act of 1974

This act was the most significant change in the congressional budgeting process since the Budget Act of 1921. It changed the basic structure, roles, and documents of congressional budgeting. While this reform is unique to Congress, it is a good way to highlight the pitfalls of reforming legislative budgeting.

As with any major reform, this was a product of compromise and those supporting its passage had many and even conflicting objectives. The basic objectives of the act as summarized by Joyce and Reischauer were to "reassert the congressional role in budgeting, to add some centralizing influence to the federal budget process, and to constrain the use of impoundments" (p. 432).[2] Its key components included:

— increasing congressional budgeting staff (CBO),
— giving Congress a more "macro" orientation,
— control of "backdoor spending," and
— control of the president's impoundment power.

By centralizing the process and extending the fiscal year to October 1, it was hoped that Congress would be better able to meet its deadlines. Finally, there were those who thought this would lead to a reduction in federal spending. As we will see, the Act had a profound effect on congressional budgeting, but has been unsuccessful in accomplishing many of its explicit objectives.

Provisions of the Act: There were two basic institutional reforms in this Act.

(1) The Budget Committees were established in each house that were to serve as the primary centralizing force in the budget process. These committees focused on the "big picture" and were to provide the guidelines to appropriation committees in much the same way as Office of Management and Budget (OMB) provided guidelines to the agencies.
(2) The Congressional Budget Office (CBO) was established as a non-partisan budget staff to provide Congress with an independent (from OMB) perspective on the budget.

The timetable of the budget process was significantly revised and provided a more centralized focus. As illustrated in Table 6.1:

(1) The President was required to submit a "current services budget" by November 10 which would indicate the expenditures required to support existing service levels;
(2) The authorization committees had to mid-March to review the budget and make recommendations to the budget committees;

[2]Joyce, P. and Reischauer, R. (1992). "Deficit Budgeting: The Federal Budget Process and Budget Reform." *Harvard Journal on Legislation*, 29, 429–453.

Table 6.1. Congressional budget process timetable, fiscal years 1977–1985.

November	
10th	President submits current services budget.
January	
14th day after congress meets	President submits his budget.
March	
15th	Committees and joint committees submit reports to Budget Committee.
April	
1st	CBO submits report to Budget Committee.
15th	Budget Committees report first concurrent resolution on the budget to their Houses.
May	
15th	Committees report bills and resolutions authorizing new budget authority.
15th	Congress completes action on first concurrent resolution on the budget.
September	
7th day after Labor Day	Congress completes action on bills and resolutions providing new budget authority and new spending authority.
15th	Congress completes action on second required concurrent resolution on the budget.
25th	Congress completes action on reconciliation bill or resolution, or both, implementing second required concurrent resolution.
October	
1st	Fiscal year begins.

Source: Congressional Budget and Impoundment Control Act, Title III, section 300 (1974); Also printed in Lee, R.D. and R.W. Johnson (1989). Public Budgeting Systems, 4th Edition. Gaithersburg, MD: Aspen Publishers, p. 163.

(3) The budget committees would then put together the first concurrent resolution which was to be passed by both Houses by May 15. This resolution provided an overall summary of the budget including budget authority, outlays, revenues, loan obligations, and debt. Although non-binding, this resolution was to provide the guidelines to the appropriations and revenue committees much in the same way as the budget guidelines in the executive branch;
(4) The process would then revert to its old procedures with the appropriations and the revenue committees considering specific appropriation and revenue legislation. These committees were supposed to remain within the ceilings proposed in the first resolution but the budget committees had no real enforcement power;
(5) Since there would undoubtedly be changes in the budget from these committee reviews, a second concurrent resolution was to serve as a final adjustment of the overall budget to these new circumstances. Once passed by both houses (by September 15) it was to bind Congress to these overall ceilings;
(6) The appropriation and revenue committees would then be instructed to modify their legislation through the process of reconciliation. This was to be completed by September 25 a week before the beginning of the new fiscal year.

Actual experience (1974–1985): On the surface, the act appeared to be a rational reform of the congressional budget process. Essentially the act attempted to install many of the major components of the executive budget process in the legislative branch. The budget committees (with support of the CBO) were to serve the same role as OMB. The first resolution was to be similar to a budget guideline and the second resolution the final budget. The bottom-up part of the process was to remain primarily in the hands of the appropriation committees.

The early years of the reform in the late 1970s seemed relatively successful. Most of the appropriations and revenue legislation were passed on time and the Presidential use of impoundments decreased significantly. However, under the surface the process was beginning to destabilize again. While the act attempted to impose executive budgeting on Congress, there was a big difference in the centralization of power. The President eventually had final say on what went in the President's budget proposal. There was no comparable source of power in Congress.

All congressmen could vote on budget legislation, and the power of the leadership of the political parties was actually becoming weaker during this time. The appropriations committees, which had served as a fiscal guardian under the old process, were increasingly turned into advocates for program expansion. The new guardian in the process, the budget committees, did not have the power to enforce their decisions on the appropriations and revenue committees.

The result was a power vacuum that left fewer constraints on spending than under the old budget process. The conflicts that were previously kept behind closed doors now erupted on the surface. The new macro-orientation of the budget left fewer options for compromise settlements of these conflicts. In summary, the increasing fragmentation of Congress conflicted with the attempt to centralize the budget process, resulting in disappointing results from these reforms.

The Reagan Administration exacerbated these conflicts. President Reagan's budget director, David Stockman, used the new budget process to press for the major budget cuts and tax reforms proposed by the President. In particular, in 1981 he helped move the reconciliation process to the first budget resolution. This resolution was made binding and an "Omnibus Budget Reconciliation Act of 1981" which contained hundreds legislative amendments was passed.

After the initial budget achievement of the Reagan Administration, however, their success in guiding the congressional budget process diminished considerably. Instead, the Reagan Administration basically took a firm stand on a few issues (taxes and defense) and let Congress hash out what to do about growing deficits. This heightened the level of conflict in Congress and further delayed the budgetary timetable. More and more of the budget was not passed on time, leaving departments funded by short-term continuing resolutions which kept funding levels the same as the previous year.

6.2 Gramm–Rudman–Hollings (GRH)

By 1985, Congress was falling farther and farther behind in its budget schedule and the federal deficit was continuing to mount. The Reagan Administration continued to remain firm on defense spending and taxes and left the deficit battles to Congress. Deficits reached $208 billion (in constant dollars) in 1983, 6.1% of GDP, the highest deficits relative to the size of the economy since World War II. It was into this highly charged atmosphere that the Balanced Budget and Emergency Deficit Control Act of 1985 was passed. In the words of Senator Rudman, GRH was "a bad idea whose time has come." As Wildavsky wrote:[3]

> "Gramm-Rudman-Hollings is as (or more) important for what it symbolizes as for what it does. The imposition of a formula for replacing the power of the purse, the most important congressional power, is an abdication of power. Congress is saying it is out of control..." (p. 236)

The process of budgeting in Congress had become so polarized that Congress could not reach compromises on important and hard decisions. The easy way out was to bind itself against its own "worst inclinations." Both parties hoped that the provisions of this act would be so "onerous" that it would force major budget reductions in either defense (democrats) or social programs (republicans).

Provisions of the Act: The act basically added two major changes to the existing budget process (Table 6.2):

(1) Speeding of budgetary timetable to allow time for the binding part of the process. The authorization committee reports and the first resolution were moved up 1 month. The first budget resolution was treated as binding (with the second dropped completely) and reconciliation was to be completed by June 15;

[3]Wildavsky, A. (1988). *The New Politics of the Budgetary Process.* (Glenview, IL: Scott, Foresman).

Table 6.2. Congressional budget process timetable, fiscal years 1989–1993.

January	
1st	Date from which deficit reduction is measured.
First Monday after January 3rd	President submits budget to Congress.
February	
15th	CBO issues annual report to Budget Committees.
25th	Committees submit views and estimates to Budget Committees.
April	
1st	Senate Budget Committee reports budget resolution.
15th	Congress completes budget resolution.
May	
15th	Appropriations bills may be considered in the House.
June	
10th	House Appropriations Committee reports last annual appropriations bill.
15th	Congress completes reconciliation.
30th	House completes action on annual appropriations bills.
July 15th	President submits mid-session budget.
August	
15th	Office of Management and Budget (OMB) and CBO estimate deficit for upcoming fiscal year; presidential notification regarding military personnel.
20th	CBO issues its initial report to OMB and Congress.
25th	OMB issues its initial report to president and Congress; president issues initial sequester order.
September	
6th	Deadline for president's explanatory message on initial order.
October	
1st	Fiscal year begins.
10th	CBO submits revised report to OMB and Congress.

(*Continued*)

Table 6.2. (*Continued*)

15th	OMB issues its revised report to president and Congress; president issues final sequester order, effective immediately. Congressional alternative to presidential order, if any, developed and adopted.
30th	Deadline for president's explanatory message on final order.
November	
15th	Comptroller general compliance report issued.

Source: *The Congressional Budget Process: An Explanation*, 100th Congress, 2nd session, Senate Committee on the Budget, p. 26, Government Printing Office, 1988; Also printed in Lee, R.D. and R.W. Johnson (1989). Public Budgeting Systems, 4th Edition. Gaithersburg, MD: Aspen Publishers, p. 174.

(2) The sequestration procedure was the real teeth in this act. By the middle of August, the CBO and OMB were to prepare separate estimates of the deficit from the budget passed by Congress. If it exceeded $10 billion over the deficit target, then the President was to submit his first sequestration order by August 25, outlining where the cuts were to be made. If Congress did not revise the budget to hit the deadline by early October, then a final sequestration order was to go into effect. Budget cuts were generally mandated by formula with some categories exempt from cuts and some not fully exposed to cuts. Overall 50% of the cuts were to come from defense and 50% from domestic programs.

Actual experience: GRH began with much less enthusiasm from Congress since in a sense it was an admission of defeat. Almost immediately after the act was passed, it was challenged on constitutional grounds. These constitutional challenges were upheld resulting in a revision to the act in 1987. This revision both changed the nature of the sequestration procedure and extended the deadline for a balanced budget from 1991 to 1993.

From 1986 to 1990, the Act clearly had an effect on Congress, but it is questionable whether most objectives had been met. The congressional budgetary timetable continued to bear only faint resemblance to when actual appropriation acts are passed. For significant portions of the year, continuing resolutions funded many agencies. The budgetary process in Congress continued to be highly polarized. If the act had any success, it was further focusing attention on the budget deficit and where possible cuts will take place.

The sequestration procedure was put into effect upon occasion; however, the cuts were often more "smoke and mirrors" than real reductions. The director of the CBO, Robert Reischauer, estimated that 45% of the cuts from FY 1988–1991 were temporary in nature, not permanent reductions. In many of these years, the GRH target has been exceeded and the actual deficit continued to grow. By 1990, the deficit had risen to $221 billion, and showed no sign of going down.

Why had this act met with limited success, even though by design it was meant to force Congress to act?

(1) Part of the problem was that the Act removed significant portions of the budget from the sequestration procedure. Wildavsky (1988) estimated that 48% of the budget was completely exempt (Social Security, interest, prior obligations, and some entitlement programs), and 24% was partially exempt (Medicare and retirement COLAs) from the process.[4] The remaining 28% was too small a base to distribute the significant cuts required by the act.
(2) Ultimately, this act failed because Congress cannot avoid hard budgetary choices by legislative handcuffs. The threat of punishment did not frighten Congress into action. When Congress found these constraints too difficult to live with, it had the power to find ways to avoid them.
(3) The inflexibility of the system could not survive in the unpredictable and volatile economic and political environment. Eventually, changes had to be made to the targets.

---

[4] *Ibid.*

6.3 The Budget Reforms of 1990

During the fall of 1990, there were heated budget battles replace Congress and the Bush Administration. Bush proposed one plan (that included tax increases) that was rejected by Congress. Finally, at the end of October 1990, one month late, a budget agreement was reached on the FY 1991 budget.

While the budget battles and tax increases received most of the attention, probably the most important part of this agreement — the budget enforcement act (BEA) — received almost no attention. As summarized in the recommended Federal Budget Report, this change was "made by a very small number of people" in "relative secrecy" and was "completed at the very last minute" (p. 2). The result was that very few people were aware of the components and importance of this reform. These components include[5]:

(1) *Revised deficit targets*: As with previous GRH changes, this change stretched out the time period for reducing the deficit and revised the deficit targets.
(2) *Appropriations limits (caps)*: The key part of the change was that it reoriented the process away from meeting specific deficit targets to controlling expenditures. At least until FY 1993, the budget was divided into three appropriations categories: defense, international, and domestic. The agreement set appropriations caps that could not be exceeded except in special circumstances. If defense spending, for example, went over their "cap," then any cuts to fit within the cap would have to be in defense. In other words, each of these categories became a separate budget that had to remain within a preset ceiling. During the 1993 budget process, President Clinton proposed and Congress passed an extension of the BEA provisions.
(3) *Flexibility*: In an attempt to avoid the stringent straight jacket of GRH, this reform provided several built-in forms of adjustment. The spending caps and the deficit targets could be adjusted a several points in the year to reflect a changing

[5]Joyce, P. and R. Reischauer. (1992). "Deficit Budgeting."

environment (e.g., inflation, recession). Provisions were made to allow exceptions to the caps in the case of an emergency declared by the president.

(4) *Pay-as-you-go provisions*: In an attempt to control for the cost of entitlement and "tax expenditures," this reform said that changes in these programs should be revenue neutral. If benefits of one entitlement went up, then the benefits of another would have to go down.

(5) *Revised sequestration*: Instead of the main focus of sequestration being to meet some deficit target, the major sequestrations would involve adjusting appropriations within each category to keep them from exceeding the cap. Also, a form of sequestration could be used to keep changes to entitlement and tax expenditures revenue neutral.

(6) *Points of Order*: Besides sequestration procedures, the budget caps and pay-as-you-go (PAYGO) procedures can be enforced by the use of points or order. A single member of Congress can raise a point of order on the floor to block legislation that violates the budget resolution. In the Senate, this mechanism can be particularly effective since it requires 60 votes to overturn.

(7) *New timetable*: The attached Table 6.3 provides the new timetable resulting from this reform. Without going into details on each change, one the major changes were the "sequestration" reports issued by the OMB. These indicate how much appropriations exceed the cap, or whether entitlement/tax expenditures are revenue neutral. If Congress is not able to stay with these limits, then 10–15 days after the adjournment of Congress, the OMB will propose the final adjustments that have to be made by the agencies within each category.

Actual experience: After BEA was implemented, the country went into a deep recession. The result was continued growth in the deficit to record levels ($290 billion) in FY 1992 despite budget caps that required a $500 billion decrease in the federal budget over 5 years. This led to another round of budget cuts in FY 1993 and significant cuts in FY 1996 and FY 1997. Some of you may remember the budget

Table 6.3. Federal budget process timetable, fiscal 2007.

Date	Action to be Completed
Between the first Monday in January and the first Monday in February	President transmits the budget, including a sequester preview report
Six weeks later	Congressional committees report budget estimates to Budget Committees
April 15th	Action to be completed on congressional budget resolution
May 15th	House consideration of annual appropriations bills may begin
June 15th	Action to be completed on reconciliation
June 30th	Action on appropriations to be completed by House
July 15th	President transmits mid-session review of the budget
August 20th	OMB updates the sequester preview
October 1st	Fiscal year begins

Source: Reprinted from the Office of Management and the Budget. 2007. *The Budget System and Concepts, Budget of The United States Government, Fiscal Year 2007: Analytic Perspectives*. Washington, DC: OMB, p. 381. Also printed in Lee, R.D., R.W. Johnson, and P.G. Joyce (2013). Public Budgeting Systems, 9th edition, ch. 10. Burlington, MA: Jones & Bartlett Learning, p. 313.

stalemate between the President and Congress in the fall of 1995 that shut down the government.

These cuts as well as an unexpectedly strong economy led to a sharp drop in the deficit in FY 1997, and for the first time in three decades budget surpluses in FY 1998–2001. However, these surpluses are somewhat deceptive since they include the "off-budget" surplus primarily from the Social Security Trust Fund. While there was an "off-budget" surplus was $160 billion in FY 2001, the "on-budget" deficit was $33 billion.

6.4 The Budget Control Act of 2011

Congress allowed the Budget Enforcement Act to expire in FY 2002. Due to a recession, tax cuts, and large new spending commitments (particularly for defense), the federal budget went into deficit in FY 2002. Then government spending in response to the Great Recession led to additional increases in the deficit. The size of the deficit reached post-WWII highs in FY 2011 of $1.6 trillion.

A new set of institutional provisions intended to help (force) Congress and the President to reduce the size of the deficit were adopted in 2010 and 2011.

PAYGO. Under the 2010 Statutory PAYGO Act, any legislative changes to taxes or mandatory spending that increase multi-year deficits must be "offset" or paid for by other changes to taxes or mandatory spending that reduce deficits by an equivalent amount. Violation of PAYGO triggers across-the-board cuts ("sequestration") in selected mandatory programs to restore the balance between budget costs and savings.

Discretionary funding caps. The 2011 budget control act (BCA) imposed limits or "caps" on the level of discretionary appropriations for defense and for non-defense programs in each year through 2021. Appropriations in excess of the cap in either category trigger sequestration in that category to reduce funding to the capped level.

BCA sequestration. On top of any sequestration triggered by PAYGO or funding cap violations, the BCA also requires additional sequestration each year through 2021 in discretionary and select mandatory programs, split evenly between defense and non-defense funding. This BCA sequestration was implemented as a result of a BCA-created congressional joint select committee's failure to propose a legislative plan that would reduce deficits by $1.2 trillion over 10 years. In the case of discretionary programs, for 2014 and after, this special sequestration reduces the appropriations caps below the level that the BCA originally set.

If budget legislation violates these statutes, the relevant sequestration penalties apply automatically, unless Congress also modifies the requirements. For example, policymakers modified the 2013 BCA sequestration requirement in the American Taxpayer Relief Act of

2012. Similarly, the Bipartisan Budget Act of 2013, worked out by Senate Budget Committee Chair Patty Murray (D-WA) and House Budget Committee Chair Paul Ryan (R-WI), reduced sequestration cuts in 2014 and 2015 while extending BCA sequestration of mandatory programs through 2023.

Lecture 7

Budget Execution and Control

7.1 Introduction

Today, we will turn to a stage in the budget process that receives less attention — budget execution. In the previous lectures on budgeting, we focused on the first two stages of the budget process — preparation and approval. Although these stages are clearly important, they represent essentially expenditure plans and revenue forecasts. It is in the execution phase of the budget cycle that the budget is turned into action.

The budget may go through significant transformations during the fiscal year. These modifications to the budget usually are a result of changes in the economy which affect revenues and expenditures. The budget office, in particular, is involved in monitoring the progress of the budget to try to ensure that the final budget will be balanced. In addition, budget offices are often involved in monitoring how agencies spend their money to assure that the money is being spent efficiently, legally, and on the programs (and in some case objects) designated in the budget legislation. In other words, the budget execution stage focuses primarily on financial control. We will review the different methods used to monitor, control, and adjust the budget.

The emphasis on financial accountability comes at a cost. Agency managers may have limited flexibility to adapt to changing circumstances through resource allocation and programmatic decisions. An alternative control system is to focus on agency performance in accomplishing their objectives and to provide managers flexibility in how they allocate the budget. The second half of this lecture will focus on fraud in government. We discuss the classifications of fraud and the role of internal controls within an organization.

7.2 Budget Execution Control

Once the new fiscal year begins in July (or January for many local governments), then the execution phase of the budget begins. Presumably, the legislative body passed its appropriations and revenue bills, which have been signed by the chief executive. If this is not the case, then some sort of "continuing resolution" has to be passed until the appropriation legislation is approved. On the surface, this phase of the budget would seem relatively straightforward. The agencies receive the money appropriated by the legislature and begin to execute their programs.

However, the agency is not the only actor involved in this phase. Because of the heavy emphasis put on accountability and control in the public sector, there are several other actors — most notably the budget office and legislature — which are actively involved in monitoring the execution phase of the budget. Much of this concern is driven at the state and local levels by the requirement for a balanced budget. Since changing economic circumstances can influence revenues and expenditures, many of the controls exercised in the execution phase are used to monitor and allow adjustments to the budget.

7.2.1 Objectives of budget execution control

(1) The primary focus of the execution and auditing phases of the budget has been on budget financial control. This emphasis on financial control is driven at the state and local level primarily by the need to assure a "balanced budget" and comply with legal

Table 7.1. Objectives/methods of financial control system.

Objectives	**Control Methods**
Adjust expenditure plan to legislative changes.	Revised expenditure plan by agency.
Hold agency accountable for type of spending.	— Pre-audit process — Position controls — Transfer controls — Requisition controls — Travel controls — Internal control system
Control expenditures to ensure balanced budget.	— Monitoring revenue and expenditures — Expenditure ceilings — Encumbrances — Contingency reserves — Impoundments
Cope with unforeseen developments	— Reprogramming funds — Transferring funds — Use contingency funds

restrictions and legislative intent. As illustrated in Table 7.1, the basic objectives of the execution control process are[1]:

(a) to adjust the expenditure plans of the agencies to reflect the changes made by the legislature and revised cost and revenue estimates,
(b) to hold the agencies accountable to the chief executive and legislature for the types of expenditures that they are undertaking. In other words, are the agencies complying with legal restrictions and legislative or chief executive intent in terms of their objects of expenditures, and prevention of fraud, waste, and abuse,
(c) to provide a regular monitoring of the budget and build contingencies which will allow adjustment throughout the year,
(d) to provide the tools to make major adjustments in the budget to cope with unforeseen developments.

[1]Donald Axelrod. (1988). *Budgeting for Modern Government.* (New York: St. Martin's Press, Inc), ch. 7.

Besides the need to "balance the budget," the heavy emphasis on control during budget execution is based partly on tradition. This was traditionally what budget directors viewed as their job and has been passed on from generation to generation. In addition, the heavy emphasis put on control and objects of expenditures by the legislature puts pressure on the budget office and the agencies to adopt this orientation. The publicity that a procurement or personnel scandal gets is another factor driving a control orientation.

(2) However, the heavy emphasis on financial control ignores the impact that programs have on society. Ideally, execution control should also attempt to hold the agency accountable for the efficiency with which services are produced, and the effectiveness of those services. Not surprisingly, there are some very basic tradeoffs between control systems focusing on financial control and service effectiveness (Table 7.1).

7.2.2 Financial control methods

We begin by discussing the traditional financial control systems used by governments. The agency is not free to spend the full appropriation as it sees fit. There is an elaborate financial control system which is usually implemented by the budget office and possibly the legislative body. This system forces an agency to get prior approval for many of its procurement and personnel decisions. A basic control mechanism is the allotment which is a process of dividing the appropriation into (usually) quarterly installments. The agency is then restricted as to what it can spend in any one quarter. This gives the central budget office a "powerful tool" to adjust expenditures to changing circumstances. Besides allotments, the other control mechanisms include:

(1) **Revised expenditure plans:** Which are essentially a revised version of the agency budget which reflects changes made by the legislature during the budget adoption phase. The agencies submit the revised expenditure plans to the budget office, which

has to approve the final apportionments to the agency. These plans serve as the basis for making allotments.

(2) **Spending controls:** Before an agency can actually commit to spending a portion of the allotment, it must submit a request to the budget office. The budget office will carry out a pre-audit to assure that this expenditure is authorized and sufficient funds are available.

There are several types of pre-audits. Position controls require agencies to get prior approval for filling vacancies or new positions. Transfer controls prevent an agency from transferring money from one object classification to another without central budget office approval. Requisition controls require central budget office approval of purchase orders. Finally, because of the political sensitivity of travel, there are usually travel controls which require central budget office approval of travel vouchers.

These accountability tools are part of an internal control system in government, which is established to protect against fraud and abuse of government financial resources, and encourage more efficient use of resources. A key principle of an internal control system is the segregation of duties for financial transactions. For instance, in the area of purchasing, segregation of duties requires that different individuals be assigned responsibility for requesting expenditures, approving expenditures, verifying receipt of the good or service, making payment for the good or services, and recording the payment in the accounting system. Segregation of duties across multiple individuals reduces the probability that fraud will go undetected. An independent internal auditor can serve as the point person in an internal control system by periodically reviewing financial transactions (see discussion below).

(3) **Budget monitoring tools:** Because the budget is just a forecast of expenditures and revenues, it is subject to significant change over the course of a year. For example, a rapid increase in inflation, or unemployment, may affect significantly the actual

revenues and expenditures during a fiscal year. The budget office (or finance department) is usually given the responsibility of monitoring revenues and expenditures during the course of the year, with the objective of identifying major discrepancies.

The budget office also has several tools that they can use to control expenditure flows to assure a balanced budget. These include the use of expenditure ceilings or contingency funds to build padding into the budget to allow for unexpected events. In addition, expenditures are usually first recorded when they are encumbered, not when they are paid for. The budget office may use encumbrances to set aside planned expenditures for a specific purpose to assure that the agency does not over-commit its resources. As a last resort, the chief executive may take the action of impounding or not spending certain appropriations as a way of assuring a balanced budget. As we discussed in the last chapter, the use by President Nixon of impoundments led to the 1974 Act which controls their use at the federal level.

(4) **Budget adjustment tools:** If the minor adjustments just discussed are not sufficient to assure a balanced budget, then the budget office or the legislature may need to take more substantial action. For the budget office, this either involves moving funds between different programs (reprogramming funds) or moving funds between different expenditure objects in the same department (transferring funds). In most cases, the executive is forbidden from transferring funds between departments.

Legislative approval may be required for some transfers or reprogramming of funds. The role that the legislature wants to play in the execution control process is really up to the legislature. When such re-adjustments are not sufficient, the agencies may be forced to ask for supplemental appropriations. These appropriations generally require the approval of the budget office and the legislature. Forrester and Mullins (1992) found that "rebudgeting" was a common event in municipal governments in the US, but appeared to be "primarily technically driven... that cities use rebudgeting to marginally adjust programs to meet management needs in a changing environment." (p. 473)[2]

7.2.3 Criticisms of the execution control

While the methods just described exist in one form or another in most governments in this country, they are not free of criticism. Several common criticisms are mounted against the focus on traditional financial control systems:

(1) Schick argues that the heavy emphasis on detailed controls has led to mountains of paperwork which are hard for the budget office to manage.[3] This leads to a routinization of the role of the budget analyst which encourages a myopic emphasis on the processing of forms and requests. Since these requests overwhelm the capabilities of the budget office, most are given only limited scrutiny. In addition, the budget analyst is prevented from doing any planning by the need to "process the paper."

(2) Hale and Douglass (1977)[4] argue that agencies find ways around the tight execution controls including: underestimating special revenue receipts to increase general revenue allocation; diverting funds from general to special appropriation accounts to avoid loss of appropriations at the end of the fiscal year; and getting around transfer or reprogramming controls to shift expenditures within a department.

(3) The focus on financial controls reduces the efficiency of government agencies by limiting the flexibility of managers to adjust to changing circumstances, and by discouraging initiative and

---

[2]Dan Mullins and John Forrester. (1992). "Rebudgeting: The Serial Nature of Municipal Budgetary Processes." *Public Administration Review* 52(5): 467–73.

[3]Allen Shick, "Control Patterns in State Budget Execution," *Public Administration Review*, 53 (September/October, 1964): 445–454.

[4]George Hale and Scott Douglass, "The Politics of Budget Execution: Financial Manipulation in State and Local Government," *Administration and Society*, 9 (November 1977): 367–378.

creativity. In addition, the inability of agencies to carry budget savings over to the next fiscal year encourages wasteful spending sprees at the end of the fiscal year.[5]

7.2.4 Control system reforms

Cothran (1993) describes how some budget reforms have focused on changing both budget preparation and control.[6] "Entrepreneurial budgeting" involves:

(1) Central decision making over the total budget amount and spending among broad categories; but
(2) Decentralized control of the budget within each agency.

> "Government managers are treated more like business managers. They might be given more discretion to move money around among line items, such as from salaries to supplies, or to move money from operations to capital spending. In addition, they might be allowed to carry over a significant portion of a year-end surplus to the next fiscal year." (p. 450)

The latter practice, often called "profit-sharing" is gaining popularity. Instead of losing any unspent funds at the end of the year, managers are allowed to shift a portion of savings to next year. Supposedly, this provides incentives to save money instead of madly spending any unspent funds at the end of the year.

(3) Accounting for results using some form of performance measures. In exchange for more autonomy, public managers must provide evidence that the mission of the agency was accomplished efficiently. However, as Cothran indicates, "To be effective, such devolution of authority must be accompanied by a clear specification of goals, authority and responsibilities." (p. 450)

---

[5] L.R. Jones and K.J. Euske. (1991). "Strategic Misrepresentation in Budgeting." *Journal of Public Administration Research and Theory*, 1 (October): 437–460.

[6] Dan Cothran. (1993). "Entrepreneurial Budgeting: An Emerging Reform," *Public Administration Review*, 53 (September): 445–454.

7.3 Control System Design

7.3.1 Factors to consider

(1) Type of good/service:

a. Is output/activity of relatively homogeneous quality?
b. Is the service demand-led (client demand for service) or led by the government (maintenance, casework, and regulation)?
c. Is the demand for the service by clients fairly regular, or very unstable?
d. Can the quantity and quality of the service be measured fairly accurately?
e. Do external factors (outside agency control) have a large influence on output or outcome levels?
f. Is the function designed to monitor the performance of others or regulate other parties?

(2) Is there already a good accounting system, and financial auditing system in place? Is corruption or financial irregularities a regular problem? Are there opportunities for corruption?

a. Is there easy access to cash?
b. Are there a number of external contracts that are difficult to monitor? (e.g., capital acquisition, consulting agreements, etc.)
c. Are there significant information asymmetries? Is this service complex or does it require significant technical knowledge? Are there any professional organizations that provide certification?

(3) How important is the service? What are the consequences of failing to provide adequate service?

a. Effect on health and safety?
b. Effect on government stability? Could loss of control significantly undermine government credibility and threaten government institutions?
c. Will government lose capacity to perform service in the future if it contracts it out?

7.3.2 Design choices

(1) *Ex ante* (before) or *ex post* (after) controls:

  a. Require approval before execution.
  b. Audit financial records or performance after execution.

(2) What do you control?

  a. Financial control.
  b. Performance — quantity or quality of inputs.
  c. Price per unit of service.

(3) Incentives for proper performance?

  a. Carrots: financial incentives, job security, recognition, advancement, and flexibility.
  b. Sticks: Loss of flexibility, job loss, negative publicity, and more *ex ante* controls.

(4) On who are controls imposed?

  a. Government manager of regular agency.
  b. Quasi-government organization (public enterprise).
  b. Private or non-profit organization.

7.3.3 Types of control systems

(1) Traditional control system:

Components:

(a) *Ex ante* control system.
(b) *Ex post* financial and performance audits.

Characteristics of service: This type of control system may be necessary if any of the following are important?

(a) heterogeneous output that is difficult to measure,
(b) significant impact of external factors on expenditures or service outcomes,
(c) poor financial control system in place now,
(d) regulating or "coercing" citizens is part of the service (e.g., police, environmental regulation etc.)

(2) Per unit contract with government agency or non-government contractor:

Components:

(a) *Ex ante* negotiation of price per unit.
(b) *Ex ante* verification of agencies capacity to meet service quantity and quality requirements.
(c) *Ex post* monitoring of service quality.

Characteristics of service: This is a viable option when all of the following exist?

(a) Homogenous output with regular demand for services.
(b) Measurable output quantity and service quality.
(c) Not a large influence of the external factors on quantity or quality of the service.
(d) Consequences of short-term failure are not catastrophic.

(3) Performance contracts:

Components:

(a) *Ex ante* specification of performance quantity and quality.
(b) *Ex ante* specification of a fixed budget total (maybe with some contingency funds or allowances for emergencies).
(c) Incentives for good performance (or poor performance).
(d) *Ex post* monitoring of contract compliance.

Characteristics of service: This is a viable option when the following exist?

(a) Homogeneous or heterogeneous output. If homogeneous then one can measure the quantity of output, if heterogeneous then one must also be able to measure quality.
(b) Difficult to game the system or manipulate measures of output quantity and quality.
(c) Not a large influence of external factors on quantity or quality (or it can be readily controlled for in the contract).
(d) Impacts of short-term failure are not catastrophic.

7.4 Fraud and Financial Accountability in Government

In the second part of the lecture, we will focus on preventing fraud and misuse of resources. The Association of Fraud Examiners (ACFE) identifies three categories of occupational fraud. Recent and very public examples of each type of fraud are included below. I encourage you to review the links to articles that provide an extensive discussion on the issues related to each type of fraud.[7] They include

(a) **Asset misappropriation:** which includes all theft or misuse of an organization's assets (e.g., skimming revenues, stealing inventory, and payroll fraud). Asset misappropriation accounts for more than 90% of all fraud detected. The most frequently misappropriated asset is cash, accounting for 93% of all misappropriation schemes which include (1) *fraudulent disbursements* (e.g., submitting for payment false invoices for fictitious goods or services, inflated invoices, using public funds to make payments on purchases that are personal, and payroll schemes by which an employer issues payment for false claims of compensation etc.) (2) *skimming* which includes taking cash before it is recorded in the books (3) *cash larceny* which includes taking cash after it has been reported on the books. The city of Dixon Illinois is a perfect example of asset misappropriation. The former city comptroller set up a series of accounts and was able to transfer more than $53 million from the town since 1990 (she was an employee since the early 1980s). While her lavish lifestyle was evident to her colleagues — no one suspected that she was skimming cash from the city's coffers.[8] The city of Bell California was also in the news recently. An audit (following investigative reporting by

[7]Summarized from the case study published by the National School Boards Association: Gregory J. Guercio and Mary M. Roach. (2005). Potential Fraud in the Business Office: Legal and Practical Issues for the School Attorney.: https://secure.nsba.org/Storefront/detail.aspx?id=1112.

[8]http://www.fbi.gov/chicago/press-releases/2012/federal-indictment-charges-former-dixon-comptroller-rita-crundwell-with-engaging-in-53-million-fraud-since-1990.

the LA times see http://www.latimes.com/local/bell/la-me-bell-scandal-a-times-investigation-20160211-storygallery.html) found the city had almost no internal controls. The audit revealed more than $5.6 million in improper sewer, property, business licensing fees and taxes, and exorbitant salaries for city leaders (e.g., city manager Robert Rizzo was paid more than $800,000, twice as much as the President of the US and three to four times more than the Mayors of the five largest American cities). The city had also mismanaged more than $50 million of bond proceeds approved by voters.

Box 1 below provides a brief description of some red flags of what one should look out for in the business office (or accounting function) of a department or organization.

(b) **Corruption:** involves the use of influence in a business transaction for the purpose of obtaining a benefit — an example of which includes accepting kickbacks. A more recent example of corruption comes from Jefferson County, Alabama. The county is currently emerging from bankruptcy that was as a result of more than $3.2 billion in debt issued by the County Commission to finance the reconstruction of its sewer system. In December 2008, the US Attorney for the Northern District of Alabama filed criminal charges against Birmingham Mayor Larry Langford and his friends William Blount and Albert LaPierre. The indictment charged that between 2002 and 2006, Langford used his position as president of the County Commission to generate $7.1 million in bond-related fees for Blount and Blount Parish Co Inc., a broker–dealer firm that in turn paid LaPierre ~$219,500 (a financial advisory firm that was supposed to serve the best interests of its client Jefferson County). LaPierre and Blount gave Langford ~$235,000 in expensive clothes, jewelry, and cash to pay off his personal debts.[9]

[9]For an extensive review of what happened in Jefferson County Alabama, see http://www.mobilebaytimes.com/alabama.pdf. Some of the SEC litigation can be found at http://www.sec.gov/litigation/litreleases/2011/lr22068.htm and http://www.sec.gov/litigation/litreleases/2008/lr20821.htm.

Box 1: Red Flags in the Business Office[10]

Most employees who commit fraud are first-time offenders, but they have been with the organization, their salary, and the higher up they are in the organizational hierarchy, the larger the dollar value of the fraud.

Red flags might be raised about people who:

- Show an extraordinary devotion to work — arrive early, stay late, never miss a day, refuse to take vacation or sick leave.
- Refuse promotion or the offer of assistance, such as additional staff.
- Are facing stressful situations at home, such as marital problems, sick children or family changes such as a wedding or college tuition that require significant funding.
- Are "control freaks" who refuse to allow anyone else near the financial center of the organization and refuse to assign any significant duties to others.
- Have a tendency to hire employees in the business office who are lax, inexperienced or extraordinarily submissive.
- Are easily annoyed or outraged by reasonable questioning or obfuscate in response.
- Express resentment at their compensation package.
- Exhibit noticeable lifestyle changes, such as expensive cars, luxury trips, jewelry, and second homes.

On an organization level look for:

- Lack of an integrated bank system.
- Missing documents or document alteration.
- Unduly close relationship with outside auditors.
- Reluctance to provide information to auditors, frequent disputes with auditors, or frequent or erratic change of outside auditors.

(*Continued*)

[10]Gregory J. Guercio and Mary M. Roach. (2005). Fraud in the Business Office: Legal and Practical Issues for the School Board.

Box 1: (*Continued*)

- Dismissal of or resistance to any tightening recommendations made by auditors.
- Attempts to direct auditors to one side or the other, revenue or expense.
- Weak internal control attitude; lax or incorrect practices tolerated.
- Lack of oversight of authority to open accounts.
- Sudden influxes of activity in dormant accounts.
- Excessive cash transactions.

(c) **Fraudulent financial statements:** includes overstating revenues and/or understating liabilities, in doing so, providing misleading information to investors. One notable recent example of fraudulent financial statements was the city of San Diego.[11] The city had created a maze of calculations and artificial devices to make it look as if the city's pension fund was sufficiently funded (i.e., that the city was making sufficient contributions to the pension fund to meet its pension obligations) when in reality it was developing a shortfall to the tune of $1.4 billion. According to the SEC, the city made misleading statements in the documents for five municipal bond offerings in 2002 and 2003 that raised over $260 million from investors. The SEC argued the city made misleading statements in the five separate bond offering documents which were intended to disclose material (or important) information to investors and were used to gauge investors' interest in a bond issuance. Second, the city made misleading statements to the credit rating agencies that gave the city its credit rating for its municipal bonds. Finally, the city made misleading statements in its "continuing disclosure statements," which described the city's financial condition and were provided by the city to investors in the municipal securities market with respect to the city's bond offerings. The SEC has

[11] www.**sec**.gov/litigation/admin/2006/33-8751.pdf.

filed similar charges against the state of Illinois and state of New Jersey.[12] In both cases the SEC alleged the governments misrepresented the true extent of the government's pension and other post-employment benefit obligations in their bond offering documents.

Even the smallest incidence of financial mismanagement or fraud can have damaging effects on government — such as reducing essential resources, causing unnecessary tax increases, decreasing the confidence of important investors and grant providers, and significantly harming public confidence in government institutions. It is therefore important to maintain a system of internal controls to ensure prudent management of fiscal resources.

7.5 Ensuring Financial Accountability Via a System of Internal Controls

The Institute of Internal Auditors defines internal control as "*a process within an organization designed to provide reasonable assurance regarding the following primary objectives*"[13]

- the safeguarding of assets,
- the economical and efficient use of resources,
- the reliability and integrity of information,
- compliance with policies, plans, procedures, laws, and regulations,
- the accomplishment of established objectives and goals of operations or programs.

Internal controls are a process — they are a means to an end, not an end itself. They are affected by people and can only provide reasonable assurance. Internal controls therefore rely on the people within the organization to assess risk, amend, and implement controls. There are five types of risk — *strategic* (risk that would

[12] http://www.sec.gov/news/press/2010/2010-152.htm and http://www.sec.gov/litigation/admin/2013/33-9389.pdf.

[13] https://na.theiia.org/standards-guidance/topics/Documents/Executive_Summary.pdf.

prevent a department from accomplishing its objectives), *financial* (risk that could result in a negative financial impact), *regulatory* (risk that could expose the government to fines and penalties due to non-compliance), *reputational* (risk that could expose the city to negative publicity), and *operational* (risk that could prevent a department from operating in the most effective and efficient manner).

Internal controls include

- separation of duties,
- authorization and approval,
- verification,
- review of operating performance,
- physical control,
- reconciliation,
- training, guidance, and monitoring.

For example, the state of Vermont recommends separate cash handling duties among different employees (see Box 2):

- In larger units, different employees should be designated to (1) receive cash, (2) deposit cash, and (3) record transactions so that no single employee has control over the entire process.
- In smaller units, with a minimal number of employees, cash operations should be reviewed and approved by someone (preferably a supervisor or manager) other than the person receiving the funds.

Box 2: Control for Cash Management: Receipts and Disbursements[14]

Receipts and deposits

Persons responsible for handling cash receipts should not participate in accounting or operating functions relative to controlling

(*Continued*)

[14]Mikesell (1999), adapted from William L. Kendig, "Cash Management in the U.S. Department of the Interior," *Journal of Cash Management* (May/June 1985): 38–44.

Box 2: (*Continued*)

accounts receivable, preparing and mailing due statements, or approving credits for returns or adjustments of amounts due. Receipts through the mail should be logged in the mailroom immediately, and receipts should be recorded within the day.

Large receipts ($1,000 federal threshold) should be deposited daily. All receipts should be deposited at least weekly.

Copies of cash receipts should be checked against the record of cash received by someone other than the person receiving the cash.

Wire transfers should be used for high-dollar cash receipts unless there are compelling reasons otherwise.

Receipt records should be maintained in a location separate from cash checks.

Disbursements

Before vouchers are certified for payment, they should be reviewed for correctness of payee and payment amount, to verify correct delivery of purchased goods or service, and to check that payment is appropriate.

Transactions should be verified, using statistical sampling procedures when transactions are numerous and other arrangements of records permit.

Procedures should accommodate exploitation of discounts when economically warranted.

Wire transfer/electronic funds transfer should be used as frequently as feasible for better control, to ease record keeping and to delay payment until actual due date.

The process should prevent duplicate payments on invoices. Advances should be controlled, being used only when necessary. Excess travel advances should be collected promptly, managers should have periodic reports of outstanding travel advances, and systems should permit withholding of overdue travel advances from employee compensation.

For purchases, the state of Vermont recommends

- Requisitions for goods and services are initiated and approved by authorized individuals (*an example of authorization and approval*).
- Purchase orders are based on valid, approved requests and are properly executed as to price, quantity, and vendor (*an example of documentation and approval procedures*).
- Received goods are secured in a safe location and inspected for quality and condition (*an example of physical control and verification*).
- Invoices are matched with purchase orders and receiving reports before approval for payment(*an example of reconciliation and verification*).
- Review invoices for accuracy by comparing charges (e.g., quantity, price etc.) to amounts indicated in purchase orders, contracts, or other source documents (*an example of verification*).
- Periodically compare recent purchases to financial and fixed asset/inventory records (if applicable) to ensure the accuracy and completeness of the transaction (*an example of monitoring*).

7.5.1 Role of internal audit and inspector general function in government

Internal auditing is an independent appraisal function established within an organization which examines and evaluates its activities as a service to the organization. The internal auditor's responsibilities may include reviewing compliance with existing financial regulations, instructions, procedures; evaluating the effectiveness of selected internal controls, reviewing reliability and integrity of record keeping, verifying claims for reimbursement for expenses, revenues, goods received, etc., and verifying inventory records etc. In government, the internal audit function is within the office of the Comptroller (or GAO, for the federal government). At the agency/department level, inspector general performs the task similar to that of an internal auditor. They not only examine financial reports, but also look for, and call attention to, instances of fraud, waste, and abuse; they work to identify the sources of these problems and make recommendations to attack their structural sources.[15]

Internal audits and/or the office of the inspector general should provide managers with analyses of the internal control shortcomings and provide recommendations for improvement. Chester County Pennsylvania provides an extensive list of management letters related to a variety of audits (see http://www.chesco.org/1856/Audit-Reports-Management-Letters). In some instances following the recommendations in the management letter, a government official or authorized personnel provide a response to the auditor concerns (see management letter and auditor response issued by the State of Michigan, Office of the Auditor General — for the Michigan State Employees Retirement System http://audgen.michigan.gov/finalpdfs/11_12/r071015112M.pdf).

Despite its relevance and importance in any organization the internal audit/inspector general's function is often underfunded and therefore unable to meet its objectives.

7.5.2 Role of external audit

While the internal audit serves to inform managers on internal control shortcomings, external audits serve to certify the financial statements of an organization. The external auditor performs, under contract, an annual audit of the financial records of the government. Their emphasis is on the fairness of information reported in the government's financial statements and compliance with Generally Accepted Accounting Principles (GAAP) as promulgated by the Governmental Accounting Standards Board (GASB). Moreover, unlike internal auditors who are employees of the government, external auditors are generally not employees of the government. However, in some states, the external auditor is the State Auditor.

[15]Irene Rubin. (2010). *The Politics of Public Budgeting*, 6th Edition. (Washington, DC: CQ Press), ch. 8.

Lecture 8

Capital Budgeting and Debt Management

8.1 Introduction

In the previous lectures, we have focused primarily on budgeting of current expenditures. Although capital expenditures are certainly part of the budgets prepared by the executive and approved by the legislature, the procedures we have discussed were developed for current expenditures.

Capital expenditures by definition are long-term commitments and accordingly require a long-term perspective. Generally, capital expenditures are defined as any object purchased by the government, which has a useful life over 1 year. Since this may involve literally thousands of small objects, such as books, desks, chairs, etc., for classification purposes in most governments, there is usually some cut-off point. For example, Hillsborough North Carolina (population 5,551) set its cut-off point at $50,000 and 1-year useful life. Largo, Florida (population 73,298) set its cut-off point at $100,000. Governments would also typically develop a recurring capital expenditure for the smaller assets with a life over 1 year that would be included in the operating budget.

Because capital assets will be around for a while, many governments have developed a different budget process to deal with capital expenditures, capital budgeting. Today, I want to give you an overview of what is typically involved in the capital budgeting process, which is used in many local governments. As part of this, we will touch briefly on the subject of cost/benefit analysis, which is an important analytic technique that can be used in capital budgeting analysis. Finally, the lecture will give you a brief introduction to the world of municipal bonds, which is the principal means by which state and local governments finance large capital expenditures.

8.2 Capital Budgeting

A capital budget is a tool which has a long tradition in local governments in this country. It was first developed in the 1940s and has slowly spread to most local governments in the country. A 1986 survey of 850 cities in this country found that 56% had a separate capital budget and 68% had a "capital improvement plan," which we will discuss shortly.[1] Although the highest use of these tools is in the large cities, this study found that around 50% of cities with a population between 10,000 and 25,000 used either a capital improvement plan and/or separate capital budget. At the state level, a survey in 1993 found that over two thirds of states had long-range capital budgets or capital improvement programs.[2] This implies that those of you going into state or local government administration will likely run into some sort of capital budget.

Why should governments have a capital budget? What is it about capital expenditures that would lead a government to treat them differently in the budget process? As we have already discussed, most budget processes in this country are short term in focus. Despite the attempt of budget reforms to increase the time frame for looking at budgets, most focus solely on next year's expenditures. While this short-term perspective may be acceptable for current expenditures, it becomes very problematic for capital expenditures.

[1] Doss Bradley Jr. (1986). "The Role of Capital Budgeting and Related Fiscal Management Tools in Municipal Government." *State and Local Government Review*, 18(3): 101–108.

[2] John P. Forrester. (1983). "Municipal Capital Budgeting: An Examination." *Public Budgeting and Finance*, 13: 85–103.

By their very definition, capital expenditures are used to acquire assets, which will be around for a number of years. Many capital expenditures are for fixed facilities (public buildings) or specialized equipment (fire engines), which is difficult for the government to resell. This implies that capital expenditure decisions tend to be irreversible, or "mistakes will be around for many years."

Because capital expenditures are usually quite large relative to the revenue in any one year, they are much more risky decisions than those over current expenditures. A bad capital expenditure can haunt a community (and a public official) for many years. Finally, capital expenditures involve the issue of intergenerational equity. What this means is that capital assets will be used by taxpayers for many years in the future and ideally the future taxpayers should pay for their use as well. All of these reasons imply that there is a need for:

— a long-term perspective,
— more careful planning and analysis,
— long-term financing of capital assets.

Capital budgeting is an attempt to bring all of these elements into the budgeting process.

8.2.1 Key steps in capital budgeting

Capital budgeting, like all of the elements of the budgeting process that we have described, varies significantly between different jurisdictions. What I want to do in this section is sketch for you some of the major components that are found in most capital budgeting systems. It is often the case that some parts of this process are used and others are not or are greatly modified. However, this section should give you a feel for what capital budgeting is all about (see Exhibit 13.2 in Lee and Johnson).[3]

[3]Ronald Lee, Robert Johnson, and Phil Joyce. 2013. *Public Budgeting Systems*, 9th edition. (Boston: Jones and Bartlett Publishers). Much of this section is borrowed from Chapter 17 of the ICMA book, *Management Policies in Local Government Finance*, fourth Edition. (Washington, DC: ICMA, 1996).

Exhibit 13.2 Capital facilities planning and budgeting.

1. Identify present service characteristics (inventory facilities and service levels)
   a. Coverage (quantity)
   b. Quality
   c. Cost per unit of service (efficiency)
2. Identify environmental trends
   a. Population growth projections
   b. Changing regulatory environment
   c. Employment and economic development trends
3. Develop service objectives
   a. Extension of service to new population or area (coverage)
   b. Improvement in quality of service
   c. Opportunities to stimulate economic growth
4. Develop preliminary list of capital projects and cost estimates
   a. Rehabilitation of existing facilities
   b. Replacement of existing facilities
   c. Addition of new facilities
5. Identify financial resources
   a. External assistance
   b. Projected growth in present revenue base
   c. Potential for direct cost recovery for individual projects
   d. Use of long-term debt
6. Select subset of projects for inclusion in 5-year capital improvement plan (CIP)
7. Identify future recurrent cost impact of CIP on operating budget
8. Include first year of CIP in annual budget estimate

Source: Lee, Johnson and Joyce (2013), p. 459.

8.2.1.1 *Long-term facilities (or master) plan*

Since the capital budgeting process involves long-term assets and may have significant effects on local finances and the economy, it is often tied into long-range planning in the community. For example, there may be "Master Plan" or "Capital Facility Plan" for the community, which lays out the proposed direction for the local economy and government. Ideally, the capital budget should be coordinated with this overall planning effort.

Typically, a master plan will include a capital facilities plan, which has an inventory of the capital stock. Such an inventory should list the amount, size and condition of the capital stock. This gives the community a foundation for deciding on what areas are in the most need of improvement and how much it will cost to address these needs.

In addition, a master plan will typically include information on past economic trends and the economic objectives in the future. What do these economic objectives imply about the necessary actions of government? Specifically, the plan should discuss the desired government services, forecast the demand for these services, and estimate the implications for capital facility requirements. For example, a master plan for sewer services would:

(1) Provide an evaluation of the condition of the present sewer facilities and when they are going to need major repair or replacement;
(2) Forecast the need for sewer services by residences and business by forecasting new households or businesses in the area, where they are going to locate, and the type of waste they are going to put in the system;
(3) Forecast the likely changes in federal and state water quality regulations that are likely to affect service needs;
(4) Estimate the least cost way to meet these demands — detail new facilities, upgrades of existing facilities, and maintenance plan.

One example of a community master plan, which is linked to infrastructure plans has been developed by the city of Cleveland (http://planning.city.cleveland.oh.us/cwp/whatis.html).

Civic Vision 2010 Citywide Plan

What is it?

- a long-term plan for neighborhood development and revitalization.
- a "guide" for use in evaluating development proposals.
- a "tool" for use in marketing Cleveland's neighborhoods for new development.

How will it be prepared?

- input from residents at community meetings
- a partnership with neighborhood groups
- collaboration with elected officials
- capitalizing on local expertise
- inter-governmental cooperation
- use of new technology

What will be its products?

- an analysis of current conditions
- goals and policies regarding neighborhood development and quality of life
- a land use plan
- a transportation and transit plan
- a zoning plan
- a capital improvements plan

How will it be implemented?

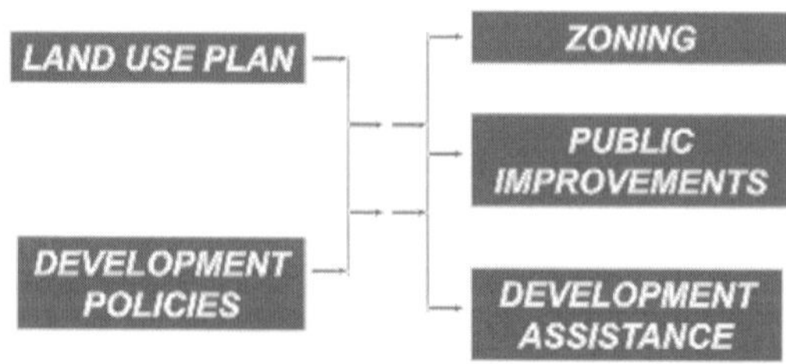

Source: http://planning.city.cleveland.oh.us/cwp/whatis.html.

Cleveland has recently updated the plan: "Connecting Cleveland: 2020 Citywide Plan," available at: http://planning.city.cleveland.oh.us/cwp/contents.html.

8.2.1.2 *Capital improvement plan (CIP)*

The first official step in most capital budgets is the preparation of what is called the "capital improvement plan." Basically, a capital improvement plan is a list of the proposed capital projects over a 5- or 6-year period.

Generally, the process involves preparation by the agencies each year of a list of capital projects that they would like to finance for the next 6 years. Typically, this involves revising the previous year's CIP and adding one more year at the end. Agency submissions will typically include a list and description of the projects, how the agency proposes that they be financed and estimated completion dates. The supporting documentation for each agency may include the results of project evaluation studies, often based on cost/benefit analysis, which we discuss next. The following details the capital planning process used in Onondaga County.

The capital planning process

Capital planning involves the County Executive, members of the County Legislature, heads of various county departments, and a citizen advisory board in a process that determines capital needs, alternatives, and priorities. The development of the CIP takes place over several months, beginning in February of each year, and includes five major phases.

1. In February, department heads begin preparation of project proposals in accordance with executive guidelines.
2. In April, proposals are submitted to the Division of Management & Budget (DMB). The proposals are analyzed by DMB in conjunction with the Syracuse-Onondaga County Planning Agency. The Law Department is consulted as needed.
3. By September, the county executive has approved a tentative CIP. It is presented to the Capital Program Committee (a committee

made up of legislators and representatives from the executive branch of county government) and the County Planning Board (a citizen advisory group).

4. In September, the Tentative CIP is presented with the County's Annual Operating Budget to the Ways and Means Committee of the County Legislature, and then to the full Legislature in October for approval.
5. From October to February, research on capital planning and management is conducted, and the prior year's process is critiqued. Revisions to forms and instructions are completed.[4]

Coordination and interaction among units of government occurs throughout the process, both formally and informally. The heads of County departments are consulted to discuss questions and recommendations regarding particular projects. Some of the major criteria for evaluating proposals are:

- relationship of the project to the goals of the county executive,
- degree of the overall need for the project,
- fiscal impact, including the County's capacity to borrow,
- non-county funding sources,
- consistency with the goals and policies in the 2010 Development Guide,
- community participation and support.

The final product of this process is a 6-year plan to improve or construct those facilities or components of county infrastructure considered necessary to provide or maintain an adequate level of public service. Approval by the County Legislature is not a commitment to fund every project in the plan, but rather it is an indication of support of the plan as a whole. Projects that require borrowing must be presented to the Legislature individually in order to secure authorization to incur debt.

Some governments have more extensive procedures for involving citizens in the capital planning process. Kansas City, for instance,

[4]http://www.ongov.net/finance/documents/CIP2014-2019BookADOPTED.pdf.

has used a fairly open (in terms of involving citizens) capital planning process. Citizens can get involved through the Community Infrastructure Committee (CIC), 16 public hearings, and they even have a website where citizens can make capital requests. The process is guided by the Capital Improvement Program Staff, and the Public Improvement Advisory Committee (PIAC). The PIAC takes the lead in evaluating the department requests, running the public hearings, and making the final recommendations to the mayor and the city council. They rate projects on some defined criteria using a numeric scale (not provided in documents I could find). The following is an illustration of the process in Kansas City.

Source: "5-year Capital Improvement Plan, Kansas City, MO," p. 13: https://data.kcmo.org/Finance/FY-2014-15-Capital-Improvement-Plan/kn9f-8g9t/data.

In both Onondaga County and Kansas City, and indeed most governments, development of the capital improvement plan begins with the agencies submitting their proposed capital projects to some central agency, either the budget office or a planning office. This central agency will review these plans much like an operating budget. Typically, they will have an idea of overall levels feasible for capital expenditures in any given year and the chief executive's priorities. Based on this, they will review and revise the agency's plan and will often force the agency to scale back or defer some projects. The resulting document will generally list:

— proposed capital expenditures by department,
— some detail on the major capital projects,
— proposed funding mechanism for these projects.

One common format for the capital plan would devote a summary page to each capital project explaining the project (including illustrations, and in some cases maps), outlining the estimated costs, and funding sources by year, and explaining how the funds are going to be used (engineering, construction, etc.). In addition, there is an estimate of the maintenance cost associated with each project. On the following page is an illustration for a park development project.

The beginning of the CIP should provide a summary of the overall capital improvement plan, funding sources, and major areas of investment. There is also typically a discussion of the operating budget impacts of the CIP in terms of additional operating spending, and maintenance spending required (or reduced) as a result of the projects in the CIP. Given that most capital and operating budgets are developed separately, formally making this link in the CIP is important.

The success of CIPs, as with other types of budgetary reforms, depends on how seriously agencies take this exercise. In many cases, CIPs can become simply unrealistic "wish lists" with little supporting documentation. However, if used properly, they serve a valuable planning tool for the chief executive and the agency in identifying major capital expenditures far enough in advance so that they can be fit into the community's resources.

8.2.1.3 *Project selection criteria*

Once a set of projects are identified by departments, the local government needs to make selection among the projects since there are usually many more projects than there is funding. Sometimes,

Sample Page

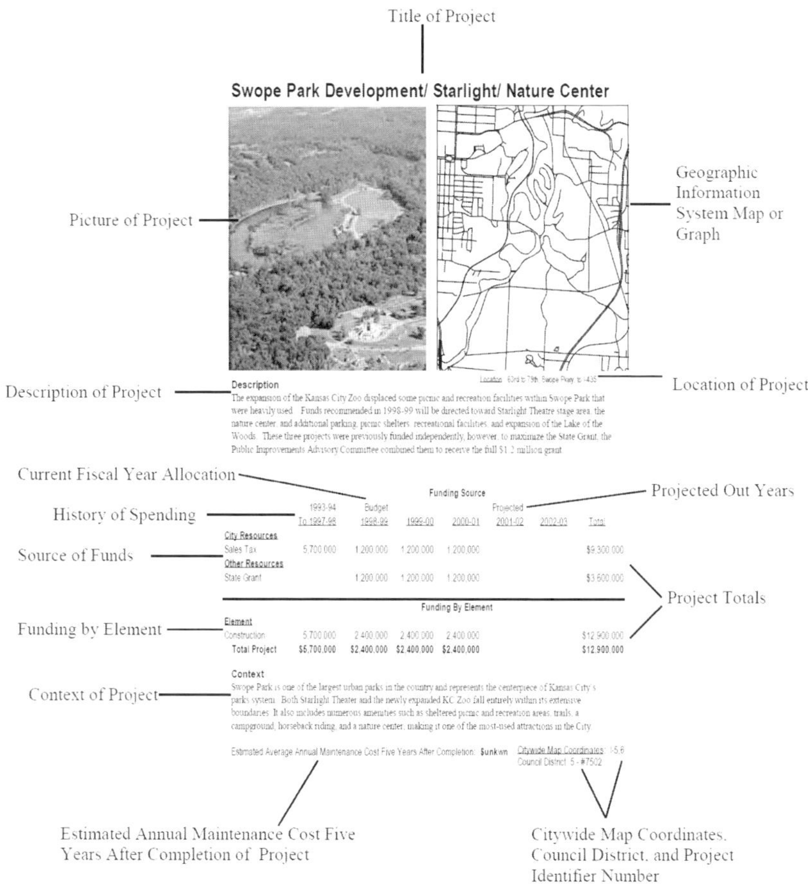

Source: "5-year Capital Improvement Plan, Kansas City, MO," p. 15: https://data.kcmo.org/Finance/FY-2014-15-Capital-Improvement-Plan/kn9f-8g9t/data.

this can be via political or geographic allocation where each part of the community gets a certain number of projects. Cleveland organizes this as a series of neighborhood plans, where each neighborhood makes its recommendations for improvements.

Beginning FY 2013, the city of Annapolis, MD prepared the CIP under a new Capital Planning and Budget Policy approved by the City Council in June, 2011. Among other things, the policy requires

Table 8.1. Evaluation criteria.

Criterion	Points
1. Health, Safety and Welfare An assessment of the degree to which the project improves health and safety factors associated with the infrastructure asset. For example, projects that result in the reduction of accidents, improved structural integrity, and mitigation of health hazards would score higher.	25
2. Regulatory or Legal Mandates An assessment of the degree to which the project is under a regulatory order or other legal mandate, or meets a federal, State or local safety requirement. For example, projects that are required by consent decrees, court orders, and other legal mandates would score higher.	25
3. Operational Necessity An assessment of the degree to which the project supports operational efficiency and effective delivery of services. Guidelines: *Improves* operational functions and services: up to 10 points *Sustains* operational functions and services: up to 5 points	10
4. Implication of Deferring the Project (opportunity costs) An assessment of the costs associated with deferring the project, such as inflationary construction costs or additional annual operating and maintenance costs for each year the project is not funded. For example, projects that would have significantly higher future costs, negative community aspects, or negative public perception, should they be deferred, would score higher.	10
5. Budget Impact An assessment of the project's budget impact, i.e., the degree to which it affects operations and maintenance costs positively or negatively. For example, a roof replacement project that reduces both maintenance requirements and energy consumption or a storm drain that reduces the need for periodic cleaning would score higher. On the other hand, a new facility that increases maintenance, energy and staffing costs would score lower.	5
6. Strategic Goals An assessment of the degree to which the project furthers thirteen (13) city's strategic goals as adopted in the Comprehensive Plan and listed in the section of the policy addressing the Comprehensive Plan.	6
7. Grant Funding Opportunity An assessment of the amount of funding in the project compared to the amount of funding provided by grant funds from outside agencies. This	7

(*Continued*)

Table 8.1. (*Continued*)

should include an assessment of the amount of funding needed to complete the current project phase and the entire project. For example, a project that would bring grant funds from an outside agency into the City would score higher, while a project that relies only on City funds would score lower.	
8. Community Demand	7
An assessment of the degree to which the project meets a community need or responds to community demand. How need/demand was assessed, measured, or recorded will be noted.	
9. Implementation Readiness	5
An assessment of the time required for a project to begin. This should include an assessment of: project complexity; internal decisions/commitments that are required; review requirements by boards/commissions; agreements or approvals required bv non-City entities; timing considerations with other capital projects (if applicable); the degree to which the project is in compliance with the Comprehensive Plan or other City-adopted plans; and level of public support. Whether a public information strategy is recommended will be noted.	
Total points possible	**100**

Source: "Capital Improvement Plan; Fiscal Year 2017–2022, City of Anapolis, Mayland," p. 3. https://www.annapolis.gov/1032/Budgets-Proposal-and-Adopted.

that all projects be scored on nine criteria to receive up to 100 points. This is to provide a measure of objectivity in the assessment of the relative priority of projects and resulting funding commitments. As expected, safety and health are the first priorities followed by how well the project fits the housing, economic development, and other city priorities (Table 8.1).

8.2.1.4 *Project evaluation: cost effectiveness*

One of the major tools for analyzing between competing capital projects is cost-effectiveness analysis. As the name implies, this technique basically involves comparing the lifetime costs of several different capital projects. You select the project with the lowest lifetime costs. Steps include:

(a) **Upfront costs:** The first part of this analysis is to develop estimates of the costs that you will spend up front for the capital project. These could include purchase of land, construction costs, major renovation costs, development of engineering and architectural plans, getting the appropriate permits, and approvals, etc. While capital project management is complicated and requires expertize and careful monitoring, the upfront costs for the project are usually the most straightforward to estimate since you have bids from realtors, contractors, architects on the project. It is important if you are using land owned by the government that you value the land at its market value. This is the concept of "opportunity costs," the value of the land in its next best use.

(b) **Operating and maintenance costs (O&M) associated with this asset:** Including O&M costs in the project analysis is important because sometimes there is a tradeoff between the upfront cost of several assets and their operating and maintenance costs. It is important that in making this comparison, you look at the full cost of this asset to the community over its full life, or commonly called lifecycle costs.

(c) **External costs:** Finally, costs should include any indirect costs or externalities caused by the project. A common indirect cost is environmental damage that the project may cause. Since many of these costs are intangible, it is difficult to come up with monetary measures. Despite this problem, it is important to document these intangible costs and to weigh them in the final project decisions.

(d) **Discounting-time value of money:** Once you have a list of costs over the life of the capital asset, the final step is to adjust these costs and benefits to reflect the time value of money. All this means is that one dollar today is worth more to you than a dollar in the future. The principal reason is that you could invest the dollar today and have more than a dollar in the future. The reason is also partially based on risk, since you may not be alive to enjoy the benefits from a dollar tomorrow. It partially reflects uncertainty about the future — are you going to need that dollar for an emergency this year, what is going to happen to inflation in the next year? This concept is illustrated by the fact that you get paid interest if you save part of your income. In general, the longer the period of savings, the higher the interest rate that people demand for this deferred consumption. The interest rate then is the price of saving.

The future value of a cost or benefit is its value in the year it was incurred. The problem is that capital projects have costs and benefits, which span many years — how do we compare costs or benefits in different years? This is basically, what the concept of present value does. It converts all future costs and benefits into what they would be worth to you today, which allows them to be directly compared.

We can then illustrate the concept of discounting. The future value next year of \$1,000 today is simply \$1,000 times one plus the interest rate. If the interest rate is 10%, then the FV of \$1 next year is \$1.1. Flipping this over then the present value of \$1 next year is equal to \$1 divided by $(1 + 10\%)$ or 0.909. Based on this, what is the future value five years from now of \$1 now. It is \$1 times 1.1 taken to the power of 5: $\$1{,}000 \times (1.1)^5 = \$1.61$. Flipping this around then the present value of \$1 in 5 years is \$1 divided by $(1.1)^5$, which equals \$0.621. We can generalize this to 'n' number of time periods as illustrated below. Future value of \$1 invested for one year at 10% interest:

$$\begin{aligned}\mathrm{FV} &= \mathrm{PV}(1 + \mathrm{r})\\ \mathrm{FV} &= \$1(1.1)\\ \mathrm{FV} &= \$1.1.\end{aligned}$$

Compounding FV of \$1 at end of 5 years

$$\begin{aligned}\mathrm{FV}_5 &= \mathrm{PV}(1 + \mathrm{r})^5\\ \mathrm{FV}_5 &= \$1(1.1)^5\\ \mathrm{FV}_5 &= \$1.61.\end{aligned}$$

Present value of \$1 received 1 year from now:

$$PV = FV/(1 + r)$$
$$PV = \$1/(1.1)$$
$$PV = \$0.91.$$

Present value of \$1 received 5 years from now:

$$PV_5 = FV/(1 + r)^5$$
$$PV_5 = \$1/(1.1)^5$$
$$PV_5 = \$0.621.$$

Present value of a stream of costs (C) over n years can be represented as:

$$PV = C_0 + C_1/(1 + r) + C_2/(1 + r)^2 + C_3/(1 + r)^2 + C_4/(1 + r)^2 + \cdots C_n/(1 + r)^n.$$

(e) Project selection: The use of discounting is illustrated in Table 8.2. Project A has lower upfront cost than Project B but higher annual costs. After discounting costs each year, we can then sum the discounted costs to get the present value of total

Table 8.2. Comparison of present value for two capital projects with different timing for costs.

Project A				
Year	**Upfront Cost**	**Annual Cost**	**Annual Discount Factor (6%)**	**Present Value of Costs**
0	1,000,000			
1		150,000	0.9434	141,509
2		200,000	0.8900	177,999
3		300,000	0.8396	251,886
4		400,000	0.7921	316,837
	1,000,000	**1,050,000**		**888,232**
			Present Value of Costs	**1,888,232**

Project B				
Year	**Upfront Cost**	**Annual Cost**	**Annual Discount Factor (6%)**	**Present Value of Costs**
0	1,500,000			
1		100,000	0.9434	94,340
2		100,000	0.8900	89,000
3		110,000	0.8396	92,358
4		120,000	0.7921	95,051
	1,500,000	**430,000**		**370,749**
			Present Value of Costs	**1,870,749**

costs. We can see that while Project A has lower upfront costs than Project B, it has slightly higher PV of total costs. All else equal we would select Project B. However, given that the PV of costs are so close, this suggests that we should probably use other criteria besides costs in selecting the project.

8.2.2 Financing the capital budget

8.2.2.1 *Develop long-range financial projections*

Ideally, the CIP should be fit into a long-range financial plan, which projects revenues and operating expenditures. Such a plan is illustrated in Table 8.3. The first step is to forecast revenue based on the present tax rates and base. This is the amount of "current revenue," which is going to be available without a discretionary change.

The next step is to forecast operating or current expenditures both with and without the proposed capital projects. This is the crucial link between the capital and operating budget, since capital projects generally have an impact on operating budgets as well. Once current expenditures and debt service payments are subtracted, then this is the present budget surplus or deficit.

Table 8.3. Example long range financial planning to support ($ thousands).

Category	2015	2016	2017	2018	2019	2020	2021
1. Projected operating revenue	6,000	6,500	7,000	7,300	7,700	8,000	8,400
2. *Less* projected operating expenditures	5,000	5,800	6,300	6,600	7,000	7,300	7,700
3. Gross cash flow from operations	1,000	700	700	700	700	700	700
4. Debt service (interest plus principal payments) on existing obligations	500	500	350	300	250	200	150
5. Gross funds flow after debt service charges	500	200	350	400	450	500	550
6. *Less* projected recurring capital expenditures	200	300	350	400	450	500	350
7. Net funds	300	-100	0	0	0	0	200
8. Less proposed major capital expenditures	1,000	1,000	1,000	500	500	500	500
9. Net new financing required.	**700**	**1,100**	**1,000**	**500**	**500**	**500**	**300**

Source: Based on example in Richard Aronson and Eli Schwartz. 2004 "Cost Benefit Analysis and the Capital Budget" in R. Aronson, E. Schwards (eds.), *Management Policies in Local Government Finance*, 5Ed. Washington DC: ICMA, Chapter 6, Table 6.2.

Finally, the impact of the proposed capital projects on the present budget needs to be calculated. This involves subtracting the additional (or reduction in) operating expenditures and the additional recurrent (small) capital, which will result from the capital projects. Finally, the proposed capital expenditures from the CIP need to be subtracted to determine the new financing requirements. This is the amount of additional revenue that will have to be found to support the proposed CIP.

8.2.2.2 *Develop financing plan*

Once it is determined how much additional revenue is needed to support the proposed CIP, then the question is from what sources this revenue will be generated. These sources can be organized by whether they are

Pay-as-you-go: Where the government will rely on current revenue sources (or accumulated reserves) to meet capital-related costs. The advantage of pay-as-you-go (PAYGO) is that it avoids interest costs and the use of debt. A government will opt for PAYGO mechanisms for projects whose costs would not distort current spending priorities (e.g., recurring capital expenditures). A school district, for example, could meet a limited amount of capital related costs directly out of current property tax revenues if the costs do not limit spending priorities in the operating budget. For instance, it might commit to buying a new school bus each year to ensure that its bus fleet is updated. It will most likely, however, rely on long-term debt if it needed to build a new school or extensively refurbish existing facilities, because those are not regularly occurring expenses.

Pay-as-you-use: The government tries to match the life of the asset to debt issued to finance the capital project. The advantage of issuing debt to finance capital projects is that it spreads the cost of the project over the project's useful life. It also matches those who use and benefit from the project with those who actually pay for the project. Debt also allows for large capital projects (e.g., highways, bridges, sewer plants, etc.) to be undertaken almost immediately. What's more, governments can undertake multiple projects simultaneously if they rely on debt, as the annual costs would be limited to maintenance on the capital project as well as principal and interest payment on any debt issues related to the project.

(a) *Current revenue*: It is certainly possible for a local government to support its capital expenditures with current revenue. Relying on current revenues for capital expenditures limits the size of the capital investment that the local government can undertake. Since major tax increases are unpopular, this system will probably lead to an under-investment in capital assets. Also, if capital projects are financed on a PAYGO basis, this will lead to large changes in tax rates as illustrated in Table 8.4. We can see that the property tax rates to support the capital plan go from one-third of a percent to 1.5% during the capital plan. One way around this problem is the establishment of "capital reserve funds," where the local government saves for future large capital investments.

One of the basic problems with this method of finance is that it is not equitable across generations. This means that you may have to pay taxes for a project this year, for which you may not receive the full benefits if you move away during the lifetime of the project. A more equitable system would be one where what you paid each year was in line with the benefits you received from the project. Despite this problem, a PAYGO system is often used for small capital investments.

Table 8.4. Example of different financing plans for capital plan.

Plan A (pay-as-you-go)

Current Revenue Financing	**2015**	**2016**	**2017**	**2018**	**2019**	**2020**	**2021**
1. Net new financing required for operations and capital budget ($000)	700	1100	1000	500	500	500	300
2. Assessed Value of Property ($000s)	70,000	73,500	77,000	80,000	83,000	87,000	91,000
3. Property Tax Rate to support Capital	1.00%	1.50%	1.30%	0.63%	0.60%	0.58%	0.33%

Source: Based on example in Richard Aronson and Eli Schwartz. 2004. "Capital Budgeting" in R. Aronson, Eli Schwartz (eds.), *Management Policies in Local Government*, 4Ed. Washington D.C.: ICMA, Chapter 17, Figure 17–12.

(b) *Capital grants*: The federal government has been a major source of grant money for capital projects, such as highways, airports, and bridges. State governments can provide significant capital grants for education facilities, local jails, local roads, and environmental infrastructure (e.g., water and sewer treatment). These capital grants typically are awarded on a competitive basis and require the local government to match the grant with their own money. Although these grants are potentially a valuable source of outside money to a local government, they are usually not given without "strings attached". It is important that you analyze the obligations associated with the grant and whether the program funded by the grant is really a high priority. The grants can be provided upfront to cover the full capital costs or can be set up to cover debt service payments.

(c) *Leasing (versus buying) the asset*: Another alternative financing mechanism, which local governments are increasingly taking advantage of is leasing. Leasing basically means that some other organization (usually private firm) buys the asset and leases it to the government to use. There are a number of types of leases but they generally fall into two types:

— true (operating) lease: where the lessor retains the ownership of the asset over its whole life,
— conditional sales (capital) lease: where the lessee will be considered an owner of the asset and the lease payment is similar to debt service payments.

Most government leases are structured as true or operating leases because it allows the private firm, which is the lessor, to take advantage of the tax benefits from ownership and to pass these on to the government in terms of lower lease payments. In addition to being a way to reduce costs, the other advantages of leases include:

— shifting the risk of ownership from the local government to the lessor. This is particularly important for assets such as computers, which are undergoing rapid changes in technology,
— a true lease may include a full maintenance contract, which for items such as a copy machine may be quite important,

— it is a way to avoid bond issue elections and the marketing costs of bonds for small capital assets.[5]

(d) *Debt payments*: For large capital projects, the most common form of financing is long-term debt. This is usually in the form of municipal bonds, which are sold for a specific project. The key advantage of debt financing as with leasing is that it is a pay-as-you-use system. This means that the debt service payments, if designed correctly, should match payment for the project to the actual beneficiaries of the project. This implies that financing should ideally be for the life of the project.

In addition, spreading out payment of the project over a number of years will lead to more stable tax rates. This is illustrated by Table 8.5, which shows the additional property tax rate required to finance a pay-as-you-use system. It is clear that pay-as-you-use system involves much less fluctuation in tax rates than the pay-as-you-go system (compare Tables 8.4 and 8.5).

Finally, for very large capital investments, there may be no alternative but to use debt financing. The capital expenditures will swamp current revenues and it may take too long to accumulate

Table 8.5. Example of different financing plans for capital plan.

Plan B (pay-as-you-use)

Bond Financing	**2015**	**2016**	**2017**	**2018**	**2019**	**2020**	**2021**
1. New debt required to finance capital budget	700	1100	1000	500	500	500	300
2. Debt: Principal paid (15 year issue)	47	117	176	197	218	236	240
3. Debt: Interest paid (5%)	35	88	132	148	163	177	180
4. Total debt service payments	82	205	308	345	381	413	420
5. Assessed Value of Property ($000s)	70,000	73,500	77,000	80,000	83,000	87,000	91,000
6. Property Tax Rate to support Capital	0.12%	0.28%	0.40%	0.43%	0.46%	0.48%	0.46%

Source: Based on example in Richard Aronson and Eli Schwartz. 2004. "Capital Budgeting" in R. Aronson, Eli Schwartz (eds.), *Management Policies in Local Government*, 4Ed. Washington D.C.: ICMA, Chapter 17, Figure 17–12.

[5]J. Marlowe, W.C. Rivenbark, A.J. Vogt. (2009). *Capital Budgeting and Finance: A Guide for Local Governments*. (Washington, D.C.: ICMA Press).

enough money in a "capital fund" to pay for the project out of cash. If a debt system is designed and managed correctly, then there are really few good reasons why debt financing should not be used, particularly for large-scale capital projects.

8.2.2.3 *Check feasibility of debt burden*

The final step before developing the final budget is to check the feasibility of the proposed financing plan. Specifically, are the debt burdens proposed in this plan within the financial capabilities of the government? Essentially this involves developing a series of debt ratios and checking these against established criteria. These ratios include:

— debt over assessed value (tax base): This is the ratio of the total outstanding debt of a government (and ideally for all "overlapping" governments as well) to the market property value. This indicates how much of the tax base is required to support the debt. (For states, the sales tax base is probably more appropriate). Normally a ratio of 10% or less is considered acceptable.

— debt service payments over current revenues: This is the ratio of total debt service payments over current own-source revenues. It indicates how much of the existing revenues are being used to pay for debt. If the ratios are below 20%, then the burden is generally considered acceptable.[6]

8.2.2.4 *Develop the capital budget*

The development of the actual capital budget is anti-climatic after the elaborate preparation of the CIP and financing plans. Basically, it involves taking the first year of the CIP and inserting it into the budget document. Although it may require some rearranging

---

[6]Richard Aronson and Eli Schwartz. 2004. "Capital Budgeting" in R. Aronson, Eli Schwartz (eds.), *Management Policies in Local Government*, 4Ed. Washington D.C.: ICMA, Chapter 17, pp. 450–451.

of information, the guts of the capital budget should already be developed.

Where communities differ is in terms of how much they connect the capital and operating budgets. The capital budget may be incorporated directly into the agency operating budgets or it may be a separate part of the budget document or even a separate document.

This raises one of the most important issues concerning the capital budget — are the operating and maintenance expenditures associated with a capital project considered in project evaluation and incorporated into the operating budget. Ideally, all expenditures over the life of a capital asset should be estimated and incorporated into the operating budget. Pagano (1984) argues that the capital budget may actually make infrastructure problems worse by separating capital and operating decisions.[7] This will lead to the approval of capital projects without the full analysis of their operating cost implications. Because these additional operating costs have not been planned for, they will not generally be funded, leading to premature deterioration of the capital assets. The key point here is that the capital and operating budgets must be connected if the capital budget is to serve as a tool to improve capital investment!

8.3 Municipal Bonds

The majority of large capital projects in this country are financed by issuing debt. In 1995, roughly 85% of capital outlays by state and local governments were financed using long-term debt.[8] In 2012, state and local governments issued over $339 billion in new debt and had total long-term debt outstanding of over $3 trillion.[9] These numbers suggest that long-term debt is the basic financing mechanism for state and local government capital projects and it is important to

[7]Michael Pagano, "Notes on Capital Budgeting," *Public Budgeting and Finance* 4 (Autumn 1984): 31–40.

[8]Calculation based on 1995 Census of Governments https://www.census.gov//govs/local/9500us.html.

[9]See p. 12 of the following Census of Governments report: https://www2.census.gov/govs/local/summary_report.pdf.

familiarize yourself with some of the types and characteristics of this debt.

Municipal bonds are the predominant form of long-term debt used by state and local governments. Municipal bonds are essentially an IOU sold by the government to an investor. In exchange for lending the government the amount of the bond, the government commits to pay the investor:

— the original or par value or the bond at the end of the bond's term, and
— an interest payment every year which is based on a fixed interest rate or coupon rate times the face value of the bond.

One of the key advantages of most municipal bonds is that the interest payments from these bonds are tax exempt. What this means is that the interest an investor may earn from municipal bonds is exempt from the federal income tax. This results in lower interest costs to governments since people are willing to buy the bonds with lower coupon rates because of the tax advantages.

8.3.1 Bond types

There are a number of different types of municipal bonds because they are used for a number of different purposes. The key differences in the types of bonds are in who or what is going to guarantee the repayment of the debt, and who is the ultimate user of the capital asset.

- General obligation bonds: These are bonds, which are backed by the "full faith and credit" of the state and local government. In other words, the government has committed to paying this bond with all of the resources available to the community. Not surprisingly, this is the safest of the municipal bond types and commands the lowest interest rate from investors. In other words, it costs the least to local governments to use this type of debt but it involves the most risk for the local government. G.O. bonds are commonly used for capital projects for general government functions such as water, sewer, fire, etc. In 2011, general obligation bond issues accounted for 46% of total state government debt issues.[10]

Another interesting variant of this is called the moral obligation bond (also known as appropriation bonds). What this means is that the chief executive is "morally obligated" to propose the tax rates to the legislative body to cover the bond. However, the legislative body is not required to pass these increases. Since this involves more risk for bondholders they will require a higher interest rate for these types of bonds.

- Revenue bonds: Revenue bonds are backed by the revenue from a proposed project. For example, if a public utility is building a new power plant it will often finance this investment with revenue bonds. Variants of these bonds include "special revenue bonds," which are financed by an earmarked general revenue source (sales tax), and a "special assessment bond," which is financed by general taxes paid by a specific group of beneficiaries. These have generally been the fastest growing type of bond, and in 2011 accounted for 54% of all long term debt issues by state governments.[10]
- Private purpose bonds: One of the fastest growing areas of municipal bonds up until the 1986 federal tax reform was "private purpose bonds." These are basically revenue bonds purchased by a government to support private firms. Private purpose bonds were used to provide low interest home loans for low-income families, to finance industrial or office parks, and to provide basic infrastructure for private firms. The capital facilities are technically owned by the government with the private party providing rental or lease payments, which pay off the revenue bond. Because the use of these bonds skyrocketed in the early 1980s and their social value is questionable in many cases, their use was significantly restricted in the 1986 Federal Tax Reform.

[10]SIFM, Municipal Bond Credit Report, First Quarter 2011, p. 7. https://www.sifma.org/wp-content/uploads/2017/05/us-municipal-bond-credit-report-2011-q1.pdf.

8.3.2 Bond ratings

A key element in the sales of municipal bonds is the credit rating given to the government. Basically, the credit rating is an evaluation of how likely the government is to repay its debt, that is, its "credit-worthiness." The ratings are typically given upon initial bond issuance and are periodically reviewed, and may be revised by changes impacting the issue or the issuer's credit position. There are three major companies, which provide evaluations of a government's credit status, Standard & Poor's Corporation, Moody's Investors Service, and Fitch Ratings.

Table 8.6 illustrates the different rating classes, which are used to classify governments. "AAA" is the top rating and indicates the least risk from the standpoint of investors. Differences in credit ratings can have a significant effect on the interest rates that a local government pays. For example, the difference between an AAA rating and a Baa rating by Moody's is around 1%. This may not seem like a lot, but on a $200 million bond issue, this is $2,000,000 per year, which is not insignificant.

What affects the credit rating given a community? The credit agencies generally list four different factors as influencing their credit rating:

(a) *Debt*: They evaluate the past debt history of the government. How have the ratios of debt over assessed value and debt service payments over current revenues changed over time, and what are their levels? Has the government paid its debts on time, or had to reschedule its debts? How have short-term debt burdens grown?
(b) *Financial*: They evaluate the revenue and expenditure position of the government since this indicates their ability to pay off their debts. Revenue measures include the overall tax burden; the growth (elasticity), stability, and adequacy of the tax base; and the government's dependence on intergovernmental aid. Expenditure measures include an assessment of the amount of fixed (uncontrollable) expenditures the government has including Medicare and Medicaid expenditures, debt service (i.e., principal and interest payment on existing debt), pension, and other-post

Table 8.6. Description of rating categories Moody's and S&P.

MOODY'S[11]		STANDARD AND POORS[12]	
AAA	Obligations rated AAA are judged to be of the highest quality, with minimal credit risk.	AAA	An obligation rated 'AAA' has the highest rating assigned by S&P. The obligor's capacity to meet its financial commitment on the obligation is extremely strong.
Aa	Obligations rated Aa are judged to be of high quality and are subject to very low credit risk.	AA	An obligation rated 'AA' differs from the highest rated obligations only to a small degree. The obligor's capacity to meet its financial commitment on the obligation is very strong.
Aa	Obligations rated A are considered upper-medium grade and are subject to low credit risk.	A	An obligation rated 'A' is somewhat susceptible to the adverse effects of changes in circumstances and economic conditions than obligations in higher rated categories. However, the obligor's capacity to meet its financial commitment on the obligations is still strong.
Baa	Obligations rated Baa are subject to moderate credit risk. They are considered medium grade and as such may possess certain speculative characteristics.	BBB	An obligation rated 'BBB' exhibits adequate protection parameters. However, adverse economic conditions or changing circumstances are more likely to lead to a weakened capacity of the obligor to meet its financial commitment on the obligation.
Obligations rated 'BB' 'B' 'CCC' 'CC' and 'C' are regarded as having significant speculative characteristics			

Source: This table is taken from N. O'Hara, T.J. Wesalo, & Securities Industry and Financial Markets Association. 2012. *The Fundamentals of Municipal Bonds.* Hoboken, N.J: Wiley, Chapter 7, Figures 7.2 and 7.3.

employment benefits. When Standard and Poor's (S&P) assigned a lower rating to bonds issued by the state of Illinois, the rating agency cited the lack of action to improve funding levels in the state-sponsored retirement plans, which increased pressure on future budgets to fund commitments to retirees. Moody's assigned a lower rating to the state of New Jersey citing that the fixed costs associated with principal and interest payments on existing debt, pension, and healthcare benefits could exceed 30% of the state budget by 2019, crowding out program-related

[11]Moody's appends numerical modifiers 1, 2, and 3 to each generic rating classification from Aa through Caa. The modifier 1 indicates that the obligation ranks in the higher end of its generic rating category; the modifier 2 indicates a mid-range ranking; and the modifier 3 indicates a ranking in the lower end of that generic rating category.

[12]Standard and Poor's ratings from "AA" to "CCC" may be modified by the addition of a plus (+) or minus (−) sign to show relative standing within the major rating categories.

spending (note debt, pension, and healthcare benefits are non-discretionary costs).[13]

(c) *Economic*: Rating firms also try to assess the overall health of the local economy. What have been the trends in employment, population, personal income? What types of industries have grown and which have declined, and how does this affect the size of the tax base. Since ultimately tax revenue must be extracted from the private economy, the assessment of economic health is quite important.

(d) *Administrative*: Finally, the rating agencies consider the financial management practices of the government. Does the government adopt Generally Accepted Accounting Principles (GAAP)? Has the government been willing to make hard financial decisions in the past (raise taxes, cut expenditures) in response to a tight financial environment? How successful has the government been in collecting revenues and its accounts payable? Rating agencies downgraded California's credit rating on numerous occasions in 2009, citing the lack of political progress around budget negotiations as a contributing factor to the state's current and projected cash position. These agencies have since taken more positive actions on California's rating following a strong economic recovery, and Governor Brown's budget proposals that put the state's budget in a more solid footing.[14]

The point of this analysis is to put together a financial profile of the government, which indicates its ability and willingness to pay off long-term debts. There have been a number of studies, which have attempted to evaluate which of these criteria seem to be the most important. It is difficult to find consistent conclusions from this research but it does suggest that all but the administrative factors probably play a major role in credit rating decisions.

---

[13] See, http://www.rockinst.org/newsroom/news_stories/2012/2012-08-25-Barron's.pdf.

[14] "History of California GO Bond Ratings" from CA Department of Finance, p. 7: http://www.dof.ca.gov/budget/summary_schedules_charts/documents/CHART-K-6.pdf.

Lecture 9

Revenue Forecasting and Evaluation Criteria

9.1 Introduction

The third part of this course will be devoted to examining government revenue sources. We will, over the course of the next few classes, try to familiarize you with the structure of some of the major taxes used in this country. Significant attention will also be devoted to the evaluation of these revenue sources. Since taxes have a significant effect on the private economy, it is important to understand their impact on private households and business firms. Much of the research on taxation has focused on evaluating the equity and efficiency effects of different government taxes. For example, do poorer taxpayers bear a disproportionately high burden of a certain tax? What impact does a particular tax have on consumer and business decisions? As a city manager or legislative staff person, you may be directly involved in making tax policy decisions. Even if you are not directly involved in tax policy or administration, many public agencies are introducing fees and charges as a means of boosting revenues. It is important that you know some of the right questions to ask in evaluating different revenues.

We begin this lecture with a brief description of the tax system in this country. The tax system — reflecting our complicated federalist system — is a complex web of different tax types used by different levels of government and revenue sharing between levels through intergovernmental grants. We will then turn to a brief discussion of revenue forecasting, which is a crucial part of the budgeting process. Finally, the bulk of the lecture will be devoted to a discussion of the criteria typically used to evaluate tax policies and government revenue sources.

9.2 Overview of the Tax System

As you are well aware, the US has a very diverse system of government, with the federal, state, and local governments each playing an important role in the provision of public goods and services. Although federal, state, and local governments spend similar amounts of the total public budget, they finance these expenditures with significantly different revenue sources. As illustrated in Table 9.1:

1. Federal revenue comes primarily from the personal and corporate income tax and the payroll tax used to finance the social security system (not included in individual income taxes in Table 9.1). Although the federal government does use various excise taxes and import duties, it does not employ either a general sales or property tax.
2. State revenue comes from a variety of sources. The major source of tax revenue is sales and excise taxes which account for half

Table 9.1. Percentage distribution of tax revenue for each level of government, FY 2010.

	Federal (%)	**State (%)**	**Local (%)**
Personal income tax	69.2[a]	33.7	4.3
Corporate income taxes	14.8	5.2	1.1
Sales and excise taxes	5.3	48.8	15.6
Property taxes	0.0	2.1	75.1
Other taxes	10.9	10.2	3.9
Total taxes	100.0	100.0	100.0

[a] *Note*: Excludes social insurance contributions.

Sources: US Bureau of Census, Governments and Budget of the US Government.

of state tax revenue. Personal income taxes are the other major source of state tax revenue. State governments do not generally use a property tax. In addition, federal aid is an important source of revenue for state governments (24% of total revenue). For New York, we see that personal income tax is the most important state source of revenue representing 46% of state revenue and almost 60% of state taxes. Consumer taxes (sales taxes) are less important in New York with 17.3% of state revenue and 23% of state taxes. This highlights the diversity across states in their tax systems. For example, four states do not have a general sales tax and seven states do not have a personal income tax.

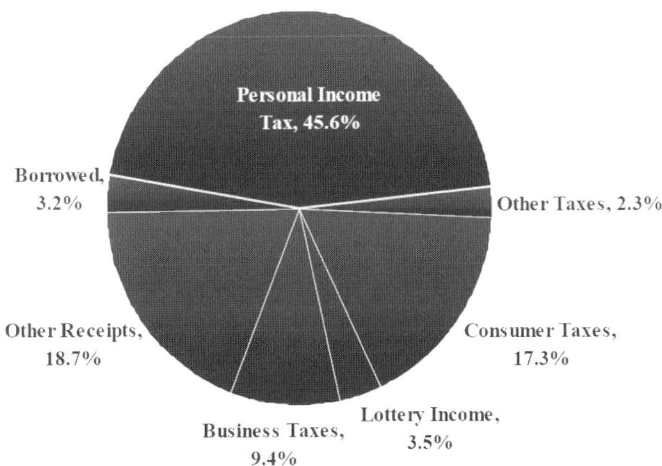

Source: Thomas P. DiNapoli, "Citizens Guide 2009: A Pocket Reference to New York State's Finances," New York State Comptroller, pg. 2. https://www.osc.state.ny.us/finance/finreports/citizens_guide/citizensguide2009.pdf.

3. Local revenue also comes from a variety of sources. The major taxes local governments employ are the property and general sales taxes. In addition, many local governments finance a portion of the cost of services such as garbage, water, sewer, transit, and

recreation with user fees. Finally, state and federal aid represent a sizeable part of the revenue of most local governments (34% on average). Aid may represent more than 50% of revenue for some local governments such as school districts. Sales taxes represent the most important revenue source for Onondaga County followed by state and federal aid and property taxes. New York State is unusual in that it allows its counties to use a general sales tax.

ONONDAGA COUNTY 2010 EXECUTIVE BUDGET

Where the 2010 Dollars Come From

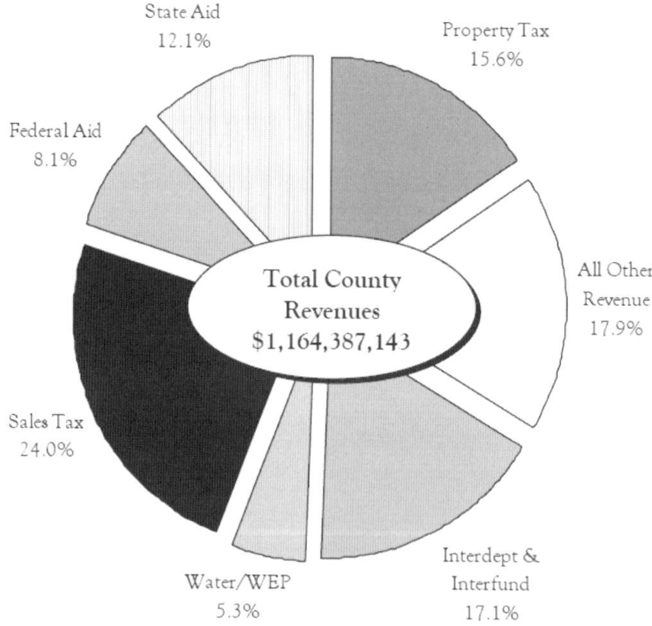

Source: Onondaga County, "Executive Budget 2010," http://www.ongov.net/finance/.

There has been a changing tax structure in the last several decades.

- At the state level, per capita individual income tax and general sales tax have been growing at 2% per year even controlling for inflation (Table 9.2.). However, relative to personal income, only income tax revenue and federal aid have shown significant growth. As we will

Table 9.2. State and local revenues in the US annual percent change.

	Revenue Per Capita (Constant Dollars)				Revenue Per $1,000 of Personal Income			
	1970–1980	**1980–1990**	**1990–2006**	**1975–2006**	**1970–1980**	**1980–1990**	**1990–2006**	**1975–2006**
State and local governments:								
General revenue	2.0	2.1	1.7	1.9	0.8	0.3	0.7	0.4
Own-source revenue	1.4	2.9	1.3	1.9	0.2	1.0	0.4	0.4
Total taxes	0.8	2.2	1.2	1.4	−0.4	0.4	0.2	0.0
Property taxes	−1.7	2.4	1.0	0.8	−2.9	0.5	0.0	−0.6
Income taxes	4.8	2.6	1.5	2.4	3.5	0.8	0.5	0.9
General sales taxes	2.9	2.8	1.0	1.9	1.7	0.9	0.1	0.4
Federal aid	4.8	−0.9	3.3	1.9	3.5	−2.7	2.3	0.2
State government:								
General revenue	2.3	2.1	1.9	1.8	1.1	0.2	1.0	0.4
Own-source revenue	2.1	2.5	1.4	1.9	0.9	0.7	0.5	0.5
Total taxes	1.8	2.0	1.1	1.5	0.6	0.1	0.2	0.1
Income taxes	5.0	2.7	1.5	2.4	3.8	0.8	0.5	0.9
General sales taxes	2.5	2.5	0.9	1.7	1.2	0.7	−0.1	0.2
Federal aid	3.0	0.6	3.4	2.1	1.8	−1.2	2.4	0.7
Local government:								
General revenue	1.9	2.1	1.3	1.5	0.7	0.2	0.4	0.0
Own-source revenue	0.6	3.2	1.2	1.6	−0.6	1.4	0.3	0.2
Total taxes	−0.7	2.6	1.3	1.2	−1.9	0.7	0.3	−0.2
Property taxes	−1.8	2.4	1.0	0.8	−3.0	0.5	0.1	−0.6
Income taxes	2.5	2.4	1.4	1.9	1.3	0.5	0.5	0.5
General sales taxes	5.8	3.9	1.7	2.8	4.5	2.0	0.7	1.4
Federal aid	13.0	−7.0	2.6	−0.7	11.7	−8.7	1.6	−2.1
State aid	2.4	1.7	1.4	1.3	1.2	−0.2	0.4	−0.1

Source: US Bureau of Census, Quarterly Summary of State and Local Tax Revenue. https://www.census.gov/govs/local/.

discuss later in the class, changes in the sales tax base have affected revenue growth (growth in services and internet sales).

- At the local level, while property tax remains the principal form of taxation, the fastest growing taxes have been income taxes and sales taxes. Only a few states permit local sales and income taxes (e.g., New York and Ohio). However, in these states, these taxes are becoming increasingly important. Property tax revenues, by contrast, have grown slowly in per capita real terms, and have actually declined relative to personal income. As we will discuss in Lecture 11, poor property tax administration can often limit its revenue growth.

State and local tax burden as a percentage of state income, Fiscal year 2010.

State	Tax Burden (%)	Rank	State	Tax Burden (%)	Rank
US	9.9	—	Mont.	8.6	38
Ala.	8.2	43	Nebr.	9.7	21
Alaska	7.0	50	Nev.	8.2	42
Ariz.	8.4	40	N.H.	8.1	44
Ark.	10.0	15	N.J.	12.4	2
Calif.	11.2	4	N.M.	8.4	39
Colo.	9.1	32	N.Y.	12.8	1
Conn.	12.3	3	N.C.	9.9	17
Del.	9.2	31	N.D.	8.9	35
Fla.	9.3	27	Ohio	9.7	20
Ga.	9.0	33	Okla.	8.7	36
Hawaii	10.1	14	Ore.	10.0	16
Idaho	9.4	25	Pa.	10.2	10
Ill.	10.2	11	R.I.	10.9	6
Ind.	9.6	23	S.C.	8.4	41
Iowa	9.6	24	S.D.	7.6	49
Kans.	9.7	22	Tenn.	7.7	48

(*Continued*)

(*Continued*)

State	Tax Burden (%)	Rank	State	Tax Burden (%)	Rank
Ky.	9.4	26	Tex.	7.9	45
La.	7.8	47	Utah	9.3	29
Maine	10.3	9	Vt.	10.1	13
Md.	10.2	12	Va.	9.3	30
Mass.	10.4	8	Wash.	9.3	28
Mich.	9.8	18	W.Va.	9.7	19
Minn.	10.8	7	Wis.	11.1	5
Miss.	8.7	37	Wyo.	7.8	46
Mo.	9.0	34	D.C.	9.3	(31)

Note: Data for years 1977 to present are available at www.Tax-Foundation.org. Payments made to out-of-state governments are tallied in taxpayer's state of residence where possible.

Source: Tax foundation calculation of state and local tax burdens, Tax Foundation Background Paper No. 65, *Annual State-Local Tax Burden Ranking* (2010).

There is substantial variation in the level of state and local taxation across the country. Tax burdens are often measured as total taxes per capita or as a percent of the total personal income in the state. If income represents a rough measure of the ability of taxpayers to pay taxes, then tax as a percent of income is probably the better measure of tax burdens. Looking at the following table, we can see that taxes range from 12.8% of personal income in New York to 7.0% of income in Alaska in FY 2010. The top three states are Northeastern states — New York, New Jersey, and Connecticut. Three of the bottom five states are in the West — Alaska, South Dakota, and Wyoming, each of which have significant natural resources (oil, gas, and minerals) that raise the level of state income.

In summary, we have a complex system of governmental finance in this country in which the federal, state, and local governments all play an important part. There has developed over our history a fairly consistent division of functional responsibility and revenue sources by level of government.

9.3 Revenue Forecasting

One of the principal roles of the budget office or finance department in a government during the budget process is the forecasting of revenue for the coming year. The revenue forecast serves as one of the principal constraints on the budget process. However, revenue forecasting should go beyond this 1-year exercise to look at the factors affecting medium- and long-run revenue growth and fiscal health.

A forecast, as defined by Stuart Bretschneider, is "any statement about the future." This definition helps to highlight how pervasive forecasts are in the public sector.[1] Many actions you take as a public manager "presupposes a forecast." Whether you consciously make the forecast or not, many of your actions will be guided by predictions of future events. For example, in deciding whether to study the need and location of a landfill, you are making judgments about the future production of garbage in your community. In deciding how much to offer the police officers in labor negotiations, you are implicitly making judgments about how this will affect negotiations with other municipal employees and the likely growth in expenditures. Forecasting, then, is a crucial element of your job as a public manager. Since you will undoubtedly at some point in your career make forecasts, even if informal, it is valuable to understand the different purposes and methods of forecasting. This will help you to select the best technique to use in a particular circumstance.

Forecasting generally involves the application of quantitative techniques to historical data, essentially extrapolating past trends into the future. While the techniques are important and may require special expertize, they are less important than many of the basic

[1]This section draws heavily from Stuart Bretschneider, "Forecasting: Some New Realities," Metropolitan Studies Program Occasional Paper # 99, Syracuse, NY, December 1985; and Larry Schroeder, "Forecasting Local Revenue and Expenditures," in *Management Policies in Local Government Finance*, Washington, DC: ICMA; 4th edition, 1996, Chapter 4.

assumptions upon which the forecasts are built. Such assumptions are generally statements about how you expect the past to relate to the future.

Technical forecasting professionals are expert in the techniques of forecasting, not in formulating or revising the core assumptions. Thus, even if you hire an expert to do your forecasting, you need to critically evaluate the assumptions upon which this forecast is built. Are they realistic? Do they reflect recent changes in your program or its clients? Do they take into account past policy changes which may have distorted the trend in the historical data?

There is a lot of room, even with the most sophisticated forecasting techniques, for subjective judgments. The more sophisticated the technique, often the greater are the number of core assumptions to be made! This implies that it is easy to manipulate forecasts to tell a number of stories. Many forecasts are made by agencies, which have a self-interest in the forecast. Even if the forecaster is not an employee of the agency, they may be a consultant, who depends on the agency for contracts. The obvious point here is that forecasts are no less open to political manipulation than any other analytic technique. As a consumer of forecasts, you need to be aware of who made the forecast and where their interests lie.

We will not spend time in this class discussing forecasting principles and techniques. However, we do want to note that it is an important part of budgeting.

9.4 Tax Evaluation[2]

Assume that you are the city manager for a local government that is facing a fiscal crisis. While some expenditure cuts will be made, the city is going to have to increase its revenues if it is going to balance its budgets. You are considering three options: (1) increasing the property taxes, (2) increasing user fees on city services (transit,

[2]This section draws heavily on Chapter 7 "Taxation: Criteria for Evaluating Revenue Options" in John Mikesell. 1999. *Fiscal Administration: Analysis and Applications for the Public Sector*, 5th edition (New York: Harcourt Brace College Publishers).

water, garbage, etc), and (3) implementing a local sales tax. What should you propose and why?

This type of question is facing more and more managers as they must cope with revenue constraints. While political considerations will always be given significant attention, there are other criteria, such as equity and efficiency, which consider the impact on households and businesses. One of the major uses of public finance theory has been to help evaluate and reform the tax system of the federal, state, and local governments. This lecture provides you a quick overview of: (1) the major criteria used in evaluating tax policy; (2) the concepts and tools used to define and measure each criterion; and (3) the tradeoffs between these criteria. Besides political feasibility, there are generally four criteria used in tax evaluation: efficiency, equity, adequacy, and administration. We will examine each in turn.

9.4.1 Efficiency

Economic efficiency is achieved when there is no way to redistribute the resources of a society to increase the welfare of at least one more citizen without making others worse off. Assuming certain assumptions hold, economists generally view the results of free enterprise (the market) as efficient since it can be shown that it allocates resources to maximize benefits to consumers and producers. (This does not imply that these resources are distributed fairly.)

What is the impact of a tax on efficiency? To illustrate this impact, let's use the example of a sales tax. Assume for simplicity that the local government has proposed to raise revenues by taxing the sale of bread. How would consumers and producers respond to this tax?

- A tax may change consumer's behavior because the tax is likely to lead initially to an increase in the price of bread (retailers pass on the tax). Consumers are likely to respond by reducing the quantity of bread they consume and substituting other products for bread, such as rice, potatoes, etc. If consumers purchase other substitutes for bread, they are not as well off as before, because these substitutes are inferior to bread (or else the consumer would have purchased them originally). The consumer has suffered a welfare loss by being pushed to change their consumption in response to the tax. Alternatively, consumers may drive to another jurisdiction to purchase bread. The heavier a consumer of bread the family is and the higher the tax rate, the more they are apt to shop in another jurisdiction. The tax on bread has caused consumers to change their shopping location and to waste gas in the process.

- Producers of bread will respond to the new tax by trying to pass on the full tax increase to consumers. If consumers do not respond by reducing their consumption of bread, then producers are not hurt by the tax. However, if consumers reduce their consumption of bread, bakeries will not be able to sell as much bread and the "after-tax" price of bread, that is the price consumers pay minus the tax, will be lower. Thus, the owners and workers at the bakery will also be worse off. If the reduction in producers' profits is large enough, some might move their bakery to another jurisdiction where bread is not taxed. If the original location was optimal from the point of view of consumers and producers, the relocation of the bakery in response to the tax makes people worse off than they were prior to the tax.

The reason that there is an efficiency loss from a tax is because you as a consumer or owner of a business firm react to the tax. If you did not change your behavior when a tax was imposed, then there would be no efficiency loss. But consumers and producers do change their behavior when a tax is imposed. In this case, with a significant tax imposed on the price of bread, consumers will switch to other foods, and consume less bread, or possibly shop somewhere else. If we assume that the distribution of resources before the bread tax was the most efficient, then the change in choices made by consumers will result in decreased efficiency.

The two crucial questions to ask when evaluating the efficiency effects of a tax are:

- What economic decisions will this tax change? All modern taxes cause some change in economic behavior.

- How much will consumers and producers change their behavior in response to this tax?

Evaluating the first question involves an understanding of how the tax operates in an economy. It is generally easy to identify who actually sends in the tax bill; however, identifying which economic actors will ultimately be affected by the tax can be more difficult. In the case of the retail sales tax, retail stores actually send in the tax bill to the government, but clearly consumer decisions are being affected by the tax. A business tax can fall not only on the owners of the business, but it can also be shifted forward to consumers (through higher prices) or backward to suppliers and workers (through lower prices paid for inputs, such as salaries).

Evaluating the second question requires an understanding of how responsive consumers and producers are to tax changes. The more responsive consumers are by switching their consumption to other commodities, the larger are the efficiency losses. Which do you think consumers are going to be more responsive to, a tax increase on gasoline or pizza? My guess is that consumers are more apt to reduce their consumption of pizza in response to a tax increase than gasoline. Why do think that might be the case? As you probably guessed the difference is that there are more substitutes for pizza than gasoline. ***The answer to the second question will depend on whether there are good alternatives or substitutes to the goods which are taxed***. The more good substitutes the more the efficiency loss from a tax.

The concept of evaluating efficiency losses may seem quite esoteric. What possible relevance could the efficiency criteria have for state and local officials setting tax or revenue policy? The importance of this concept for policymakers can be summarized in two words, **economic development**. Attempts to promote economic development and growth are receiving increasing attention at all levels of government. While taxes are usually not the major factor affecting business location across regions, they can be important determinants within regions. Taxes can also affect where households locate, where they spend their money, and where and how much they choose to work. All of these decisions can affect economic growth within a community.

9.4.2 Equity

Another important criterion for evaluating the effects of a tax is equity. Is a particular tax fair and what does fair mean? While the notion of fairness or equity would seem straightforward, defining and measuring equity is not as simple as it seems. Two principles are frequently used to evaluate tax fairness — the benefits principle and the ability to pay principle.

(1) **Benefits principle:** An equitable tax system is one in which each taxpayer contributes in line with the benefits they receive from the service.

In other words, your taxes should be based on the benefits you receive from the public service. This would imply that a family with two kids should pay a higher property tax for education than one with no kids. The advantage of this equity principle is that it would encourage people to conserve public resources since they would be charged for everything they use. The disadvantages are that the benefits principle:

- cannot be used in the case of general taxes such as the income or sales taxes since you cannot link taxes to a specific public service; and
- does not do anything to improve income distribution, and will most likely make it worse since it encourages governments to collect revenue in the form of user charges for many basic services.

Although it is not typically used to evaluate taxes raised to support government services generally, the benefits principle has been used as a justification for local user fees for services such as water, sewer, garbage, etc.

(2) **Ability to pay principle:** People should contribute to the cost of government in line with their "ability to pay." There are

generally two different standards used in judging the equity of a tax based on this principle:

(a) **Horizontal equity:** This standard implies that people with same ability to pay should pay equally. This seems like a reasonable standard and is certainly consistent with most of our views of fairness. But measuring horizontal equity is not an easy task. Income is often used as the measure of ability to pay. However, income is not the only factor that influences ability to pay. Other factors that might influence "ability to pay" include:

— wealth
— number of children
— medical expenses
— lifetime earning potential.

(b) **Vertical equity:** This standard implies that people with different abilities to pay should pay differently. This also seems like a reasonable standard and certainly fits most people's view of fairness. But by itself, this standard does not tell us very much. All this suggests is that higher income taxpayers should pay more total tax than low-income taxpayers. But how much more? Most of you probably associate an inequitable tax with one that is regressive. But what does regressive (or progressive) mean?

To find the progressivity or regressivity of a tax, you need to calculate something called the effective tax rate (ETR). This is simply defined as the total taxes collected from a household from a particular tax divided by that household's ability to pay, usually defined as income. By comparing the level of the ETR for typical households by income class indicates whether a tax is progressive or regressive. For example, an effective tax rate of 20% for the income tax for taxpayers with incomes between \$20,000 and \$30,000 implies that households with this income generally pay 20% of their income in income taxes. If a typical household with an income of \$100,000

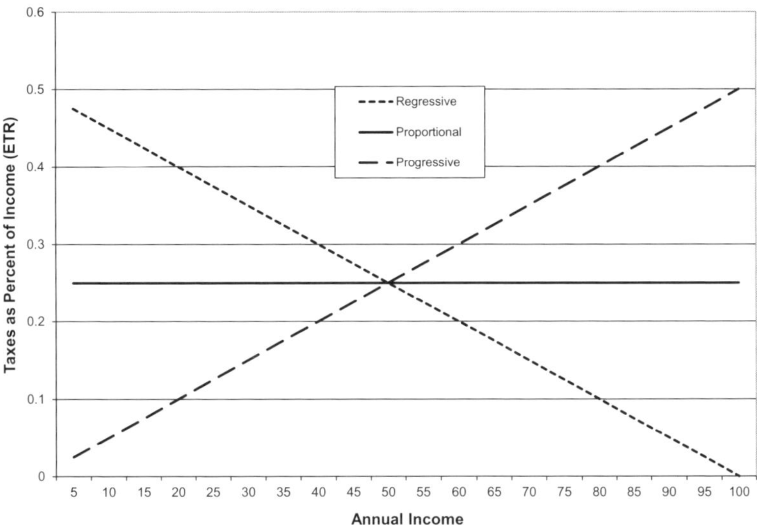

Figure 9.1. Vertical equity of a tax.

pays 30% of their income in income taxes, this would be called a progressive tax.

ETRs by income class can be plotted to determine if a tax is progressive. As you can see in Figure 9.1, a progressive tax is one where the ETR goes up as income goes up. A proportional tax is where the ETR stays the same, and a regressive tax is where the ETR goes down. The ability to pay principal alone does not tell you which of these is the most equitable since total taxes for higher income classes may be higher even with a regressive tax.

How do you measure tax equity? To calculate the effective tax rate for a tax involves several steps. There is not adequate time in this course to go into these steps in detail but the following is a brief summary. Determining vertical equity involves asking two questions:

(1) Who pays the tax? (Tax Incidence): The first step is deciding who actually pays the tax. This is called finding the incidence of the tax. At first glance, this seems rather easy — all you need to do is find who pays the bills. A property tax is paid by the property owner, a retail sales tax is paid by the retail store, etc. However,

as we discussed in evaluating efficiency, taxpayers do not sit idly by and absorb the full tax — they react by adjusting their behavior. The more they adjust their behavior, the less of the tax they will have to pay — and the more they will be able to shift the economic burden of the tax onto someone else.

In the case of the bread tax, how do we determine the incidence of the tax? In a formal economics course, you would examine the concept of tax incidence using supply and demand curves. Here, we will focus on intuitive explanations of this concept. Let's say that bread costs $1.00 per loaf and the sales tax rate is 10 cents per loaf. Producers of bread will have to pay 10 cents to the government for every loaf of bread they sell. Of course, producers will attempt to pass on this tax increase in the form of higher prices, raising bread prices initially to $1.10 per loaf. If consumers have poor substitutes for bread, they may react little to this tax, and instead absorb the price increase. In this case, consumers will "bear the full burden" of the tax in the form of higher prices and less income to spend on other commodities.

However, we would expect that at least some consumers will react by substituting other grain products for bread. By reducing their consumption of bread, they are causing a glut in the bread market-bread remains unsold at present prices. What happens when there is a glut? Producers begin to lower their price. Assume that bread producers have to lower the price to $1.06 per loaf to sell all the bread. Since they also have to pay a tax of $0.10 per loaf, the price they are receiving after tax is now $0.96. The price they have received has dropped by 4 cents. In this case, the 10-cent loaf tax is paid 60% by consumers in the form of higher prices and 40% by producers in the form of lower "after tax" prices they receive.

What effects tax incidence? The responsiveness of consumers to price increases will affect how much of the tax they will pay. As discussed previously, the responsiveness of consumers and producers depends on the alternatives open to them. What other products can a consumer replace this good with that is, availability of good substitutes? What other kinds of investments can producers channel their money into?

(2) How does the tax affect income distribution? Once you know who actually pays the tax, then you need to determine what income classes are most apt to be affected by this tax — who is the typical consumer or producer of this good?

Going back to the bread example, how do you think the percent of your income spent on bread changes as your income goes up? Bread is likely to be a "necessity" — a product that represents a higher percentage of the income of low-income individuals than high-income individuals. This implies that the impact of the tax on the income of lower and middle-income consumers will be greater than the impact on high-income consumers — a bread tax is likely to be regressive.

Who are the typical producers of bread? They probably range from small local bakeries to large national companies. We would expect that producers or stockholders in bread companies are likely to be middle to upper income. This would imply that the portion of the bread tax paid by producers is likely to be progressive.

The total equity effects of the bread tax will depend on whether producers or consumers are more likely to pay the tax. We will discuss the equity effects of different taxes in the next couple of lectures.

Generally, the political rhetoric would suggest that most of us favor a mildly progressive tax system. However, state and local tax systems are generally not progressive. Estimating tax incidence is difficult and requires certain assumptions. The assumptions about tax incidence (tax shifting) can have a significant effect on estimates of how progressive or regressive a tax is. In one of the most comprehensive reviews of the equity of the tax system in this country, Pechman (1985) concluded that over most income ranges that tax system is proportional.[3]

While the overall tax burden on taxpayers may be proportional, the vertical equity of taxes varies significantly between the federal government, state governments, and local governments. As indicated in the following table produced by the Tax Policy Center, the

[3] Joseph Pechman. 1985. *Who Paid the Taxes 1966–85.* (Washington, DC: The Brookings Institution).

Table 9.3. Effective federal tax rates under current law, by cash income percentile, 2010.

	Average Effective Tax Rate				
Cash Income Percentile	**Individual Income Tax**	**Payroll Tax**	**Corporate Income Tax**	**Estate Tax**	**All Federal Tax**
Lowest Quintile	−4.5	8.4	0.8	N/A	4.6
Second Quintile	−0.4	10.3	0.8	N/A	10.8
Middle Quintile	5.4	10.9	0.8	N/A	17.1
Fourth Quintile	8.5	10.6	1.0	N/A	20.2
Top Quintile	15.7	5.8	4.3	N/A	25.7
All	10.9	7.9	2.8	N/A	21.5
Addendum					
80–90	11.5	10.2	1.4	N/A	23.1
90–95	14.1	8.7	1.9	N/A	24.6
95–99	17.2	5.4	3.4	N/A	26.0
Top 1%	18.3	1.5	8.1	N/A	27.9
Top 0.1%	18.2	0.7	10.4	N/A	29.3

Source: Jeffrey Rohaly. 2008. "The Distribution of Federal Taxes, 2008–11." Washington, DC: Tax Policy Center, June 11. Available at: http://www.taxpolicycenter.org/publications/url.cfm?ID=1001189.

incidence of federal taxes is progressive, due in large part to the individual income tax. Taxpayers in the lowest 40% of income do not pay any federal personal income tax on average while individuals in the top 1% of income pay 18%. The effective tax rate for all federal taxes drops from 29% for the top 1% of income to 4.6% for the bottom 20% of income (Table 9.3).

By contrast, a recent estimate by the Institute on Taxation and Economic Policy of the tax incidence of state and local taxes shows that overall, these taxes are regressive.[4] (These estimates of the total take into account the fact that state income and local property taxes are deductible on the federal income tax, the so-called "federal offset"). State income taxes are, on average, progressive. State sales and excise taxes are very regressive, and property taxes are regressive

[4]Institute on Taxation and Economic Policy. 2009. *Who Pays? A Distributional Analysis of the Tax Systems in All 50 States*. Washington, DC: Author.

at low and high incomes, and the tax is proportional for most middle-class households. The Institute on Taxation and Economic Policy also calculated the tax incidence for each state. The most regressive state tax systems are Washington, Florida, South Dakota, Tennessee, and Texas. Not surprisingly, none of these states have a state income tax. The most progressive state tax systems include Delaware, New York, and Vermont, which rely heavily on the state income tax. It should be noted, however, that no state tax system is estimated to be progressive across all income ranges.

State & Local Taxes in 2007, All States

State and local taxes imposed on own residents, as shares of income

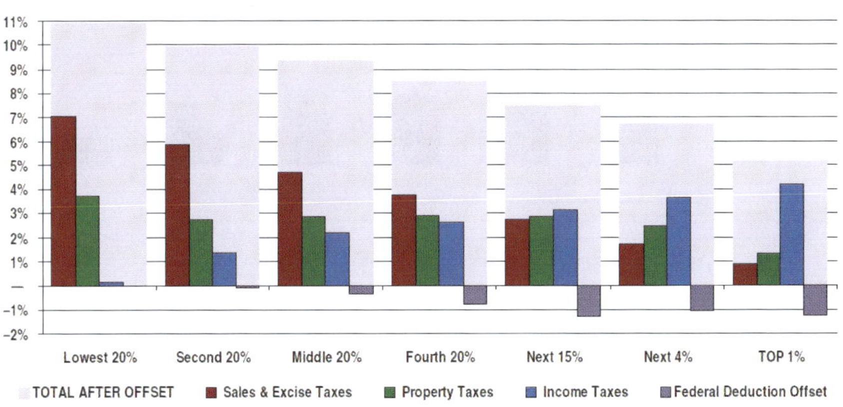

Source: Institute on Taxation and Economic Policy. 2009. *Who Pays? A Distributional Analysis of the Tax Systems in All 50 States*. Washington, DC: Author.

The following chart provides an estimate of tax incidence for state and local taxes in New York.[5] Overall (including the federal offset), state and local taxes are slightly progressive up to the 60th percentile of income and then is mildly regressive except at the very highest income classes when it becomes very regressive. A similar pattern exists for total taxes without the offset, but the regressivity in the highest income classes is less pronounced. As expected, the individual income tax is very progressive over most income ranges. The sales and excise taxes are regressive over all income ranges, and

[5]Institute on Taxation and Economic Policy. 2009. *Who Pays? A Distributional Analysis of the Tax Systems in All 50 States*. Washington, DC: Author.

this applies to both the general sales tax and excise taxes (such as gas taxes). The property tax in New York is quite regressive at low-income and high-income levels and fairly proportional in between (ignoring the federal offset).

New York

State & Local Taxes in 2007

Shares of family income for non-elderly taxpayers

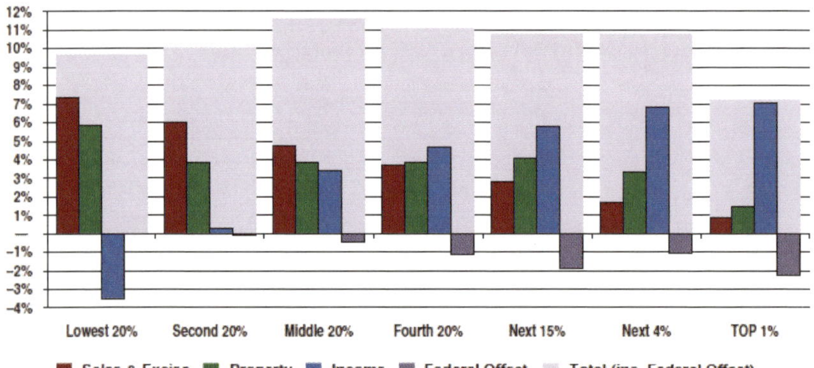

Income Group	Lowest 20%	Second 20%	Middle 20%	Fourth 20%	Top 20%: Next 15%	Next 4%	TOP 1%
Income Range	Less than $16,000	$16,000 – $33,000	$33,000 – $56,000	$56,000 – $95,000	$95,000 – $209,000	$209,000 – $633,000	$633,000 or more
Average Income in Group	$9,600	$24,400	$43,800	$73,100	$133,000	$338,100	$3,065,800
Sales & Excise Taxes	**7.3%**	**6.0%**	**4.7%**	**3.7%**	**2.8%**	**1.7%**	**0.9%**
General Sales—Individuals	3.6%	3.34%	2.8%	2.3%	1.8%	1.1%	0.6%
Other Sales & Excise—Ind.	1.5%	0.9%	0.6%	0.4%	0.3%	0.1%	0.0%
Sales & Excise on Business	2.2%	1.8%	1.4%	1.0%	0.7%	0.4%	0.2%
Property Taxes	**5.8%**	**3.8%**	**3.9%**	**3.8%**	**4.1%**	**3.3%**	**1.5%**
Property Taxes on Families	5.3%	3.3%	3.4%	3.4%	3.6%	2.6%	0.6%
Other Property Taxes	0.5%	0.5%	0.5%	0.5%	0.5%	0.8%	0.9%
Income Taxes	**–3.5%**	**0.3%**	**3.4%**	**4.7%**	**5.8%**	**6.8%**	**7.0%**
Personal Income Tax	–3.5%	0.3%	3.4%	4.6%	5.7%	6.6%	6.7%
Corporate Income Tax	0.0%	0.0%	0.0%	0.1%	0.1%	0.2%	0.4%
TOTAL TAXES	**9.6%**	**10.1%**	**12.0%**	**12.2%**	**12.7%**	**11.8%**	**9.4%**
Federal Deduction Offset	–0.0%	–0.1%	–0.5%	–1.1%	–1.9%	–1.1%	–2.2%
TOTAL AFTER OFFSET	**9.6%**	**10.0%**	**11.6%**	**11.0%**	**10.7%**	**10.8%**	**7.2%**

Note: Table shows 2007 tax law updated to reflect permanent changes in law enacted through October 2009.

Source: Institute on Taxation and Economic Policy. 2009. *Who Pays? A Distributional Analysis of the Tax Systems in All 50 States*. Washington, DC: Author.

As you might expect in many cases, there is a tradeoff between the equity and efficiency effects of a tax. Using the sales tax example, a tax which is more progressive (or less regressive) tends to fall relatively more heavily on producers than consumers since producers generally have higher incomes. This implies that consumers have good substitutes and react to the tax by reducing their consumption of the taxed item. However, the more consumers react, the higher the efficiency losses from the tax.

9.4.3 Adequacy/elasticity/stability

The major criteria that most government officials use to judge tax types is how much revenue are the taxes going to produce. After all, taxes are first and foremost a means to pay for expenditure programs. Politicians are interested in the adequacy, the elasticity, and the stability of the tax.

(1) *Adequacy*: Refers to how much revenue can be generated at reasonable tax rates. Generally, it is desirable to find taxes with a broad base, such as the income, sales, or property taxes, since a lot of revenue can be generated from the tax at reasonable rates. The interest in reasonable tax rates arises for two reasons:

- It is politically unpopular and horizontally inequitable to tax one segment of the economy much higher than others. Using our bread tax as an example, if the state of New York tried to raise most of its revenue from a bread tax, this would unduly burden consumers and producers of bread; and
- Raising tax rates may actually lead to thc case where total tax revenue goes down as tax rate increases cause more and more people to make choices that allow them to avoid the tax.

(2) *Elasticity*: Since raising tax rates every year is unpopular, political leaders are generally interested in taxes where the revenues automatically keep up with inflation and growth in the income of residents. This is because the costs of public services will also go up with inflation, and people's demands for public services generally go up with their income. The most

common measure of this revenue growth is something called the tax elasticity.

Definition: Tax elasticity (E) is the percent change in tax revenue from a 1% change in the community's income, holding the tax structure constant.

$$E = \% \text{ change in TR}$$
$$\% \text{ change in real income.}$$

An elasticity of one indicates that a 1% increase in real income (income adjusting for inflation) would lead to a 1% increase in tax revenue. Generally, we would like an elasticity of about one since this implies that taxes would just keep up with real income growth. Over the next several classes, we will discuss the elasticity of several of the most common taxes in this country.

One estimate of state and local tax elasticity for the state of Washington indicates just how different tax elasticities can be across different types of taxes. The sales, use tax, and business and occupation (B&O tax is another type of sales tax) have short-run elasticities of 1.4. In other words, a 1% increase in income in the state is associated with an increase in 1.4% in tax revenue. By contrast, the property tax is estimated to have an elasticity of 0.2, which implies very little response to income growth. The overall tax elasticity is greater than one, indicating Washington's tax system is quite responsive to income growth (Table 9.4).

(3) *Stability*: Since it is difficult for governments to make dramatic changes in their expenditure programs, ideally, public officials would like revenue sources that are stable.

Definition: Tax Stability is measured as the change in tax revenue in a given year over the tax revenue of the previous year.

For example, public officials would be alarmed if the property tax revenue fluctuated by 20% every year. It would be very difficult to come up with firm budgets, and the government

Table 9.4. Estimates of short-run elasticities.

Tax Base	Short-run Elasticity
Sales and Use	1.4
B&O	1.4
Property	0.2
Public Utilities	−0.2
All Taxes	1.2

Source: Washington State Tax Structure Study Committee. 2002. "Tax Alternatives for Washington State: A Report to the Legislature." Available at: http://dor.wa.gov/content/aboutus/statisticsandreports/wataxstudy/final_report.htm# Complete%20Report.

may be forced to borrow or cut back on services if there was a significant drop in revenue.

As you may have guessed, there may be a tradeoff between the stability of tax and its elasticity. A tax, which is elastic, is one which is responsive to changes in its tax base. However, this implies that tax revenue will not only go up with the tax base, it will go down when the tax base goes down. In other words, an elastic tax may also be an unstable tax. Ideally, you want to find a tax which grows with its base (elastic) and where the tax base itself experiences stable growth.

9.4.4 Tax administration

Finally, a tax can be judged on the ease of its administration. Generally, there are two objectives which are important in examining tax administration:

Fairness: Are taxpayers with the same tax base treated the same under this tax? As you will notice, this is very closely related to the concept of horizontal equity. An unfair administration of the tax is one of the principal ways to decrease the horizontal equity of the tax.

Administration costs: Another important criterion is how much does it cost to administer the tax fairly. These costs involve both the administration costs of the government and the compliance costs of the taxpayer. The compliance costs of tax administration are the foregone resources or time given up by the taxpayer to comply with the tax. The time you spend filling out your income tax form (or the amount you pay H.R. Block), is a compliance cost. It is important to account for both. For some taxes (income and sales taxes), compliance costs are much larger than administration costs, while for others (property taxes), most of the costs fall on governments.

As you might expect there is an important tradeoff between fairness in tax administration and its costs. The fairer a tax, generally the more the administration costs. Table 9.5 in Mikesell (1999) summarizes estimates of the administrative costs as a percent of revenue for several different types of taxes.[6]

A study by the Washington State Department of Revenue (2002) found[7]:

Table 9.5. Administrative-cost estimates for major taxes.

Tax Base (Data Source)	**Administrative Costs as a Percentage of Revenue**
Income tax	
Colorado (individual and corporate)[a]	0.7
Michigan (individual)[b]	0.64
Michigan (single business tax)[b]	0.42
General sale and use tax	
California[c]	0.84
Colorado sales[a]	0.4

(Continued)

[6]John Mikesell. 1999. *Fiscal Administration: Analysis and Applications for the Public Sector*, 5th edition (New York: Harcourt Brace College Publishers), Chapter 11.

[7]Washington State Department of Revenue, *Tax Alternatives for Washington State: A Report to the Legislature*, November 2002. Available at: http://dor.wa.gov/Content/AboutUs/StatisticsAndReports/WAtaxstudy/Final_Report.htm.

Table 9.5. (*Continued*)

Tax Base (Data Source)	**Administrative Costs as a Percentage of Revenue**
Colorado use[a]	3.6
Idaho[d]	0.8
Mississippi[d]	1.0
North Carolina[d]	0.68
North Dakota[d]	0.5
South Dakota[d]	0.41
Washington[d]	0.7
Other taxes	
Federal luxury excises[e]	0.3
Twelve OECD value-added taxes[f]	0.32–1.09
GAO estimated for 5% broad US value-added tax[g]	1.2–1.8
Taxes administered by IRS[h]	0.56
California alcoholic beverage[c]	0.73
California cigarette tax[c]	0.32
California motor vehicle fuel tax[c]	0.27
Colorado alcoholic beverage[a]	4.8
Colorado cigarette and tobacco[a]	0.4
Colorado mileage and fuels[a]	1.1
Colorado death and gift[a]	0.7

Sources: Mikesell (1999), Chapter 11, Table 11-2.
[a]Colorado Department of Revenue. *Annual Report*, 1990 (Denver: Department of Revenue, 1992). [b]Michigan State Treasurer, *Annual Report*, 1977–78 (Lansing: State Treasurer, 1980). [c]California State Board of Equalization, *Annual Report*, 1991–92 (Sacramento: Board of Equalization, 1993). [d]John F. Due and John L. Mikesell. *Sales Taxation* (Washington, D.C.: Urban Institute, 1994). [e]US General Accounting Office, *Annual Report on the Tax-Related Studies* (GAO/GGD-93-68) (Washington, D.C.: General Accounting Office, Mar. 1993). [f]Organization for Economic Cooperation and Development. *Taxing Consumption* (Paris: OECD, 1988). [g]US General Accounting Office, *Value-Added Tax: Administrative Costs Vary with Complexity and Number of Businesses* (GAO/GGD-93-78) (Washington, D.C.: General Accounting Office, May 1993). [h]US Internal Revenue Service, *Annual Report*, 1991 (Washington, D.C.: Government Printing Office, 1993).

> "Most of Washington's taxes are relatively simple to administer for both government and households. The average Department of Revenue cost of collection is 69 cents per $100 of collections. The main reason is that households do not have to file tax returns. While the retail sales tax is very cost effective for the government to administer, a significant cost of administration is shifted to retailers who act as uncompensated collection agents. Costs of collecting sales tax are estimated to be $6.47 per $100 of total state and local sales tax collected for small retailers (those with annual Washington gross sales between $150,000 and $400,000) and 97 cents per $100 for large retailers (those with annual Washington gross sales over $1.5 million)." (p. 27).

There are several important steps in tax administration. I have simplified Mikesell's list to four basic steps:

(1) *Tax registration*: Who should pay the tax? This involves developing lists of potential taxpayers, such as property owners, employees, and retail businesses. Generally, the more taxpayers there are the more costly it is to develop these lists, or tax rolls.
(2) *Tax assessment*: What is their tax base? This involves assessing what the tax base is for each taxpayer. In some cases such as the income tax, taxpayers themselves are responsible for assessing their tax base. In other cases such as the property tax, this is a major role of the government. Generally, the more complicated the tax system, the more difficult and complicated it is to assess the tax base.
(3) *Tax collection and appeal*: How much is owed by the taxpayer? This is the process of collecting the revenue from the taxpayer. In some cases, the taxpayer is responsible for estimating what is owed and sending it in (income tax) and in others the government sends out tax bills (property tax). Built into this process usually is the ability of the taxpayer to appeal the tax bill to the government. The fewer the number of taxpayers, the fewer the appeals, and the less costly the collection process.
(4) *Audit and enforcement*: Finally, to ensure taxpayer compliance, the government generally has some program to determine who has not paid and who has under (or over) paid their tax bill. This will be followed by some legal mechanism for coercing the

taxpayer to pay the bills. In the case of a tax such as the income tax, the IRS carries out a program of "spot checks" on tax returns ("Tax Compliance Measurement Program") to try and catch those avoiding tax payments. There is a clear tradeoff here between administrative cost and the fairness of the enforcement program. The more complicated and the greater number of taxpayers the more the enforcement costs will generally be.

9.4.5 Conclusion

In summary, there are a number of criteria, which can be used in assessing a revenue source. I have outlined the four most common criteria used by public finance economists. Frankly, most public officials probably concentrate on the adequacy of the tax with some attention given to equity and administration costs. As was clear in this discussion it is not possible to achieve all of these criteria simultaneously. There are tradeoffs between:

— efficiency and vertical equity
— tax elasticity and stability
— administrative costs and horizontal equity.

In the next several lectures, we will use these criteria to examine several of the most common revenue sources in this country: income, sales, and property taxes.

Lecture 10

Consumption Taxes

10.1 Introduction

The sales tax has continued to be a major source of revenue for state and local governments. Sales taxes represented in 2009–2010[1]:

- 23% of state and local own-source revenue and 34% of state and local taxes,
- 34% of state own-source revenue and 46% of state taxes,
- 10% of local own-source revenue and 16% of local taxes.

Sales taxes at the federal level are a much smaller share of taxes than most other developed countries. Taxes on goods and services in the US were 17% of total tax receipts in 2010, compared to an OECD average of 32%.[2] The US is one of the few developed countries without a value-added tax (VAT) as a major source of central government revenue.

There are two basic types of sales taxes: general sales taxes and taxes on individual commodities (excise taxes). We are going to review briefly the structure of each and then evaluate how they stack up on the criteria presented in the last lecture.

[1] US Bureau of the Census. 2010. "State and Local Government Finance."

[2] Tax Policy Center, "Tax Facts." Available at: http://www.taxpolicycenter.org/taxfacts/displayafact.cfm?Docid=308&Topic2id=95.

10.2 Structure

On the surface, the sales tax used in this country is structurally simple. The tax revenue from the sales tax is found by multiplying the amount of sales of a commodity by its tax rate. The question is what sales are taxed? Deciding at what stage of production to tax and what to include in the base makes this tax more complex than commonly believed.

10.2.1 Stage of production

Although we think of general sales tax as a retail sales tax, retail sales is only one of several possible forms of sales tax. Taxes can be applied to resource suppliers (e.g., mining or farming), manufacturers, and wholesalers, as well as retailers. These represent the possible stages of production. Some of the key questions in evaluating a sales tax are:

- To what stage of production is it applied?
- Does it cascade through all stages of production?

A tax cascading through all stages of production is one in which the tax accumulates at each part of the production process, resulting in a higher tax at the end (retail level) than at the earlier stages.

There are basically two types of sales taxes:

(1) A single-stage tax is a tax, which is applied to only one stage of the production process. Since it strikes only one stage, it does not cascade through the process. The two most common forms include:

   (a) *Manufacturers' taxes*: This tax applied only at the manufacturing stage. The problem with this tax is that it encourages a firm either to reduce the amount of "manufacturing" *per se*, or to move to another state without such a tax. Both possibly results in significant efficiency losses.

   (b) *Retail sales tax*: This tax applies to the final (retail) sale of the product. This is clearly the main form of the general sales tax used in this country. By striking only the final stage, this does not provide much incentive for a firm to alter its behavior.

(2) A multiple stage tax is a tax that hits several stages of the production process. The two most common forms include:

   (a) *Turnover or gross receipts tax (business and occupation tax)*: Generally a tax on the sales at each stage of the production process. A similar form of tax is used in three states in this country and in many developing countries.

   (b) *VAT*: It has received increasing attention lately as one option considered for financing the federal government. The VAT is the principal sales tax used in Europe and Japan. The VAT is also a multi-stage tax, which will strike most stages of the production process. But the tax is specifically designed to avoid cascading. Specifically, the tax is based on the value added or the net receipts of a firm. This means that the firm pays a tax on the difference between its total sales and the cost of purchasing inputs to produce its product. By taxing only net receipts, there is no cascading of the tax rate over each stage of production, and no incentive for the firm to change how it is organized.

To illustrate the different types of sales taxes, we will use a simple example of the production of bread. Assume for simplicity that a farmer does not buy any inputs to grow wheat and sells this wheat to a miller for \$100. The miller grinds the wheat into flour and sells the flour to a baker for \$150. The baker produces the bread and sells it to the retail store for \$300, which in turn sells it to consumers for \$400 (for 400 loaves). The first column of Table 10.1 shows the sales at each stage, and the second column shows the "value added" defined in terms of the value of outputs minus value of purchased inputs.

The third column shows that a 5% retail sales tax will be multiplied only by sales at the last (retail) stage, and will produce \$20 in revenue. A 5% VAT will be multiplied by the value added in each stage, and will also produce \$20 in revenue. By contrast, a turnover tax is multiplied by the gross sales at each stage, and will require only a tax rate of 2.1% to produce \$20 in revenue. A manufacturing tax will be imposed only at the two stages where manufacturing takes place.

Table 10.1. Comparison of sales taxes by stage of production. Production of bread.

Stage of Production	**Sales**	**Value Added**	**Retail Sales Tax (Rate = 5%)**	**VAT (Rate = 5%)**	**Turnover Tax (Rate = 2.1%)**	**Manufacturer Tax (Rate = 4.5%)**
Farmer	100.0	100.0		5.0	2.1	
Miller	150.0	50.0		2.5	3.2	$6.75
Baker	300.0	150.0		7.5	6.3	$13.50
Retail store	400.0	100.0	20.0	5.0	8.4	
Total tax			20.0	20.0	20.0	$20
Tax if vertical monopoly			20.0	20.0	$8.40	$13.50

Source: This table is adapted from *Benedict C. Cabaltica, Comparing the Value-Added Tax to the Retail Sales Tax*, THE TAX ADVISER. (Sept 1, 2008).

From an efficiency standpoint, you do not want the type of sales tax adopted to affect the organization of the production process. The key question is: Can a business reduce their tax burdens by changing how they produce? Let us take the extreme case and assume that they become a vertical monopoly (control all stages of production). What would the tax be under this structure? For the retail sales tax and VAT, nothing changes since the value added equals the retail sales of $400. For the turnover tax, the tax burden with a vertical monopoly would be $8.4 (2.1% × $400), which is a reduction of 58% in the tax burden. The new tax under the manufacturing tax would be $13.5 (32.5%) reduction. It is clear that these two taxes could provide powerful incentives for firms to consolidate the stages of production (Table 10.1).

10.2.2 Coverage of the tax

The coverage of a sales tax involves identifying which types of goods and services are taxable. As I said, there are basically two types of sales taxes used in this country:

(1) Excise taxes are taxes on individual commodities. There is heavy use by both the federal and state governments of excise taxes. The most common commodities for such taxes are gasoline, alcohol, cigarettes, and luxury items such as jewelry. The stated reasons for such taxes are either to:

- Discourage consumption of some types of products — alcohol and cigarettes. These are called sumptuary taxes;
- Act as a substitute for a benefit charge (gasoline tax) to fund a public program (highway maintenance and construction);
- Increase equity by taxing a luxury item.

You can see in Table 10.2 that all states use some form of cigarette, alcohol, and gasoline tax. Rates, particularly for the cigarette and beer taxes, vary considerably. In addition, in many states, the general sales tax also applies to most cigarette purchases, which leads to an even higher tax rate.

(2) A general (retail) sales tax is on retail sales of all goods and services. Almost all state governments use the retail sales tax and, in 31 states, local governments have access to the tax. However, the base of this tax is usually reduced for several types of sales:

(a) Food and other commodities: Most states exempt food, electricity and gas utilities, personal services, and intermediate sales to manufacturers (Table 10.3). However, there is

Table 10.2. State excise tax rates (2008).

Type	Number of States	Tax Rates (per unit)		
		Median	Low	High
Gasoline (gallon)	50	\$0.21	\$0.08 (AK)	\$0.36 (WA)
Cigarette (pack)	50	\$1.00	\$0.17 (MO)	\$2.58 (NJ)
Alcohol (beer — gallon)	50	\$0.19	\$0.02 (WY)	\$1.07 (AK)

Source: Federation of Tax Administrators, *State Excise Taxes*, http://www.taxadmin.org/fta/rate/tax_stru.html, accessed June 29, 2009.

Table 10.3. State sales tax exemptions.

Major Exemptions	**Number of States**
Food	33
Prescription drugs	46
Non-prescription drugs	13

Source: Federation of Tax Administrators, *State Sales Taxes — Food and Drug Exemptions*, http://www.taxadmin.org/fta/rate/sales.html, accessed June 29, 2009.

Table 10.4. Average number of taxed services (2007).

Service Category	**Number in Each Category**	**Minimum (%)**	**Maximum (%)**	**New York (%)**
Utilities	16	0.0	100.0	25.0
Personal	20	0.0	100.0	20.0
Business	34	0.0	100.0	38.2
Computer	8	0.0	100.0	12.5
Entertainment	15	0.0	93.3	40.0
Professional	9	0.0	100.0	0.0
Fabrication, repair, installation	19	0.0	100.0	73.7
Other	47	0.0	91.5	31.9
TOTAL	164	0.6	95.2	33.9

Source: Federation of Tax Administrators, *State Sales Taxation of Services*, http://www.taxadmin.org/fta/pub/services/services.html, accessed June 29, 2009.

significant variation across states in what items are exempt from taxation.

(b) Services are often exempted supposedly for administrative reasons since it is difficult to identify and collect tax on many services. The number of services, which are exempt, also varies widely across states (Table 10.4).

(c) Production inputs are usually exempted since they are inputs used in the production of some final output. To not exempt them would lead to tax cascading and possible

Table 10.5. Percent loss of sales tax revenue. Due to electronic commerce.

	Percent Loss of Tax Revenue			
Type	**Average** (%)	**Low (Alaska)** (%)	**New York** (%)	**High (Louisiana)** (%)
Percent loss of tax revenue:				
2007	2.4	0.6	2.8	3.8
2009	2.3	0.5	2.7	3.6
2012	3.8	0.9	4.4	5.9

Source: Don Bruce, William Fox, and LeAnn Luna. 2009. "State and Local Government Sales Tax Revenue Losses from Electronic Commerce." Center for Business and Economic Research, The University of Tennessee. Available at: http://cber.utk.edu/ecomm/ecom0409.pdf.

efficiency losses. Most states exempt sales to manufacturers, but a much smaller share exempt sale to contractors (Table 10.3).

(d) Interstate mail order/internet sales: Sales taxes on purchases in other states are called use taxes. States can attempt to impose use taxes, but their success in collecting these taxes will depend on whether and how the tax is collected. Vendors without a physical presence in a state do not have to register with the state as a use tax collector. Since it is unlikely that individuals will voluntarily send in their use tax, states stand to potentially lose between 1% and 6% of state tax revenue in 2012 (Table 10.5).

The result of these exemptions is a sizeable loss in the total tax base. For example, if both food and all services are exempt, this is a potential loss of over 70% of the potential tax base (Table 10.6). If food, medical care and household gas, and electric are removed, there is a loss of one-third of the tax base. These potential losses have increased slightly between 1992 and 2004.

10.3 Evaluation

As one of the most common and most popular state and local taxes, it is important that you have a basic understanding of how this

Table 10.6. Potential sales tax bases, 1992 and 2004.

Category	Percentage of Personal Consumption 1992 (%)	2004 (%)
Personal income	123.5	117.7
Disposable personal income	108.2	105.1
Personal consumption	100.0	100.0
Consumption expenditures on		
Food	15.4	14.0
Clothing	5.4	4.0
All services	56.8	59.0
Housing	14.7	15.1
Medical care	15.5	16.9
Household gas and electric	2.6	2.2
Consumption less expenditures on food and all services	27.8	27.0
Consumption less expenditures on food, medical care, and household gas and electric	66.5	66.9
Consumption less expenditures on food, medical care, household gas and electric, and 50% of other services	47.2	47.0

Source: US Department of Commerce, *Survey of Current Business*, July 1993, and July 2004.

tax compares to others in terms of the evaluation criteria we have discussed.

10.3.1 Efficiency

The key questions to ask in evaluating efficiency are what prices does the tax distort and by how much?

(1) *Excise taxes*: Excise taxes are the case of a bread tax we discussed in the last lecture. An excise tax distorts the price between the taxed good and all other goods. This encourages consumers to substitute non-taxed commodities for this taxed good. The size of the efficiency loss depends on how many good substitutes there are for this product.

— In the case of gasoline, alcohol, and cigarettes, there appear to be relatively few good substitutes either because of our heavy dependence on automobile transportation or because of the addictive nature of the product. This implies that the efficiency loss from taxing these items is not likely to be large.
— In the case of luxuries such as jewelry, there are probably some non-taxed luxury items that are good substitutes. Consumers may respond by reducing their consumption of this luxury item, causing a greater efficiency loss.

However, there may actually be some efficiency gains from imposing taxes on harmful substances, such as alcohol and tobacco. As you can learn (or have learned) in an economics course, consumption of these items can have harmful effects on others (drunk driving, secondary smoke). The government may be justified in trying to discourage these behaviors.

Another potential for efficiency loss is due to resources (time and transportation costs) spent by some individuals to purchase the goods in other states or local jurisdictions. While in general, we would not expect large border effects for sales taxes, they could be sizeable if the tax rates are very high, there are large differences across states, and the commodity can be purchased in bulk. These conditions can apply to the case of cigarettes and alcohol.

Several studies have looked at the relationship between excise tax rates and "cross-border sales" of beer and cigarettes.[3] For both commodities, studies have found a significant relationship between cross-border sales, and the differential in tax rates across state borders. As illustrated below for beer sales, states with significantly higher beer tax rates experience a significant loss of in-state sales of beer.

[3]Patrick Fleenor, "How Excise Tax Differentials Affect Cross-Border Sales of Beer in the United States." *Tax Foundation Background Paper*, No. 31, May 1999; Patrick Fleenor, "How Excise Tax Differentials Affect Interstate Smuggling and Cross-Border Sales of Cigarettes in the United States." *Tax Foundation Background Paper*, No. 26, October 1998.

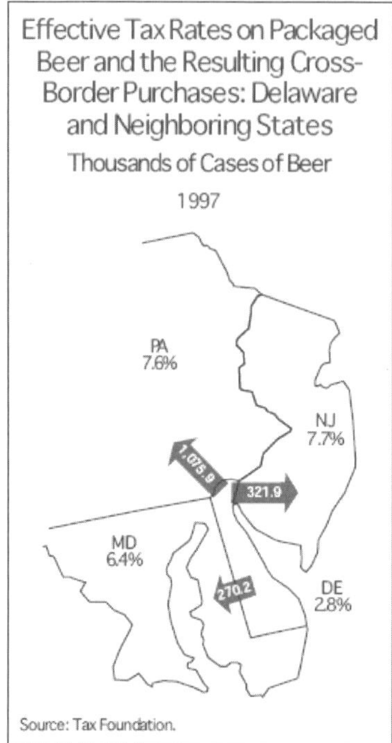

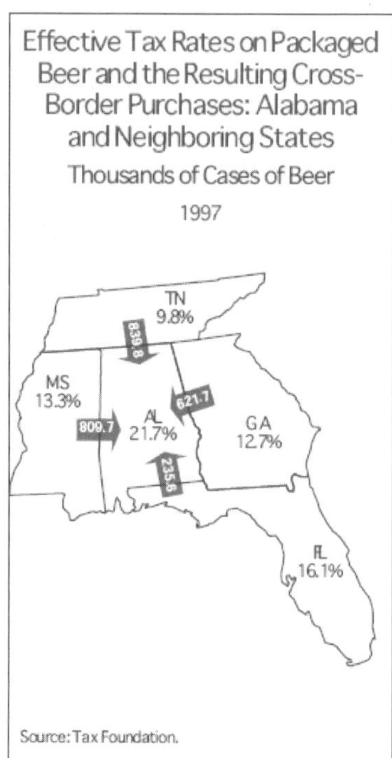

(2) *General (retail) sales tax (and VAT)*: In the case of a truly general sales tax the price distortions are less clear cut since most goods are taxed at the same rate. It is less likely that you will make major changes in your consumption patterns because of the tax.

However, there is one form of consumption that is not taxed — leisure. Using time for recreation instead of work is a form of consumption. All of you as students can appreciate the importance of time and the luxury of being able to take a day off to relax. Because leisure is not taxed, the general sales tax may encourage you to consume more leisure, that is, to work less. To the extent this happens, there is an efficiency loss.

Finally, because sales tax rates vary between states and even some local governments, there may be a tendency for people to travel outside of a community to purchase certain major items, for example, cars. The expenditure on this transportation is also an efficiency loss to society. We illustrated this for excise taxes. The studies for general sales taxes "are quite consistent in finding that a disadvantageous sales tax rate differential leads to a statistically significant but relatively small reduction in sales in the higher-tax jurisdictions." (p. 400)[4] The Table 10.7 illustrates just how different from each other are state and local general sales tax rates in the US.

10.3.2 Equity

(1) *Horizontal equity*: The sales tax has a simple structure, which does not take into account differences in the ability of taxpayers to pay. Excise taxes penalize those consumers who are relatively heavy consumers of these products. Also, such a tax does not control for differences in special circumstances between households, such as the number of children or high medical expenses. Special needs are controlled for somewhat in the exemption of food and medicine, but differences in clothing and other forms of consumption are not.

(2) *Vertical equity*: Sales taxes do not tax an individual household, but a commodity purchased by a household. Consequently, the incidence of the tax is complicated.

   (a) *Tax incidence*: For an excise tax, whether consumers or producers pay for this tax depends on how many substitutes they have. Since there are few legal substitutes for gas, alcohol, and cigarettes, the consumer will probably pay for most of the tax in terms of higher prices. For luxury items, such as jewelry, which have substitutes, it is likely that producers bear a portion of the tax as well consumers.

   For the general sales tax, determining incidence is more complicated since most relative prices do not change. Will consumers change their behavior by consuming more leisure or going to lower-tax states? The general consensus is that consumers probably will not alter their behavior much, in other words, they will bear most of the burden of the retail sales tax (or VAT).

[4]Ronald Fisher. 1996. *State and Local Public Finance*, Second Edition. (Boston: Irwin).

Table 10.7. Combined State and Local Tax Rates.

State	Average Local Rate (%)	Combined Rate(a) (%)	Rank (%)	State	Average Local Rate (%)	Combined Rate(a) (%)	Rank (%)
Tenn.	2.41	9.41	1	Utah	0.66	6.61	26
Calif.	0.81	9.06	2	Nebr.	1.01	6.51	27
Wash.	2.28	8.78	3	N.M.	1.40	6.78	28
Okla.	3.94	8.44	4	Mass.	None	6.25	29
La.	4.43	8.43	5	Pa.	0.22	6.22	30
Ill.	2.15	8.40	6	Ala.	2.15	6.15	31
N.Y.	4.30	8.30	7	Conn.	None	6.00	32
N.C.	2.32	8.07	8	Idaho	None	6.00	32
Ariz.	2.32	7.92	9	Ky.	None	6.00	32
Ark.	1.79	7.79	10	Md.	None	6.00	32
Nev.	0.74	7.59	11	Mich.	None	6.00	32
Tex.	1.14	7.39	12	N.D.	1.00	6.00	32
Colo.	4.34	7.24	13	Vt.	None	6.00	32
Minn.	0.34	7.22	14	W.Va.	None	6.00	32
Mo.	2.95	7.18	15	S.D.	1.52	5.52	40
S.C.	1.04	7.04	16	Wis.	0.42	5.42	41
Ga.	3.02	7.02	17	Wyo.	1.38	5.38	42
Fla.	1.01	7.01	18	Maine	None	5.00	43
Ind.	None	7.00	19	Va.	None	5.00	43
Miss.	None	7.00	19	Hawaii	0.38	4.38	45
N.J.	None	7.00	19	Alaska	1.13	1.13	46
R.I.	None	7.00	19	Del.	None	1.92	47
Kans.	1.65	6.95	23	Mont.	None	None	—
Iowa	0.94	6.94	24	N.H.	None	None	—
Ohio	1.33	6.83	25	Ore.	None	None	—

(a) Local county and municipal rates vary. We weight them by population to compute a statewide average.

(b) California and Virginia both mandate and collect a 1% "local rate" and Utah mandates a 1.25% "local" add-on rate. These rates are included only in the state and local combined rank because localities do not have the authority to change it.

Source: *Tax Foundation Fiscal Fact*, No. 196, "Updated State and Local Option Sales Tax." As of September 29, 2009.

(b) Income distribution: The income distribution of consumers depends obviously on the item being taxed.

— For most excise taxes, including gas, tobacco, and alcohol taxes, lower to middle-income consumers probably spend a higher percentage of their budget on the taxed items. This implies that these taxes will tend to be regressive. Excise taxes on luxury items, which are designed to be a form of progressive taxation, are one exception.

— For the general sales tax, effective tax rates depend on what is included in the tax base. For a general tax without any exemptions, it is likely that the tax would be regressive over most income ranges. Since most sales taxes have exemptions, their vertical equity depends on the exemptions.

Table 10.8 provides information on the percent of income spent on various consumption items by households in particular income classes.[5] For example, households with incomes between 5,000 and 10,000 dollars spend 24% of their income on food, 79% on housing, and 213.4% of their income on total consumption. The fact that the percent is above 100% implies that the household receives transfer payments and/or is in debt.

— since the percent spent on food drops dramatically as incomes rise, exclusion of food is likely to reduce the regressivity of the tax,

— the effect that exclusion of services has on regressivity depends on the nature of the service. For medical services, their exclusion will probably reduce regressivity, since the percent of income spent on medical care drops with income. The exclusion of other professional services, personal services, repair services, and entertainment services may actually increase its regressivity.

[5] Ronald Fisher. 1996. *State and Local Public Finance*, Second Edition. (Boston: Irwin). Chapter 15, Table 15.4.

Table 10.8. Personal consumption expenditures as a percentage of income, 2002.

Income Class[a]	Total Personal Consumption	Food at Home	Utilities and Fuel	Housing	Medical Care
5–9.99[b]	213.4	23.8	20.2	78.6	14.7
10–14.999	168.3	18.6	15.2	57.1	14.9
15–19.999	144.4	14.3	11.9	49.3	12.2
20–29.999	117.7	11.3	9.5	39.2	9.3
30–39.999	101.9	8.7	7.3	32.7	6.9
40–49.999	94.0	7.3	6.2	29.6	5.8
50–69.999	85.5	6.0	5.3	25.9	4.8
70 and over	66.3	3.9	3.3	20.5	2.8
All consumers	86.1	6.5	5.4	27.3	4.9

[a]In thousands of dollars.
[b]Data for consumer units with income less than $5,000 are not meaningful.
Source: US Department of Labor. *Consumer Expenditure Survey*. 2002.

Given the distribution of total personal consumption as a percent of income in Table 10.4, we would expect that the general sales tax would be regressive. The estimates of tax incidence for the sales tax by the Institute on Taxation and Economic Policy indicate that both general sales taxes and excise taxes are very regressive.

10.3.3 Adequacy/elasticity

(1) *Adequacy*: The adequacy of sales taxes depends on the size of their tax base. For the general sales tax, the tax base is quite broad so that the tax rate can be kept relatively low-between 4% and 7%, usually. However, the exclusion of items, such as food and services can significantly reduce the size of the tax base and increase the required rate.

For excise taxes, the base is much narrower and not surprisingly, the tax rates are much higher.[6] However, since many

[6]Ronald Fisher. 1996. *State and Local Public Finance*, Second Edition. (Boston: Irwin). Chapter 10, Table 10.3.

Averages for All States

State & Local Taxes in 2007

Shares of family income for non-elderly taxpayers

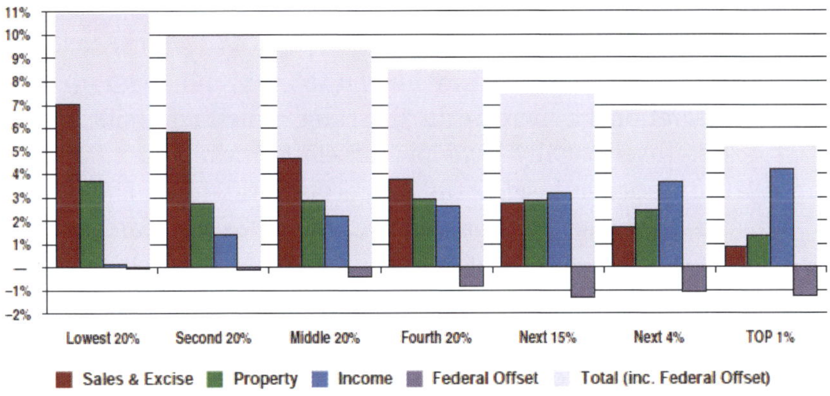

Income Group	Lowest 20%	Second 20%	Middle 20%	Fourth 20%	Top 20%		
					Next 15%	Next 4%	TOP 1%
Income Range	Less than $18,000	$18,000 – $33,000	$33,000 – $54,000	$54,000 – $90,000	$90,000 – $185,000	$185,000 – $476,000	$476,000 or more
Average Income in Group	$10,700	$25,500	$42,900	$69,900	$122,400	$277,900	$1,768,000
Sales & Excise Taxes	**7.1%**	**5.9%**	**4.7%**	**3.7%**	**2.8%**	**1.7%**	**0.9%**
General Sales—Individuals	3.3%	3.0%	2.5%	2.1%	1.6%	1.0%	0.5%
Other Sales & Excise—Ind.	1.6%	1.1%	0.8%	0.6%	0.4%	0.2%	0.1%
Sales & Excise on Business	2.1%	1.8%	1.4%	1.1%	0.8%	0.5%	0.3%

Source: Institute on Taxation and Economic Policy. 2009. *Who Pays? A Distributional Analysis of the Tax Systems in All 50 States*. Washington, DC: Author.

of these are sin taxes there is generally not a lot of political grumbling. It does, however, significantly increase the horizontal and vertical inequities from such taxes.

(2) *Elasticity*: The elasticity of the sales tax again depends crucially on what is in the sales tax base. If the item is considered a necessity, then it is likely that increases in community income will not lead to a proportionate increase in consumption. If the item is a luxury, then a 1% increase in income will most likely lead to a greater than 1% increase in consumption and tax revenue.

- For excise taxes, elasticity obviously depends on the item taxed. For goods such as alcohol, tobacco, and gasoline, their tax elasticities are likely to be low since consumption of these commodities does not increase significantly with income. For luxury items such as jewelry, we would expect that the elasticity would be greater than one. However, the elasticity of most excise taxes is further dampened by the fact that they are typically per unit taxes rather than *ad valorem* taxes. In other words, the only way for the tax per unit to go up is for a discretionary increase in the rates. The end result is that excise taxes usually have low tax elasticities.

- For the general sales tax, the elasticity depends on what is in the base. In general, we would expect an elasticity below one. Exclusion of food and medicine should increase the elasticity, while exclusion of most services will probably have little effect. **A good rule of thumb is that exclusion of a necessity from the sales tax will increase elasticity, while exclusion of a luxury will decrease the elasticity of a sales tax.** Based on a survey of state fiscal staff, Gold (1995) found that state staff reported elasticities between 0.80 and 1.2, with most elasticities approximately equal to one.[7]

(3) *Stability*: Besides tax elasticity, the issue of tax stability can be important. Because the general sales tax is tied directly to retail sales, its stability depends on the stability of retail sales in general. This can depend on the particular state and business cycle. Compared to some state taxes (corporate income and severance taxes), retail sales taxes, and most excise taxes are considered to moderately stable, with average fluctuation in revenue of 5–7%.[8]

Looking at annual percent change in sales tax revenue for New York from 1972 to 2010, we can see that retail sales tax revenues typically fluctuate between 5 and 10% (Figure 10.1). Excise taxes in

[7]Steven Gold, "The Income Elasticity of State Tax Systems: New Evidence." *State Tax Notes*, May 1, 1995.

[8]Oskar Harmon and Rajiv Mallick. 1994. "The Optimal State Tax Portfolio Model: An Extension." *National Tax Journal*, 47(2): 395–401.

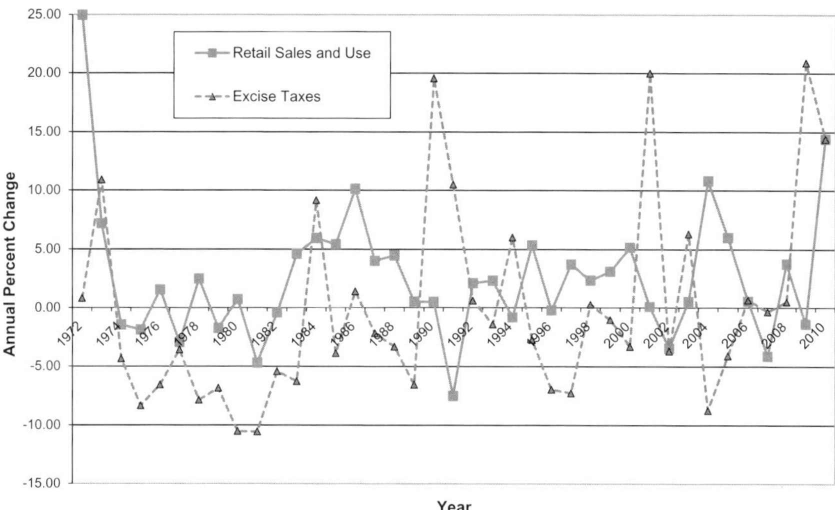

Figure 10.1. Comparison of trends for state sales tax revenue, New York state (inflation adjusted dollars).

Source: New York State, *Department of Taxation and Finance*, 2010.

New York, on the other hand, have been much less stable, and in some years have fluctuated by as much as 20%. The reason for this fluctuation is not clear, but the large increases in 1991, 2001, and 2009 are probably due primarily to increases in excise tax rates.

10.3.4 Administration

The sales tax is considered to be an average tax in terms of administrative costs.

(1) *Registration*: For the general sales tax, this involves keeping records of the thousands of retail outlets in most states. This is a difficult task but has generally been accomplished without too much trouble in this country. Multi-stage taxes, such as the VAT, would require a record of all producers and sellers of all products, which would greatly expand the registration costs.
(2) Assessment is basically accomplished by the firm themselves. It does require significant paperwork for the firm.
(3) *Collection*: This is accomplished by the firm.

(4) *Enforcement*: This probably represents a fairly significant expense for state and local governments for the retail sales tax. One advantage of the VAT is that it tends to be self-enforcing since each firm has an incentive to keep good records on transactions with other firms.

In general, the estimates of the administrative costs of the sales tax are between 0.5% and 1% of total tax revenue. Including compliance costs significantly increases the overall administrative costs.

Lecture 11

Local Property Taxes

11.1 Introduction

The property tax is the most important tax used by local governments. In 2003, the property tax accounted for[1]:

— 73% of local tax revenue (TR) and 25% of total revenue,
— 56% of city taxes and 21% of revenue,
— 69% of county taxes and 24% of revenue,
— 96% of school district taxes and 34% of revenue.

The property tax also is politically unpopular. Proposition 13 in California and Proposition 2½ in Massachusetts were property tax limitation measures passed at the state level, which severely reduced the future potential growth of the property tax in these states. Over 40 states have some form of property tax restrictions in place, including New York which recently adopted a new law limiting local property tax.[2] Why is the property tax such an unpopular tax? Undoubtedly, part of its unpopularity is based on the visibility of the tax. Unlike the sales tax, which is paid in small amounts, the

[1]US Census Bureau. Governments Division, *Annual Finances of Governments: State and Local Governments.*

[2]Anderson, N. B. 2006. Property Tax Limitations: An Interpretative Review. *National Tax Journal*, 59(3), 685–694.

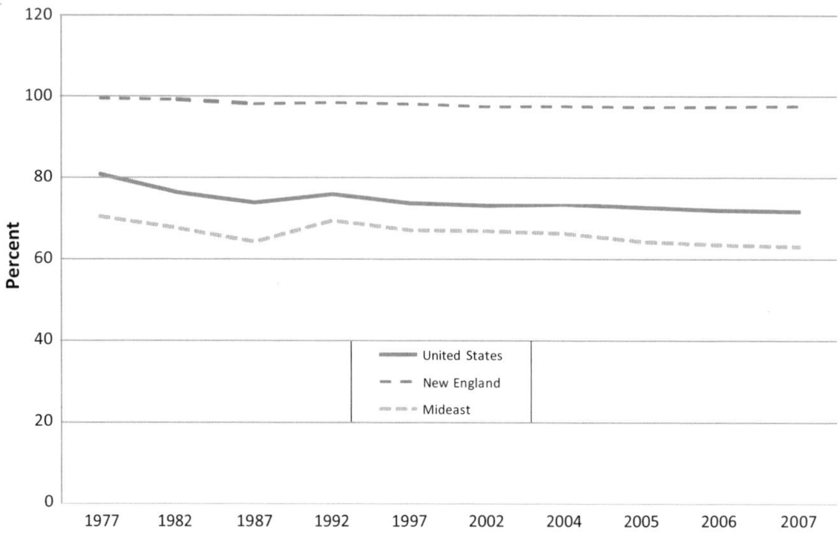

Figure 11.1. Property taxes as a percent of local tax revenue.
Source: Tax Policy Center, "Tax Facts," Available at: http://www.taxpolicycenter.org/taxfacts/displayafact.cfm?Docid=518.

property tax is typically paid in an annual lump sum, which makes tax increases more visible.

Although the property tax remains a significant source of revenue for local governments, it has declined in importance over the last 30 years (see Figure 11.1). More elastic taxes, such as income and sales taxes, have become more important, as have user fees at the local level. There are significant differences in the importance of property taxes across states and regions. For the New England states, property taxes are the only significant source of local tax revenue. By contrast, in the Mideast states, including New York, the property tax has dropped to about 60% of total local TR (54% in New York) by 2007. We will discuss in this lecture some of the other reasons, besides political unpopularity, that has affected the growth of property TR.

As illustrated in Table 11.1, there are also large differences in the level of property taxes per capita across the country. Property

Table 11.1. State and Local Property Tax collections, FY 2007.

State	Per Capita	Rank	State	Per Capita	Rank
US Total	$1,278	—	Montana	$1,163	25
District of Columbia	$2,584	—	Washington	$1,151	26
New Jersey	$2,485	1	California	$1,151	27
Connecticut	$2,312	2	Nevada	$1,141	28
Wyoming	$2,311	3	North Dakota	$1,097	29
New Hampshire	$2,222	4	Oregon	$1,067	30
Vermont	$1,984	5	South Dakota	$1,036	31
New York	$1,963	6	Georgia	$1,010	32
Rhode Island	$1,859	7	Arizona	$993	33
Massachusetts	$1,710	8	South Carolina	$984	34
Illinois	$1,595	9	Indiana	$973	35
Maine	$1,565	10	Missouri	$898	36
Alaska	$1,528	11	Hawaii	$891	37
Wisconsin	$1,506	12	North Carolina	$817	38
Florida	$1,482	13	Utah	$776	39
Texas	$1,449	14	Mississippi	$759	40
Michigan	$1,444	15	Idaho	$754	41
Nebraska	$1,351	16	Tennessee	$733	42
Virginia	$1,307	17	Delaware	$665	43
Kansas	$1,250	18	West Virginia	$628	44
Pennsylvania	$1,247	19	Kentucky	$612	45
Iowa	$1,215	20	Louisiana	$605	46
Minnesota	$1,185	21	Oklahoma	$538	47
Colorado	$1,180	22	New Mexico	$517	48
Maryland	$1,167	23	Arkansas	$479	49
Ohio	$1,165	24	Alabama	$455	50

Source: US Census Bureau, 2007 Census of Government Finance; Tax Foundation Calculations.

taxes range from almost $2,500 per capita in New Jersey to under $500 per capita in Arkansas. As expected, many of the New England states have high property tax burdens, but so do several Mideast states, such as New York. Given that property taxes represent less than 55% of local taxes in New York, this will give you some idea of how high local tax burdens are in New York.[3]

11.2 Property Tax Structure

At first glance, the property tax used in this country is a simple tax. TR is equal to the assessed property value (AV) in a community times a flat tax rate (r). This can be represented as:

$$\text{TR} = \text{AV} \times r.$$

However, when you go to sell your house, you do not sell it at the government's assessed value but at the highest price you can receive in the market, i.e., the market value (MV). What is the relationship between the assessed value and the actual and estimated MV? The relationship between the estimated MV and assessed value can be represented by the concept of an assessment ratio (AR):

$$\text{AR} = \text{AV}/\text{MV}^*.$$

The TR can now be represented as:

$$\text{TR} = \text{MV}^* \times \text{AR} \times r,$$

where MV^* is the MV estimated by the government. While it is certainly possible that the AR is 1, generally the assessed value is less than the government's estimate of MV. Why don't governments set the $\text{AV} = \text{MV}^*$? In some cases, this is done to favor some types of property more than another. For example, in the state of Kansas, non-profit and residential properties have an assessment rate that is lower than for other types of properties. Another reason may be to limit property tax appeals and increase acceptance of property tax increases. If the assessed value is below their MV, then homeowners may be less apt to complain when the assessed value goes up.

[3]Property Taxes and Assessment. Department of Taxation and Finance, New York State.

Official Assessment Rates in Kansas.

Description	Assessment Rate (%)
CLASS 1 — REAL PROPERTY	
Residential (e.g., single or multiple family dwellings)	11.50
Commercial properties (e.g., apartments, convenience stores, malls)	25
Public utility real properties (a)	33
Vacant lots	12
Not for profit properties (e.g., churches)	12
Land used for agriculture (b)	30
All other urban or rural real property not otherwise specifically classified	30

Assessment Rates from Art. 11, §1 Kansas Constitution, available at: http://www.leavenworthcounty.org/documents/appraiser/forms/assessment_rates.pdf.

Much more important is the relationship between the government-estimated MV (MV*) and the actual MV. This relationship depends on the frequency and the accuracy of property tax assessments. The property TR can now be represented as:

$$\text{TR} = \text{MV} \times (\text{MV}^*/\text{MV}) \times \text{AR} \times r.$$

The ratio (MV*/MV) is added to measure the accuracy of the assessment — the ratio of government-estimated MV to actual MV. If assessment was perfect, then this ratio would be one. As you can see, we have already added two complications — the AR and the ratio measuring the accuracy of the government's estimate of MV. In addition, in an article on property tax administration in Kenya, Kelly (2000) adds several other ratios to this (which we will discuss in the section on administration)[4]:

- *Coverage ratio*: which measures the amount of the actual property that is included in the tax records (often called cadastral records). In other words, how complete is the list of taxable properties.

[4]Roy Kelly. 2000. "Designing a Property Tax Reform Strategy for Sub-Saharan Africa: An Analytic Framework Applied to Kenya." *Public Budgeting & Finance* (Winter): 36–51.

• *Tax collection ratio*: which measures the share of property tax levy (property tax bills sent to taxpayers) that is actually paid.

This formulation of property TR helps to highlight the important parts of the property tax structure.

11.2.1 Tax base

The property tax is called a wealth tax because it taxes a stock of wealth as opposed to a flow of income or consumption which is the case for the income and sales taxes. What this means is that the property tax taxes the value of your property at a certain point in time, i.e., it is based on a "snapshot" of the property wealth of the community at one point in time. This differs from the income and sales taxes which measure the amount of income you make or the amount you consume over a period of time.

(1) *Composition*: Ideally, a comprehensive property tax would include all forms of wealth such as:

- tangible property such as real estate (real property), and personal property such as cars, boats, etc.,
- intangible property such as stocks, bonds, annuities, etc. Generally, these are the financial assets held by the individual.

Unfortunately, it is difficult and costly to tax all these sources of wealth. For example, most forms of personal property are both hard to identify and their value is difficult to measure. For example, imagine how much more complicated the property tax would be if the appraiser had to appraise the value of your television, VCR, appliances, clothes, etc. Because of these difficulties, the base of the local property tax has been reduced primarily to real property — land and improvements. It is not surprising, as indicated in the following table, that the value of personal property assessed by local governments has decreased.

In the case of intangible property, it is generally easy to value such property since there is a clear market price; however, the cost of locating and taxing all these financial assets would be prohibitively expensive for most local governments. For example,

Table D. **Percent Distribution of Net Taxable Property Assessed Value: 1961, 1971, 1981, 1986, and 1991**

Assessed value type	1961	1971	1981	1986	1991
Total net assessed value (net locally taxable)	**100.0**	**100.0**	**100.0**	**100.0**	**100.0**
State assessed property	7.9	7.7	5.6	5.3	4.3
Locally assessed property	92.1	92.3	94.4	94.7	95.7
Real property	76.2	79.6	84.8	84.6	86.9
Personal property	16.0	12.7	9.6	10.1	8.8

Source: US Bureau of the Census, *1992 Census of Government*, "Assessed Valuations for Local General Property Taxation," Available at: http://www.census.gov/prod/2/gov/gc/gc92 2_1.pdf.

a local government, such as Syracuse, N.Y., would have to have detailed records on where you placed all your financial investments and be able to find out their value at a given point of time.

The distribution of the tax base in Michigan is fairly typical of other states in the US (see Table 11.2). As you can see, real property can be divided into residential, commercial, and other types of property. The most important category of real property is clearly residential property (65.7% in Michigan), and typically the vast majority of residential property value is single family homes. Commercial property is also an important part of the local property tax base (13.7% of real property).[5]

(2) *Exemptions*: Even the real property tax base is not entirely taxable. There are a number of exemptions or other forms of tax reductions which are implemented because of administrative necessity or for equity or other social goals.

- Exemption of the property of religious institutions, governments, schools, and non-profit and charitable organizations.
- Homestead exemption — exemption from taxation of a certain amount of the property value of single-family homes. This is usually done to help low-income families or the elderly or veterans.
- Special assessments — this is a reduced AR which acts to reduce the property taxes usually on farm land, usually as a way of preserving farmland in urban areas.

[5]Fisher, Ronald C. 2007. *State and Local Public Finance*. Chicago, Ill: Irwin. Chapter 13.

Table 11.2. Assessed value by type of real property, Michigan, 2002.

	Real Property		**Personal Property**		**Total**
Type of Property	**Billions of Dollars**	**Percentage of Total (%)**	**Billions of Dollars**	**Percentage of Total (%)**	**Billions of Dollars**
Agriculture	\$7.9	2.9	\$0.0	0.0	\$7.9
Commercial	\$37.6	13.7	\$11.0	4.0	\$48.7
Industrial	\$18.1	6.6	\$11.4	4.2	\$29.5
Residential	\$180.6	65.7	\$0.2	0.1	\$180.8
Utility	\$0.0	0.0	\$7.6	2.8	\$7.6
Other	\$0.5	0.2	\$0.0	0.0	\$0.5
Total	\$244.8	89.0	30.2886	11.0	\$275.0

Source: Fisher, 2007. Chapter 13, Table 13.4.

Table 11.3 provides the geographical areas in New York with the highest and lowest incidence of exempt value (AY 2009 Assessment Rolls).

As illustrated in Table 11.3, there are wide variations in New York in the amount of exempt property. The top 10 towns have 75% or more of their property value exempt from taxation and for the top 10 cities over 50% is exempt. In contrast, there are 10 towns with less than 4% of property value exempt. Much of this difference is represented by both exempt government and non-profit property.

11.2.2 Tax rates

On the surface, the property tax rate would seem to be relatively straightforward since it is generally a uniform rate applied to all property. However, this simple generalization is not always correct. There are a number of jurisdictions where different property tax rates are applied to different types of property. This is called a classified

Table 11.3. Geographic areas with the highest and lowest incidence of exempt value, 2009 assessment rolls.

A. TEN WITH HIGHEST INCIDENCE

Rank	Counties	Percent Exempt	Cities	Percent Exempt	Towns	Percent Exempt
1	Seneca	39.9%	Ogdensburg (St. L.)	64.1%	Harrisburg (Lew.)	88.4%
2	Tompkins	39.3%	Ithaca (Tom.)	62.1%	Ashford (Cat.)	87.2%
3	Oswego	38.4%	Troy (Ren.)	60.2%	Scriba (Osw.)	85.8%
4	St. Lawrence	38.1%	Salamanca (Cat.)	59.9%	Martinsburg (Lew.)	84.7%
5	Cattaraugus	37.4%	Geneva (Ont.)	59.2%	Romulus (Sen.)	81.0%
6	Lewis	37.0%	Albany (Alb.)	55.5%	Alfred (All.)	79.4%
7	Allegany	34.5%	Watervliet (Alb.)	54.6%	Clinton (Cli.)	77.8%
8	Niagara	33.2%	Dunkirk (Cha.)	53.9%	Athens (Gre.)	76.5%
9	Oneida	32.0%	Olean (Cat.)	52.1%	Eagle (Wyo.)	75.9%
10	Clinton	31.8%	Oneonta (Ots.)	51.7%	Marcy (One.)	74.9%

B. TEN WITH LOWEST INCIDENCE

Rank	Counties	Percent Exempt	Cities	Percent Exempt	Towns	Percent Exempt
1	Hamilton	6.9%	Long Beach (Nas.)	11.3%	Benson (Ham.)	1.1%
2	Putnam	10.6%	Mechanicville (Sar.)	15.9%	Arietta (Ham.)	2.0%
3	Warren	10.7%	Lockport (Nia.)	16.0%	Hope (Ham.)	2.3%
4	Ulster	12.5%	Tonawanda (Eri.)	17.1%	Inlet (Ham.)	2.7%
5	Saratoga	14.1%	Rye (Wes.)	17.3%	Wayne (Ste.)	2.7%
6	Rockland	14.6%	No. Tonawanda (Nia.)	17.4%	Ohio (Her.)	2.9%
7	Columbia	16.1%	Sherrill (One.)	18.1%	Pittsfield (Ots.)	3.0%
8	Schuyler	16.2%	Glen Cove (Nas.)	18.4%	Olive (Uls.)	3.4%
9	Fulton	16.6%	Sara. Springs (Sar.)	18.8%	Ellicottville (Cat.)	3.6%
10	Washington	16.8%	Kingston (Uls.)	20.6%	Horicon (War.)	3.6%

Source: New York Office of Real Property Services (ORPS), "Exemptions from Real Property Taxation in New York State: 2009 County, City, & Town Assessment Rolls." Available at: https://www.tax.ny.gov/pdf/publications/orpts/reports/exempt/exemptrpt2009.pdf. pg. 4.

property tax system. Usually, residential property is taxed at a lower rate than business and utility property. As we will discuss when we look at property tax incidence, this will not necessarily lower the tax burden on lower or middle-income households.

The property tax is also unique in how its rate is set. First, the local government approves the level of expenditures (E). It then subtracts out the amount of anticipated revenue from non-property tax sources (NPR) such as a sales tax, user fees, and state and federal aid. Finally, the government will take the remaining deficit between revenues and expenditures and divide it by the AV. This is the required property tax rate, r, to balance the budget. This process can be represented as:

$$r = (\text{E} - \text{NPR})/\text{AV}.$$

Example: Let's illustrate this rate-setting process with an example. Assume that the county of Skandia wants to pass a total budget of \$3,000,000. The community receives \$500,000 in state and federal aid and \$250,000 in revenues from other sources. If the assessed value is \$45 million, what will the nominal (official) property tax rate need to be for the budget to balance? If AR = 40%, what percent of the MV of property will be paid in taxes?

$$r = (\$3{,}000{,}000 - \$750{,}000)/\ \$45{,}000{,}000$$
$$= 5\%\ \text{nominal tax rate to balance the budget.}$$

Since AV = MV × AR, then the percent of MV paid in taxes (t) is:

$$t = 5\% \times 40\% = 200\%.$$

Mills: In property taxes, you will often see the term **mills** used in reference to the property tax rate. Mills simply means that the property tax rate is expressed as the dollars paid per 1,000 dollars in assessed value. For example, 10 mills means that for every \$1,000 of assessed value the taxpayer pays \$10, which is just equivalent to a 1% tax rate.

One of the unique features of the use of property taxes by local governments in the US is that it is not uncommon for you to be paying property taxes to several local governments at the same time. Often these are combined into one bill sent to you by the county government. The following table is an example of property tax statement for St. Johns County, Florida. A taxpayer in this county would pay property tax to the County, St. Johns County School District, St. Johns Water Management District, and several other special districts. The total tax rate for all of these property taxes combined is 17.6 mills or 1.76%.

Market value	Assessed value	Exemptions	Taxable Value
$274,784	$274,784	$25,000	$249,784

Taxing Authority	Millage	Property Tax $
St. Johns County:		
General Fund	4.2214	$1,054.44
Transportation	0.7652	$191.14
Fire District — Special District	1.0954	$273.61
County Health Department	0.0171	$4.27
Subtotal	6.0991	$1,523.46
St. Johns County School District	7.7210	$1,928.59
Subtotal	7.7210	$1,928.59
St Johns Water Management District	0.4158	$103.86
Subtotal	0.4158	$103.86
Independent Special Districts:		
Anastasia Mosquito Control	0.1344	$33.57
Airport Authority	0.1807	$45.14
Florida Inland Navigation District	0.0345	$8.62
Subtotal	0.3496	$87.32
Total Taxes	**17.5855**	**$3,643.23**
St. Johns County Taxes (41.8%)		$1,523.46
All Other Taxes (58.2%)		$2,119.77

Source: St. Johns County Tax Collector, St. Johns County, Florida. http://www.sjctax.us/DataFiles.aspx.

11.2.3 Assessment of property value

The final element in the structure of the property tax is the assessment of property. As we will discuss throughout this section, this is the "Achilles heel" of the property tax and leads to many of the equity and elasticity problems.

(1) *Cycle*: Again on paper, this would appear to be a relatively straightforward task — simply estimate the MV of the property in your community each year. However, as you might imagine, going out once a year to make an accurate estimate of the MV of every piece of property in the community would be prohibitively expensive. To make this task manageable, governments generally use three different assessment schemes:

   (a) *Cyclical assessment*: all property is assessed in the same year and then not updated for several years (usually 5–10). The problem with this method is that it requires massive assessment manpower in one year and then few people until the next assessment.
   (b) *Segmental assessment*: the more common technique is to assess a certain segment of the jurisdiction, every year. This way every parcel will be reassessed at the same interval, e.g., 3 years. However, with this approach, if there is a big jump in values in a particular year, there will be inequities between those properties reassessed that year and those not.
   (c) *Annual assessment*: this is the ideal situation where all property is reassessed every year. Due to cost, usually an annual assessment system involves carrying out full reassessments every couple of years, and computer estimates of assessed value in off years. In New York State, as illustrated with the following map, very few assessing units have annual assessment.

(2) *Method*[6]: The heart of reassessment is the method used to determine the value of properties. As you can imagine, it is not easy to assess the MV of certain properties, especially commercial

[6]This discussion of assessment methods is based on the discussion in John L. Mikesell. 2011. *Fiscal Administration: Analysis and Applications for the Public Sector*, Eighth Edition. (Boston, MA: Wadsworth Cengage Learning), pg. 503–504.

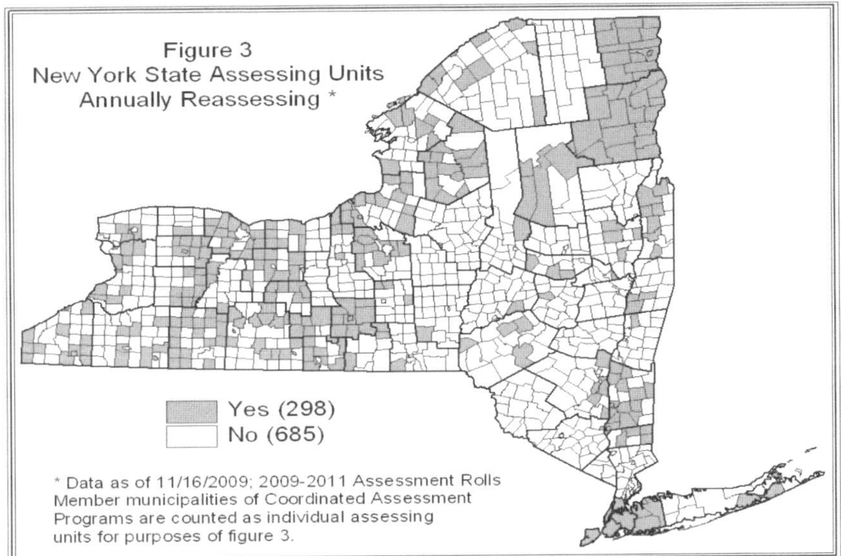

Source: New York Office of Real Property Services. 2010. *Assessment Equity in New York: Results from the 2009 Market Value Survey*. Albany, NY: State of New York. pg. 11.

and industrial property. There are generally three methods used to assess property:

(1) *Comparative Sales Approach*: This approach, which is used almost exclusively for residential property, uses data on the selling price of similar houses in similar areas which are then applied to estimating MVs for a property.
(2) *Cost Approach*: This approach is used primarily for industrial and some commercial properties. It involves the estimation of the cost of replacing an existing facility — labor, materials, etc., and then adjusts for the depreciation of the building since construction.
(3) *Income Approach*: This approach is usually used for commercial property with a steady source of income such as restaurant, hotel, or movie theater. The approach involves using information about the annual net income (income minus cost of doing business) to construct an estimate of the MV.

As you can imagine, the estimates from these approaches are often crude at best and leave open the possibility for unintended horizontal inequities in the property tax payments of households or firms. Since property tax assessment is relatively expensive for local governments to carry out and politically controversial, governments are often slow to reassess their property. For example, Syracuse, NY., prior to 1995, had not carried out a comprehensive reassessment since the 1930s — over 60 years. In New York State, over 10% of assessing units have not been assessed in over 25 years.[7]

11.3 Evaluation

As we will briefly review, the local property tax is actually a very complicated tax to analyze, because it is actually several taxes. Evaluation of the incidence of the property tax is controversial. The objective of the lecture is not to provide the answer on how the property tax does on standard tax evaluation criteria but an appreciation for the issues and tradeoffs involved in evaluating the property tax.

11.3.1 Efficiency

As we have discussed, the efficiency effects of a tax are caused by distorting the price of some good or service. This change in price causes consumers or producers to react by changing their behavior. The more options you have, i.e., the more good substitutes you have the more you will change your behavior. If we assume that the original consumption and production levels were efficient, then these changes in behavior represent efficiency losses.

(1) The first question we need to answer is what prices (or economic decisions) are being distorted by a property tax? It is possible to identify several economic decisions which might be affected:

[7]New York State Department of Taxation and Finance, "Assessment Equity in New York: Results from the 2009 Market Value Survey," New York State.

(a) Housing for most of us is, at least partially, a form of **consumption**. We make tradeoffs in how we spend our income between better housing and other forms of consumption (e.g., food, automobiles, etc.). The property tax may distort our consumption decisions between housing and other commodities.

(b) Most of us also purchase houses as a form of **investment**. Instead of putting our savings in stocks, bonds, or other forms of investment, we invest in a house. When we sell the house, we hope to make a "capital gain." The property tax may also distort our investment decisions between property and other assets.

(c) For the business firm, the property tax also distorts **business investment** decisions between real property and non-taxable property and investments. For example, it would encourage firms to invest in areas such as training of their workers instead of office space.

(d) Last, but certainly not least, property taxes may affect the **locational decisions of individuals and firms**. It is quite likely in a metropolitan area that there will be significant opportunity for movement by households and firms.

(2) The second question is how much consumers and producers will respond to these potential price distortions by changing their behavior? This depends on the availability of good substitutes or alternatives.

(a) While estimating the effects of the distortion on **housing consumption** is complex, housing consumption may not have any close substitutes.

(b) As a form of **investment**, housing does have some good alternatives. You certainly have a number of other choices of investment. Despite the availability of substitutes, housing investment may still not be affected all that strongly due to the very favorable treatment that housing receives under the income tax system. Landlords reduce their investment in housing by cutting back on maintenance of their rental units.

(c) It is not likely that **business investment** will be dramatically affected by an increase in property taxes because it is difficult for business to substitute away from investment in plant and equipment, at least in the short-run.

(d) One area where the property tax may lead to significant efficiency losses is its impact on **locational decisions of individuals and firms**. Renters and homeowners and business firms may try to relocate to communities with lower tax rates. There are several factors that complicate this decision.

— **Land and most improvements are immobile:** You can't pick them up and move them. Instead, homeowners and business that own their property will have to find someone to purchase the property. There is a significant "transaction cost" to moving.

— **Tax competition** between communities implies that any differential in property taxes between communities in the same area may be short-lived.

— **Property tax capitalization:** The fact that individuals and businesses move in response to taxes and public services affects the price of houses (and commercial/industrial property). In a world of perfect information, a 1% point increase in the property tax rate (assuming no improvement in public services) should be reflected exactly in the price of the house. The buyer of the house should now offer a lower price for the house since he or she is going to have to pay the increased property tax in the future. There has been significant research (much of it by John Yinger, Professor of Economics and Public Administration at the Maxwell School, Syracuse University) on how complete property tax capitalization is, and how it affects the evaluation of the property tax. Generally, Yinger has found close to complete capitalization, implying that movers are very responsive to tax changes in making their residential location decisions. Full property tax capitalization implies that the property tax may not cause significant efficiency losses from the locational decisions of households, because present homeowners will not be able to escape property tax increases by moving.[8]

11.3.2 Equity

The property tax has long had the reputation as an unfair and inequitable tax. This helps partially explain why it has consistently come up as one of the most unpopular government taxes. As we will see, such unequivocal conclusions are not so easily made.

11.3.2.1 *Horizontal equity*

As we reviewed last week, this standard requires that the tax system treats taxpayers with an equal ability to pay equally. This is clearly one area where the property tax often falls short. There are often large differences in the relationship between estimate MV and actual MV in a community which leads to two houses of equal MV paying significantly different taxes. In Syracuse in the early 1990s, for example, there had been differences as high as 300% between taxes for similar houses.

Because the property values can be difficult to assess and changes in assessments can be controversial, local governments may be slow in reassessing their property. The longer between reassessments the greater the possibility of significant differences in assessed value for homes that are of equal MV. State government departments responsible for monitoring local property taxes may on a regular basis estimate just how serious the horizontal equity problems might be.

One statistic that is commonly calculated as a measure of the horizontal equity of property tax assessment is the **coefficient of dispersion (COD)**.

[8]Yinger, John. 1982. "Capitalization and the Theory of Local Public Finance." *Journal of Political Economy* 90(5) (September): 917–943; Yinger, John, Howard S. Bloom, Axel Börsch-Supan, and Edwin S. Mills. 2013. *Property Taxes and House Values: the Theory and Estimation of Intrajurisdictional Property Tax Capitalization.* (Burlington: Elsevier Science).

Definition of COD: Average deviation around the median assessment ratio as a percent of the median. In other words, it shows the average percent variation in the assessment ratio around the median. The calculation of the COD is illustrated with the following example from the New York State Office of Real Property Services.

(a) Calculate the median. The median (middle) AR in this example is 0.8.
(b) Calculate the deviation in AR for each house from the median. For example, the AR for the first house is 1.2, so the deviation is 0.4. Take the absolute value of each deviation. (Turn it into a positive number.)
(c) Calculate the average deviation. Add up the deviations for each house and divide by the number of houses ($1.2/5 = 0.24$). This is the average deviation from the median.
(d) COD is equal to the average deviation divided by the median AR. COD $= 0.24/0.8 = 0.30 = 30\%$. For this example, the average deviation in the AR was equal to 30% of the median AR. This is a very high level of deviation and would indicate a property tax system with significant horizontal inequity.

Example 1. Coefficient of Dispersion of 30 Percent: Low Uniformity

Parcel #	Assessed Value	Market Value	AV/MV Ratio	Absolute Deviation from Median
1.	$120,000	$100,000	1.20	.40
2.	110,000	100,000	1.10	.30
Median 3.	80,000	100,000	.80	.00
4.	58,000	100,000	.58	.22
5.	52,000	100,000	.52	.28
			Total Deviation	**1.20**

$$\frac{\text{Total Deviation}}{\text{No. Parcels}} = \frac{1.20}{5} = .24 \text{ average deviation from median}$$

$$\text{COD} = \frac{\text{Avg. Deviation}}{\text{Median Ratio}} = \frac{.24}{.80} = 30 \text{ percent}$$

Source: New York Office of Real Property Services. 2010. *Assessment Equity in New York: Results from the 2009 Market Value Survey.* Albany, NY: State of New York. pg. 3.

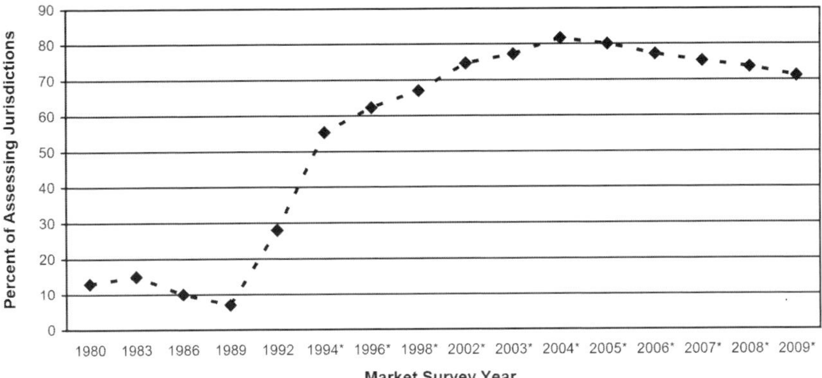

* In measuring assessment equity for survey years 1994 through 2009, acceptable levels of the coefficient of dispersion (COD) statistic were increased for the more rural assessing units. Recent reassessment programs that were reviewed and verified for the 1996 and subsequent surveys were deemed uniform.

Figure 11.2. Percent of county, city and town assessing jurisdictions with assessment uniformity, 1980–2009.

Source: New York Office of Real Property Services. 2010. *Assessment Equity in New York: Results from the 2009 Market Value Survey*. Albany, NY: State of New York. pg. 9.

New York recommends different COD levels depending on the type of property and level of urbanization of the assessing unit. For urban residential property, a COD of 10% is recommended. The number of assessing units with acceptable levels of horizontal equity (uniformity) increased dramatically in the 1990s. In 2009, about 70% of assessing units in New York had acceptable levels of uniformity (Figure 11.2).

11.3.2.2 *Vertical equity*

This standard implies that households of different abilities to pay should pay differently, and many people believe that the incidence of the tax should be progressive. As we reviewed, there are two key steps in assessing vertical equity.

(a) *Tax incidence*: First, we must determine who actually pays the tax. In the case of the property tax, this is very complicated.

The general consensus is that:

(1) Tax on land is borne by landowners. The reason is that unimproved land cannot be moved! If landowners cannot adjust their behavior by moving the land, then they are stuck paying the full tax. There is no one they can pass these taxes on to someone else.
(2) Tax on owner-occupied housing is borne by homeowners. Less clear is whether the tax increase is borne by present homeowners or those purchasing the house. If we assume that future purchasers of homes are aware of the tax increase, then we can expect that they will reduce the amount they are willing to pay for the house to reflect the tax increase, i.e., the tax increase will be capitalized into the housing price. In other words, if relative property taxes go up while you own a house, you are likely going to have to absorb most of the tax increase in terms of a lower sales price for the house.
(3) Tax on commercial and industrial improvements is borne both by property (capital) owners, employees and consumers. The incidence of the property tax on rental, commercial (e.g., restaurant), and industrial property is very complex. When the property tax on a restaurant goes up, what choices does the owner of the restaurant have? The owner can raise the prices of the meals or the owner can try to reduce its costs, particularly the wages it pays its workers. How much the owner can shift the tax onto **consumers** or **labor** depends on the options that these groups have.

    - Consumers can avoid the tax by eating in restaurants outside the taxing jurisdiction or substituting in home meals for restaurant meals.
    - Workers can quit the job and go somewhere else to work.

    In the case of rental housing, either landlords can pass the burden onto renters in the form of higher rents, or they will have to absorb a portion of the tax. Their ability to shift the tax onto renters depends on:

- The choices that renters have. If the rental market is very tight (high occupancy rate) and/or the options outside the community are slim, then renters may have little choice but to absorb most of the rent.
- Landlords can reduce their investments in rental housing as well by reducing the money spent on maintenance of the property. This money can be shifted to different investments or communities. The result will be a decrease in the quality of rental housing in this community, which will raise the rents on remaining rental units of similar quality. Remaining tenants will end up paying the tax through increased rents.

What does the evidence suggest about the incidence of the property tax? While there is no definitive answer to this question, most public finance economists probably would argue that property taxes on commercial property falls more heavily on the consumer and to a lesser extent on property owners and labor. Renters, in particular, may have relatively few good substitutes.

(b) *Income Distribution*: The second part of assessing vertical equity is determining the income distribution of landowners (capital), homeowners, consumers, and labor.

- Commercial and industrial property owners are likely to be middle to upper income. If so, then the tax would be progressive.
- Homeowners are generally middle to upper income so the tax on them is likely to be proportional over most ranges of income.
- Consumers and renters (and labor) are generally lower to middle income so the tax on them is likely to be regressive.

Because the distribution of property tax burdens across these groups and the income distribution within each group is uncertain, assessing the vertical equity of the property tax is very difficult. Pechman (1985) has presented two estimates for the vertical equity of the property tax, which are represented in Table 11.4 based on different assumptions about tax incidence. The effective tax rate on the property tax in the "most progressive" estimate is slightly regressive

Table 11.4. Effective rates of property taxes, by adjusted family income, 1981.

Adjusted Family Income	Most Progressive	Least Progressive
0–5,000	1.0	7.9
5,000–10,000	0.6	3.0
10,000–15,000	0.9	2.4
15,000–20,000	0.9	2.1
20,000–25,000	1.0	2.1
25,000–30,000	1.2	2.1
30,000–50,000	1.4	2.2
50,000–100,000	2.2	2.3
100,000–500,000	3.9	2.2
500,000–1,000,000	5.2	2.2
Overt 1,000,000	5.8	2.3

Source: Pechman, J.A. 1985. *Who Paid the Taxes, 1966–1985*? Brookings Institution Press: New York. Table 4.9.

at low income, proportional in middle incomes and then progressive in upper incomes. For the "least progressive" case, the property tax is very regressive at low incomes and fairly proportional during middle income ranges. These results would suggest that the property tax, while not progressive, is closer to a proportional tax than is generally believed!

11.3.2.3 *Property tax relief*

In order to improve the vertical equity of the property tax many states have adopted property tax relief programs. There are three main types of programs.

(1) *Homestead exemption.* As discussed above, this form of tax relief exempts part of the assessed value of owner-occupied homes from the property tax. The exemption is usually a fixed dollar amount, and thus, reduces the effective tax rate on lower-priced homes by a larger percentage than higher priced homes. In this way, a homestead exemption can help make the incidence

Table 11.5. Property tax relief programs, number of states.

Type	All States	Applies Only to Seniors	Applies to Renters and Homeowners	Applies to All Taxpayers
Homestead exemption	41	12		26
Circuit breaker	34	20	29	14
Tax deferral	20	18	0	2

Note: Does not include local option program or homestead exemption programs restricted to special groups, such as veterans and the disabled.
Source: National Conference of State Legislatures. 2002. A Guide to Property Taxes: Property Tax Relief. Denver, CO: Author. Available at: http://www.leg.state.nv.us/73rd/otherDocuments/PTax/NCSL-gptrelief.pdf.

of the property tax more progressive. However, the fact that the exemption is limited to owner-occupied homes means that renters, typically a lower income group, do not receive any property tax relief, which reduces the effect of this type of program on vertical equity. Forty-one states use a homestead exemption, but in 12 of these states, the exemption is limited to elderly households (see Table 11.5).

(2) *Circuit breaker.* This is a tax credit applied to the state income tax which is designed to provide property tax relief. Because it works through the income tax system, a circuit breaker can target relief to low-income households with excessive property tax burdens, and can also be extended to renters as well. Thirty-four states had some form of circuit breaker in 2002, and in many states, this form of tax relief is limited to the elderly.

(3) *Tax deferral.* One way to allow for groups that have high property taxes relative to their income, such as the elderly, is to allow them to pay a lower tax while they own the house but the tax is deferred until the time they sell the house (or until their death). On vertical equity grounds, this is superior to the homestead exemption since it treats two households with the same income but different values of their home to pay similar taxes while they own the house but differential taxes at the time the property is

sold. Twenty states have this program, with almost all of them limiting it to seniors.

11.3.2.4 *Impact of assessments on equity*

As discussed previously, communities are often slow to reassess property. This not only affects horizontal equity but can affect vertical equity as well! The reason has to do with how property values grow. Let us illustrate this point with an example. Assume that we have two houses in Syracuse in different neighborhoods each worth $10,000 in 1950. Assume the assessed value was set at the MV. House 1 is in a wealthier neighborhood, so has enjoyed strong growth in property values. Assume the house's value has gone up 15 times in the last 60 years to $150,000. House 2 is in a neighborhood which has undergone a transition to lower-income residents. Because of poorer public services (schools) and higher crime rates, property values have grown more slowly, increasing by only seven times to $70,000.

If there were no reassessment of property values, the assessed value of these two houses would not have changed and the households living in the two houses would be paying the same taxes. Assume that the tax rate is 20% of assessed valued so that each household is paying $2,000. What is the effective tax rate for both households? For the property tax, the effective tax rate is the actual property tax payment divided by the MV. While both houses had the same effective tax rate in 1930, they now have very different rates.

— House 1: ETR: $2,000/$150,000 = 1.3%.
— House 2: ETR: $2,000/$70,000 = 2.9%.

The household in the poorer neighborhood is paying over twice the effective rate as the wealthier household purely because of the lack of reassessment! While this example may seem extreme, it is not far from the truth in some places. In the town of Granby just a few years ago, two homeowners each paid ~$470 in property taxes even though one house had a full MV of $364,600 and the other house a MV of $15,600. The effective tax rates for these two homes were 0.13% and 3.0% respectively, a 23 times difference. The elected assessors in the town conceded that they were not able to keep up with rising property values.

11.3.3 Adequacy/elasticity/stability

The criteria probably of most interest to local officials are how much revenue they can raise from a revenue source at a reasonable rate (tax adequacy). In the case of the property tax, the tax base is usually considerable and the rates are generally relatively low, particularly if there are some large tax-paying commercial and industrial properties in the community.

In addition, local officials would like a revenue source which will grow with inflation and the growth of real income. In other words, they want an elastic tax. In the case of the property tax, there are two factors that influence elasticity:

(1) How much MVs grow as income increases.
(2) How well do estimated MVs and assessed values keep up with changes in MV.

The first issue is whether property value tends to keep up with income growth. In general, this has been the case in most communities. A study of residential property values for Minnesota and Kansas found that a 1% increase in non-farm income was associated with a 1–1.2% increase in residential property values.[9] The second is whether the assessment process is able to keep the AR from falling. Unfortunately, this is often not the case with ARs steadily declining over time. The State of Washington estimated the short-term elasticity of the property tax as only 0.2, suggesting that assessments were very slow to change in that state.

Although the property tax is not as elastic as other broad based taxes such as the sales tax and income tax, which increase automatically as income and spending in a community increase, the property tax has proven to be a more stable source of revenue than the sales or income tax.

[9] Terri Sexton and Richard Sexton, 1986. "Re-Evaluating the Income Elasticity of the Property Tax Base." *Land Economics* 62(May): 182–191.

11.3.4 Tax administration

(1) *Registration*: This involves keeping a "cadastral" record of all taxable property in a community. Although keeping track of properties has been a problem in many developing countries, it is not a problem for most US communities. The "coverage ratio" used by Kelly (2000) is a measure of efficiency in registering property. In Kenya, the coverage ratio averages between 30 and 70%.
(2) *Assessment*: As I indicated, this is the "weak link" in the property tax. There is a clear tradeoff between horizontal equity and the administrative costs associated with assessment. As discussed previously, the variability in the ARs in many communities is commonly measured by the "coefficient of dispersion." Over 50% of all US communities had coefficients of dispersion greater than 0.20 in 1981.[10] Close to 11% of all communities had dispersion rates of over 0.50. With improvements in assessment practices, coefficients of dispersion are smaller in many places today. Nevertheless, poor assessment practices can still lead to drastic differences in the tax payments of two households with the same house value.
(3) *Collection*: This is generally not too much of a problem in the US. However, as indicated by Kelly (2000), this is a problem in some developing countries such as Kenya, where the collection ratio averages between 20 and 60%.

Total estimates of the percent of property TR spent just on administering the tax are 1.5%. This is 2–3 times higher than for the sales or income taxes.[11] However, these comparisons only include costs to the government, and do not take into account taxpayer compliance costs which will generally be much higher for these other taxes!

---

[10]Pechman, J.A. 1985. *Who Paid the Taxes, 1966–1985?* Brookings Institution Press: New York.

[11]Mikesell, John L. 2011. *Fiscal Administration: Analysis and Applications for the Public Sector*, Eighth Edition. Boston, MA: Wadsworth Cengage Learning. Chapter 10.

Lecture 12

User Fees and Charges

12.1 Introduction

One of the fastest growing sources of revenue for state governments over the last decade is user charges. While taxes grew by 4.41% per year from 1998 to 2010, revenue from user charges grew by 6.09% (see Table 12.1). Combined with miscellaneous revenues,[1] user charges, and fees[2] are a substantial source of revenue for state (and local) governments (more than 22% of revenues).[3]

Why have these non-tax revenue sources grown so fast in the last two decades? Part of the answer lies with the anti-tax climate, which has existed in this country since the late 1970s. The unpopularity of the property tax (major local tax) and income tax (major state tax) led to several "tax revolts" in the late 1970s and early 1980s, Proposition 13 in California and Proposition 2½ in Massachusetts being two of the most visible results. With pressure not to increase property taxes, many local governments have begun to search for

[1]The Bureau of Census classifies miscellaneous revenues as revenue from interest earnings, special assessments, the sale of property, and other general revenue.

[2]The Census Bureau defines user charges and fees as charges levied to support one of the following program categories — education, hospital, highways, air transportation, parking facilities, sea and inland port facilities, natural resources, parks and recreation, housing and community development, sewerage, and solid waste management.

[3]US Census Bureau. State and Local Government Finance. https://www.census.gov/govs/local/.

Table 12.1. State and local government finances: 1998–2010.

(Dollar amounts in thousands)	**2010**[4]		**1998**[5]		**Annual % Change (1998-2010)**
Revenue	2,655,550,993	100%	1,446,888,470	100%	**5.2%**
Intergovernmental revenue	**623,732,004**	**23.5%**	**255,048,096**	**17.6%**	**7.74%**
General revenue from own sources	**1,878,323,148**	**70.7%**	**1,110,713,868**	**76.8%**	**4.48%**
Taxes	***1,269,649,543***	***47.8%***	***773,963,195***	***53.5%***	***4.21%***
Property	441,660,815	16.6%	230,150,058	15.9%	5.58%
Sales and gross receipts	431,176,366	16.2%	274,883,406	19.0%	3.82%
General sales	284,910,393	10.7%	188,752,895	13.0%	3.49%
Selective sales	146,265,973	5.5%	86,130,511	6.0%	4.51%
Motor fuel	37,879,755	1.4%	29,246,986	2.0%	2.18%
Alcoholic beverage	6,028,119	0.2%	4,047,022	0.3%	3.38%
Tobacco products	17,267,568	0.7%	7,956,232	0.5%	6.67%
Public utilities	28,290,741	1.1%	16,796,302	1.2%	4.44%
Other selective sales	56,799,790	2.1%	28,083,969	1.9%	6.05%
Individual income	260,338,250	9.8%	175,630,035	12.1%	3.33%
Corporate income	42,860,067	1.6%	34,411,615	2.4%	1.85%
Motor vehicle license	22,498,381	0.8%	14,884,049	1.0%	3.50%
Other taxes	71,115,664	2.7%	44,004,032	3.0%	4.08%
Charges and miscellaneous general revenue	***608,673,605***	***22.9%***	336,750,673	***23.3%***	***5.06%***
Current charges	409,580,071	15.4%	201,554,212	13.9%	6.09%
Miscellaneous general revenue	199,093,534	7.5%	135,196,461	9.3%	3.28%
Utility revenue	**145,706,824**	**5.5%**	77,019,180	**5.3%**	**5.46%**
Liquor store revenue	**7,789,017**	**0.3%**	4,107,326	**0.3%**	**5.48%**

Source: US Census Bureau. State and Local Government Finance. https://www.census.gov/govs/local/.

alternative revenue sources. User charges and lotteries are often sold as revenue sources that are not taxes. It is important in evaluating user-related revenue to distinguish between government fees and user charges.

(1) *Government licenses or fees*: These are usually fees charged to an individual or business for the right to partake in a particular activity. For example, to operate a vehicle, to hunt or fish, to operate a business, etc. While in some instances they are proxies for a user charge (motor vehicle license), a crucial distinction is that they are not tied to the volume of usage.
(2) *User charges*: These are the closest thing in the public sector to private sector prices. They are charges tied to the frequency of usage of a government service (pool tickets, transit fares, etc.) This implies that for user charges to work, the government service

[4]Data from US Census Bureau. State and Local Government Finance. https://www.census.gov/govs/local.

[5]Data from US Census Bureau. State and Local Government Finance. Historical Data, 1998. https://www.census.gov/govs/local/historical_data_1998.html.

must be like a private service — it must be **feasible to exclude people** from consuming the service.

12.2 User Charges

12.2.1 Design of user charges

At first glance, the design of user charges would seem relatively straightforward, develop prices similar to those in the private sector. However, governments have generally not been in the business of selling their services, and have been expected to focus on other objectives besides maximizing profit. The design of user charges then is more complicated because governments need to balance what are often competing objectives, such as efficiency and equity.

(1) What types of services? What types of services should be financed with user charges? User charges are best suited for what has been called "private services." Private services have three characteristics that are crucially important[6]:

 (a) *Can measure output*? For a user charge to be feasible, it must be possible to measure the output or activity of the service. While measuring output for some services is certainly feasible, such as water supply and garbage collection, it is not always feasible or possible to measure output for other services provided by government. For example, what are the outputs provided by a police department, is it arrests, miles patrolled, and/or cases solved? This is similar to the challenge of developing good performance measures for public agencies.
 (b) *Exclusion is feasible*: What this means is that it is feasible to exclude people who do not pay from using the service. If exclusion is not feasible, then governments cannot

[6]Selma J. Mushkin and Charles L. Vehom. 1980. "User Fees and Charges" in Charles S. Levin (Ed.), *Managing Fiscal Stress: the Crisis in the Public Sector* (Chatham, N.J.: Chatham House Publishers).

realistically charge for the services. What is possible and what is feasible in a particular context can be different? For example, it is clearly possible to charge people tolls for using city streets; however, the cost of implementing such a system may be cost prohibitive. (Both London and Singapore have developed systems for charging drivers entering their central city.)

(c) *There is rivalry in consumption*: If my consumption of a service will prevent you from consuming it, then there is rivalry in consumption. If I drink a gallon of water, you will not be able to consume the same gallon. In contrast, my sitting in a classroom will not necessarily prevent you from enjoying the full benefits of the class. We would ideally not charge for goods, which are "non-rival," because we want everyone to take advantage of the service (since allowing others to take advantage creates additional benefits without creating any additional costs). Realistically, classrooms are non-rival only to a degree.

Goods that generally fall into the private good category are listed in Table 12.2. You can see that many of these services are commonly what we would call public enterprises or utilities (e.g., water, sewer, bus service, etc.). However, there are some public service areas, such as police and fire protection, where charges can be used for some of the services provided by these departments.

(2) What is the cost of providing the service? If user charges are meant to cover at least some of the cost of providing the service, then it is important to understand the costs of providing the service. Ideally, you would start by developing a cost accounting system, if it does not already exist, for the service. It is important to identify:

(a) *Direct and indirect costs*: The level of the charge will depend on not only the direct resources that the service uses but also what overhead costs of the parent government are "assigned" to this service.

Table 12.2. Types of local government charges and fees.

Sewerage	Parks and recreation
Sewerage service charges	Green fees
	Permit charges for tennis courts, etc.
Storm sewers	Stadium fees and tickets
Runoff fees	Park development fees and land dedications
Sanitation	Transportation
Trash collection charges	Subway and bus fares
Landfill charges	Bridge and road tolls
Refuse hauler licenses	Landing and departure fees
	Dockage fees
Public utilities	
Water meter or connection charges	Development
Water service charges	Streetlight installation charges
Electricity charges	Convention center charges
	Tract map filing fees
Health and hospitals	Special housing rental fees
Inoculation fees	
Hospital charges	Police and fire protection
Ambulance charges	Charges for special events
Concession rental fees	Fire inspection fee
Parking	Social control licenses
Meter fees	Merchant licenses
Parking lot fees	Animal control tags

Source: Adapted and condensed from Mushkin and Vehom. 1980. "User Charges and Fees," Figure 13.2, pg. 233.

(b) *How costs vary with the level of service*: Understanding how costs vary with service will allow you to estimate with a fair degree of accuracy the total cost and unit costs at different levels of output.

(3) How much should be charged? Once the decision is made to charge for a service, the next question is how much, and how should the charge be set.

(a) *Supply and demand*: In the private sector, the charge would be set by producers to maximize profits. The market price for a product is the result of both consumer (demand) and producer (supply) decisions. Governments tend to focus on the cost of providing the service (supply side). It is equally as important to consider how consumers of the services are likely to react to different user charges (demand side). If the service has few good substitutes (e.g., water supply), then consumer demand may be fairly inelastic to changes in the user charge. If there are good substitutes (e.g., parks and recreation), then small increases in the user charge could have substantial effects on demand.

(b) What are the main objectives of the charge?[7]

(1) The main objective of user charges is to cover the costs of providing the service. This is commonly called "full-cost" pricing since the goal is to set a charge that results in total revenue equaling total cost. However, there may be other objectives, besides covering costs that the government is trying to accomplish.

(2) Closely related to covering costs is the objective of **encouraging conservation of the resource**. For example, a user charge can help encourage users to conserve water and electricity. The closer the charges are to covering the full cost, the more users are likely to conserve.

(3) The charge may be set below costs to encourage people to use this resource. If the use of the service helps to reduce other problems, then below-cost pricing would provide an incentive to increase consumption. For example, one of the justifications for subsidized public transportation is to encourage people to stop driving, to relieve traffic congestion.

(4) The charge may be set below costs to reduce the burden on low-income households who are heavy users of the service. As discussed below, it is usually better to target subsidized charges to low-income households, rather than subsidize the service for all users.

---

[7] Bierhanzl, Edward J. and Paul B. Downing, "User Charges and Special District" in Aronson, J. Richard, and Eli Schwartz. 2004. *Management Policies in Local Government Finance*, 5th Edition. (Washington, D.C.: ICMA).

With the exception of parking, user charges for most services are not sufficient to cover expenditures for the service. Local governments cover a higher share of their spending with user charges than state governments for most types of services. Programs/services including natural resources, parks and recreation, and higher education — are particularly heavily subsidized.

(4) How should the user charge be designed? While user charges should be linked to costs, there are other decisions that need to be made in the design of user fees[8]:

   (a) Flat rate versus variable rate user charge

      (1) A flat rate user charge implies that only one rate (dollars per unit of output) is applied to all levels of consumption. For example, the same rate per gallon of water would be charged whether 100, 1,000, or 10,000 gallons of water were used. For full-cost pricing, the rate would be set at the unit cost for the expected level of demand. This type of user charge is simple to administer but it will be difficult to determine the required charge to cover full costs?

      (2) *A variable rate user charge*: With this charge structure, there is typically a fixed "connection fee" that is the same no matter what the level of consumption. In addition, there is a variable rate part of the charge, which is structured as a price (dollars per unit of output). This type of charge is easier to match to the underlying costs of providing the service since it can capture both fixed costs and variable costs. A common variant on a variable rate charge is a block rate charge, where the variable part of the charge is allowed to vary across different levels of service.

         (a) *Increasing-block charge*: Where the variable rate goes up with the level of consumption? This type of charge would help to encourage conservation.

[8]Fisher, Ronald C. 2016. *State and Local Public Finance.* (New York: Routledge), Chapter 9.

   (b) *Decreasing-block charge*: Where the variable rate goes down with the level of service? This type of charge might better match the cost structure if there are "economies of scale" in the production of the service.

(b) *Peak-period pricing*: If the service experiences large variation in demand across periods of time (day, week, month), this can make it very difficult to provide adequate capacity to meet demand and still cover costs. If the capacity is matched to peak periods, then there will be significant over-capacity during other times. One way to solve this problem is to encourage people to use the service during non-peak times by charging more for peak times than for non-peak times. This approach is very frequently used in developing user charges for mass transportation services.

(c) *Pricing by classification of user*: Another factor a government may have in setting a user charge is whether certain users should be charged different rates than other users. Two common examples include:

   (1) *By group*: To have lower charges for low-income households or for special groups (e.g., elderly, disabled, children). Typically, the lower charge is justified on equity grounds (e.g., low-income households) or greater dependence on the service (e.g., elderly bus riders).
   (2) *By residence*: For some services, it is common to see lower rates for residents of the community than for non-residents. Justifications for residential-based rates can include: (1) higher costs of providing services to non-residents (e.g., expand water distribution system); (2) partial subsidization of the service with general taxes paid only by residents; and (3) to assure adequate capacity for residents by discouraging non-resident use. However, it is important that the design of the charge cannot be construed as a way to refuse service groups based on race, religion, and gender.

The following is an example of the water charge rate structure for the City of Englewood, California. This fee has several components we have talked about. First, there is a fixed charge (by meter size) and a variable charge (usage fee) per gallon of water. This is an example of a "decreasing block" rate structure since the usage fee goes down with the level of water consumption. Finally, there is a differential connection fee for residents and non-residents.

City of Englewood California

Connection Fee:

Inside City		**Outside City**	
Meter Size	**Connection Fee**	**Meter Size**	**Connection Fee**
5/8″ or 3/4″	$1,000	5/8″ or 3/4″	$1,500
1″	$1,800	1″	$2,700
1–1/2″	$4,000	1–1/2″	$6,000
2″	$7,200	2″	$10,800
3″	$16,000	3″	$24,000
4″	$28,800	4″	$43,200
6″	$64,000	6″	$96,000
8″	$115,000	8″	$172,800

Usage Fee:

Quarterly Consumption	
First 400,000 Gallons	$2.69
All Consumption Over 400,000 Gallons	$1.68

There can be significant variation in the type of rate structures that governments use even for the same type of service. The following table indicates the number of metropolitan agencies providing sewer services using a particular type of rate structure. While the majority of agencies use a two-part rate structure (flat charge + volume charge), a significant number of agencies use volume rate only.

Rate Structure	Number of Agencies			Percent of Agencies (%)		
	2002	1999	1996	2002	1999	1996
– Flat/Fixed Charge Only	14	18	14	12.3	18.0	14.9
– Volume Rate Only	39	34	24	34.2	34.0	25.5
– Flat Charge + Volume Charge (no tax rate)	49	36	44	43.0	36.0	46.8
– Tax Rate (alone or with other charges)	12	12	12	10.5	12.0	12.8
– Total	114	100	94	100	100	100.0

Association of Metropolitan Sewerage Agencies. "2002 AMSA Financial Survey" Presentation in Santa Fe, NM, 2/7/2003. Available at: archive.nacwa.org/getfile.cfm?fn=Final%202002%20AMSA%20Financial%20Survey.ppt.

Developing and implementing a user fee can require expertize and adequate staff. Not surprisingly, larger local governments are more apt to implement more complex rate structures, such as increasing block rates, as illustrated in the following table about water systems in the US (see Table 12.3).

12.2.2 Evaluation — user charges

(1) *Efficiency*: One of the major advantages associated with the use of user charges is that they can improve the efficiency of both the consumption and production of public services by:

   (a) Encouraging consumers to conserve government resources. You are much more apt to use water carefully or recycle your garbage if you are charged for these services. However, to be effective, these user charges must vary with the amount of the service you use. For example, charges by the gallon for water, by the can for garbage, or by the trip for public transit.

   (b) If user charges are the primary form of financing to cover the cost of providing a service, then the government agency has a strong incentive to improve the efficiency of their operation. They also may be more sensitive to the demands

Table 12.3. Residential rate structure and billing profile by ownership. (Percent of systems with each structure).

	System Service Population Category							
Ownership Type Public Systems	**100 or Less**	**101–500**	**501–3,300**	**3,301–10,000**	**10,001–50,000**	**50,001–100,000**	**100,001–500,000**	**Over 500,000**
Metered charges								
Uniform rate	11.6	52.2	52.9	55.1	45.4	45.4	51.1	39.4
Declining block rate	0.0	14.1	29.0	31.4	32.1	21.7	21.0	18.4
Increasing block rate	2.6	10.2	14.3	12.4	16.7	29.3	24.1	34.1
Seasonal rate	0.0	0.0	0.4	2.3	0.6	8.9	8.9	9.7

Source: US EPA, "Community Water System Survey, 2000" December 2002. Available at: http://www.epa.gov/safewater/consumer/pdf/cwss_2000_volume_ii.pdf.

of consumers by tailoring the service to better meet their needs.

(c) Exceptions to the rule of full cost pricing on efficiency grounds would be the case where this service helps to remove other possible efficiency problems (e.g., traffic congestion).

(2) *Equity*: Assessing the equity of user charges depends heavily on whether one applies the benefits principle or the ability to pay principle. Some would argue that whenever a private service is provided (as defined above by excludability and rivalry), whether it is provided by a government or for-profit firm, the benefit principle should apply. Others, however, argue that for services that satisfy basic needs or that we believe people should have equal access to, the ability to pay principle is a more appropriate standard.

(a) *Benefits principle*: As we reviewed earlier, this equity principle stresses that a "fair" tax or revenue source is one where the taxes people pay are in line with the benefits that they receive from government services. User charges obviously do well on this principle since users are charged directly for the amount they use of the service.

(b) *Ability to pay principle*: That people should pay taxes or revenues in line with their "ability to pay."

(1) *Horizontal Equity*: That people with the same ability to pay should pay the same. User charges impose a heavier burden for financing a public service on heavy users of the service. Two households with the same ability to pay can pay significantly different amounts to support a service if one of them is a heavier user of the service. Only some government services are amenable to user charge financing, which implies that heavy users of one type of government service may be paying more taxes/charges, than heavy users of another type of service.

(2) *Vertical Equity*: That people with different abilities to pay should pay differently. This is one area that

user charges generally do not fare well, since lower to middle-income households spend a higher portion of their income on basic services such as water, sewer, electricity, and public transportation. This implies that user charges for these services fall disproportionately on the poor, that is, they are regressive. However, they are not necessarily more regressive than other state and local taxes, for example, general sales and excise taxes. Also, it may be possible to provide reduced charges or "vouchers" for low-income households. It is better on equity and efficiency grounds to use selective reductions in user charges for low-income households than an across-the-board reduction.

(3) Adequacy

(a) *Adequacy*: In general, user charges are a relatively small source of revenue for state governments. However, for local governments, user charges do account for 22% of own-source revenue, on average.
(b) *Elasticity*: How responsive are user charges to growth in community income? The growth of user charge revenue depends crucially on whether the government can increase these charges to keep up with income growth and inflation. Since significant increases in user charges may be politically unpopular, it is likely that growth in this revenue source will not keep up with income growth in the long-run, that is, there is an elasticity of less than one.
(c) *Stability*: Since there are few good substitutes for many of these basic services (garbage, water, sewer, and electricity), people probably do not change their usage of these services very much as user charges go up, that is, they are price insensitive. This means that user charges are likely to be a stable source of revenue for these services. However, for other services with good substitutes, such as recreation facilities, user charge revenue may be more unstable.

(4) Administration

(a) *Tax registration*: It is easy to identify the users of this service since charges are used for private type goods or services.

(b) *Tax assessment*: In this case, this simply means identifying the price to be charged and the quantity that has been used. Public sector pricing can actually be a complicated topic. While charging for a bus trip is relatively easy, identifying the amount of water used, or garbage or sewer service used may be more difficult. Communities may need to set up metering systems for water or record keeping on the number of cans of garbage produced.

(c) *Tax collection*: This is probably the most difficult part of administering user charges. You have to have a system for collecting them. This can vary from a toll booth (for a highway), a fare box (for a bus) to monthly billing for water and sewer services. In addition, if subsidies are to be given to certain groups (senior citizens or low income), then this can increase the collection cost.

(d) *Tax enforcement*: Ultimately, the government has to have some system for enforcing the payment of these charges. If someone does not pay the bus fare, what recourse does the bus driver have? What types of fines or additional charges should be assessed on people who are late paying their water bill? Is the local government willing to turn off the water and power if a household does not pay the bills?

Lecture 13

State Government Lotteries

13.1 Introduction

One of the fastest growing sources of revenue for state and local governments over the last decade is revenue from government lotteries. While total taxes in state and local governments grew by 6.4% per year from 1992 to 2008, lottery revenues grew by 12%, respectively (see Table 13.1). Despite the rapid growth in lottery revenue, they remain a very small source of revenue, on average (1.4% of total revenue). User charges and lotteries are often pitched to the public as revenue sources that are not taxes.

Lotteries share many traits with government monopolies, which involve the government receiving revenues from the direct provision of a good. These are usually for certain "sin goods," such as alcohol and state-run gambling (lotteries). While part of the reason for government involvement may be to regulate the usage of these "sins," their primary justification is to raise revenue.

13.2 State Monopolies (Lotteries)[1]

Another form of revenue that some state governments use is profits from government-run monopolies. Since lotteries represent the fastest

[1]For a good overview of lotteries, see Alicia Hansen. 2004. "Lotteries and State Fiscal Policy." *Tax Foundation Background Paper*, No. 46, October. Available at: http://www.taxfoundation.org/publications/show/65.html.

Table 13.1. Revenue by source state and local governments in the US.

Type of Revenue	Annual % Change (1992–2008)	Percent of Total (2007–2008)
Total Revenue	5.94%	100.0%
General revenue	6.73%	91.2%
Intergovernmental revenue	7.31%	18.1%
General revenue from own sources	6.59%	73.1%
Taxes	6.40%	50.0%
Property	6.09%	15.4%
General sales	6.16%	11.4%
Selective sales	7.07%	5.4%
Individual & Corporate Income	5.74%	13.6%
Other taxes	1.32%	3.3%
Lottery	**11.96%**	**1.4%**
Current charges	**7.44%**	**14.0%**
Education	**7.71%**	**4.2%**
Hospitals	**6.99%**	**3.7%**
Miscellaneous general revenue	6.40%	9.0%
Interest earnings	3.81%	3.5%
Utility revenue	**6.33%**	**5.2%**
Liquor store revenue	**5.08%**	**0.3%**
Insurance trust revenue	-3.62%	3.3%

Source: US Bureau of the Census, *State and Local Finances*, 1991–1992 and 2007–2008.

growing and largest source of such revenues, this is what we will focus on in this lecture. Almost all lotteries were passed after 1970. While New York and New Hampshire had lotteries in the 1960s, they were generally poor sources of revenue. It was the success of the New Jersey lottery in the early 1970s which got state governments interested in lotteries as a source of revenue.

By 2008, 42 states used lotteries, with 29 added since 1980. Lottery revenues reached $77 billion by 2008, and lottery revenues grew by 12% per year from 1993 to 2008. Despite this rapid growth, lottery revenue (sales net of prizes and administration) still accounted for only 1.4% of total state revenue. This implies that lotteries, while a fast-growing source of revenue, are still relatively

Table 13.2. Lottery revenue (profits) as a percent of total state own-source revenue fiscal year 2008.

State	Percentage	Rank	State	Percentage	Rank
Total US	1.4%				
Rhode Island (b)	7.7%	1	Kentucky	1.4%	22
West Virginia (a) (c)	7.6%	2	Texas	1.2%	23
South Dakota (b)	7.4%	3	Indiana	1.0%	24
Oregon (a) (c)	5.5%	4	Maine	1.0%	25
Delaware (a) (c)	4.7%	5	North Carolina	0.9%	26
Georgia	3.1%	6	Louisiana	0.8%	27
Florida	2.6%	7	Arizona	0.8%	28
Michigan	2.6%	8	Wisconsin	0.8%	29
New York	2.5%	9	California	0.7%	30
Maryland	2.5%	10	Idaho	0.7%	31
Massachusetts	2.2%	11	Kansas	0.7%	32
New Jersey	2.0%	12	Vermont	0.6%	33
Connecticut	1.7%	13	Colorado	0.6%	34
New Hampshire	1.7%	14	Oklahoma	0.5%	35
Pennsylvania	1.7%	15	Nebraska	0.5%	36
Tennessee	1.6%	16	Minnesota	0.5%	38
Missouri	1.6%	17	Iowa	0.5%	39
South Carolina	1.6%	18	New Mexico	0.5%	40
Virginia	1.6%	19	Washington	0.5%	41
Illinois	1.5%	20	Montana	0.2%	42
Ohio	1.4%	21	North Dakota	0.2%	43

(a) Includes net VLT sales (Cash in less cash out).

(b) Include gross VLT sales (Cash in).

Therefore, the figures for these states are not strictly comparable to other states with or

Source: North American Association of State and Provincial Lotteries; US Census Bureau; Tax Foundation calculations.

small in the scheme of things. However, as indicated in Table 13.2, there is significant variation in the importance of lottery revenue by state. For three states, lottery revenue is over 7% of their total revenue. For eight states, lottery revenue is 0.5% or less of state revenue.[2]

As Mikesell and Zorn (1986) emphasize, the most positive aspect of lotteries from the standpoint of state political leaders is that they are generally politically popular.[3] Seldom have lottery referenda been turned down and many political candidates have found that

[2]US Census Bureau, 2008 "Income and Apportionment of State Administered Lottery Funds" from the 2008 Annual Survey of State Government Finance.

[3]John Mikesell and Kurt Zorn, 1986. "State Lotteries as Fiscal Savior or Fiscal Fraud: A Look at the Evidence," *Public Administration Review* 46 (July/August): 311–320.

supporting lotteries is good politics. The political popularity of lotteries makes a thorough evaluation of their effects even more important. As Mikesell and Zorn have summarized:

> Has something changed to make them productive and acceptable sources of revenue or does the growth of lotteries across the United States represent the expansion of a bad idea? (p. 311).

13.2.1 Voluntary activity or tax?

Governments earn profits from running lotteries, otherwise they would not be sources of revenue. In fact, because states prohibit private firms from running lotteries, they effectively have a monopoly. As a result, the profits governments take from lottery programs are well in excess of what they could expect to earn in a competitive market. Most public finance experts view these excess profits as a tax on playing the lottery. As Alicia Hansen explains:

> Lottery proponents often argue that a tax is a mandatory or compulsory payment and lottery purchases are voluntary, so the lottery cannot be a tax. This argument overlooks the fact that the purchase is voluntary, not the tax, just as a sales or excise tax is compulsory on a voluntary purchase. A mandatory tax on a voluntary purpose is still a tax. In fact, all taxed purchases and activities are technically voluntary. The same argument applies to the sale of alcohol or tobacco. (Hansen, 2004, p. 24).

An important question, then, is why do state governments maintain a monopoly over lottery programs rather than allowing private firms to run lotteries? One possible justification for state-run lotteries is that they increase government control of gambling. Prior to 1960, lottery gambling was illegal in most places in the US. Not surprisingly, a sizeable illegal gambling business emerged, often operated by organized crime. It is quite possible that there are a number of negative effects associated with illegal gambling (violent crime, bribery and extortion, connection with drug distribution). One of the potential advantages of state-run lotteries is that it will attract people away from illegal gambling, and reduce many of these negative effects. Unfortunately, the empirical evidence on this issue is scarce. One study found that the use of lotteries is actually associated with an increase in property crime rates.[4] Perhaps more fundamentally, legalizing gambling activities is likely to have the same impact on illegal gambling and the crimes associated as running public lotteries. In others words, the benefits of legalizing gambling do not depend on creating a government monopoly.

Another possible justification for government provision of these services is that government is able to control an industry, which would on its own become a monopoly. Government can dampen the harmful effects of monopolies by keeping prices down. The evidence is pretty weak that gambling would become a monopoly if left to the private sector. More importantly, however, most state governments run lotteries exactly as we would expect private, unregulated monopolists would. In order to maximize revenues, governments use their monopoly power to keep payout rates low, that is, by returning a relatively small percent of sales in prizes. Table 13.3 provides information on what percent of total lottery sales (minus commissions) is paid out in prizes. On average, about 73% of lottery sales are paid in prizes, and, in some states, this payout percentage is less than 60%.

13.2.2 Tax evaluation

If lotteries are some form of tax, what are they closest to? Most analysts argue that lotteries are closest to other forms of excise taxes, such as cigarette or alcohol taxes. This parallel is particularly close for alcohol taxes since some states actually own and operate liquor stores. The tax is the difference between total sales and the total costs, i.e., the profits from operating this service. As an excise tax, lotteries can be evaluated with the standard tax criteria.

(1) Adequacy/elasticity/stability

  (a) *Adequacy*: The adequacy criteria deals with whether this is a broad-based, significant revenue source. In other words, can a significant amount of revenue be raised with fairly low tax

[4] John Mikesell and Maureen Pirog-Good. 1990. "State Lotteries and Crime: The Regressive Revenue Producer is Linked With a Crime Rate Higher by 3 Percent." *American Journal of Economics and Sociology* 49 (January): 7–19.

Table 13.3. Income and apportionment of state-administered lottery funds, 2008.

State	Income -- Ticket Sales Excluding Commissions (000s)	Percent of Income		
		Prizes	Administration	Proceeds available
United States	$77,313,909	73.4	3.1	23.5
Alabama	$0			
Alaska	$0			
Arizona	$441,624	59.4	8.0	32.5
Arkansas	$0			
California	$2,837,449	57.1	5.6	37.4
Colorado	$467,422	67.1	7.2	25.7
Connecticut	$942,198	64.6	4.4	31.0
Delaware	$7,975,968	95.2	0.6	4.2
Florida	$3,939,125	62.9	3.9	33.2
Georgia	$3,045,616	67.3	4.5	28.2
Hawaii	$0			
Idaho	$126,349	64.5	6.9	28.6
Illinois	$2,057,270	58.3	2.9	38.8
Indiana	$763,345	65.9	6.6	27.5
Iowa	$233,568	61.9	13.6	24.5
Kansas	$222,898	59.7	10.9	29.4
Kentucky	$728,069	67.7	5.5	26.8
Louisiana	$352,781	54.7	8.7	36.7
Maine	$214,337	67.2	9.5	23.4
Maryland	$1,555,214	61.5	3.7	34.7
Massachusetts	$4,417,538	77.4	2.3	20.3
Michigan	$2,330,198	58.0	2.9	39.2
Minnesota	$411,031	71.8	5.7	22.5
Mississippi	$0			
Missouri	$934,633	68.6	3.8	27.6
Montana	$41,263	55.3	18.0	26.6
Nebraska	$114,501	60.5	13.1	26.4
Nevada	$0			
New Hampshire	$246,853	62.7	6.9	30.4
New Jersey	$2,397,091	59.8	3.2	37.0
New Mexico	$140,762	59.3	12.1	28.6
New York	$6,839,951	57.8	4.4	37.8
North Carolina	$1,002,711	61.7	4.8	33.5
North Dakota	$21,074	53.9	17.5	28.5
Ohio	$2,181,214	64.0	5.0	30.9
Oklahoma	$200,851	56.2	7.7	36.1
Oregon	$2,881,537	73.5	2.6	23.8
Pennsylvania	$2,841,028	65.0	2.9	32.2
Rhode Island	$2,185,073	83.7	0.1	16.3
South Carolina	$922,060	67.3	4.4	28.4
South Dakota	$589,574	78.2	1.2	20.6
Tennessee	$995,186	68.0	5.2	26.8
Texas	$3,485,754	65.4	4.8	29.8
Utah	$0			
Vermont	$96,016	67.4	9.2	23.3
Virginia	$1,386,413	57.2	5.2	37.6
Washington	$488,712	64.4	8.6	26.9
West Virginia	$13,797,828	95.1	0.2	4.7
Wisconsin	$461,824	62.1	7.0	31.0
Wyoming	$0			

Note: An amount of 0 indicates that the state government did not administer a lottery program.

Source: US Bureau of the Census, State Government Finances. Available at: http://www.census.gov/govs/state/07lottery.html.

rates? The answer on both of these counts for most states is no.

As illustrated in Table 13.2, on average lotteries produced only 1.4% of state revenue in 2008. Only six of the 42 states with lotteries generated more than 3% of revenue from this source.

In addition, to extract this amount of revenues lotteries have very high implicit tax rates. The Tax Foundation has calculated an implicit tax rate on lottery sales, which is defined as the net sales (sales minus prizes and administrative cost) as a ratio of prizes and administrative costs. Nationally, the average implicit tax rate was 42% in FY 2008, and the rate ranged from 17.4% to over 100% in Oregon. These tax rates are as high as or higher than other state excise taxes.

(b) *Elasticity/stability*: Because lotteries are constantly changing the games that are being offered, it is difficult to evaluate them with the traditional concept of elasticity (which is supposed to control for discretionary rate and base changes in the tax). What we can look at is how lottery revenues have grown over time. Lottery revenue from 1992 to 2008 increased by 12%, which is faster than most other state taxes.

Lotteries, however, have not been a stable source of revenue. Mikesell and Zorn (1986) examined lottery revenue from 1978 to 1988 and found that 13 states experienced a year in which the lottery revenue actually dropped, often by over 10%. The instability of lottery revenue is illustrated for New York over a 30-year period in Figure 13.1. While lottery revenue has become more stable in the last decade, fluctuations in revenue of 10% are not uncommon. Fluctuations are much higher in New York than the personal income of the population. A lottery is potentially an elastic and unstable source of state revenues.

(2) Administration

(a) *Types*: The types of lotteries used by states have evolved over time as states try to provide new and exciting gimmicks to

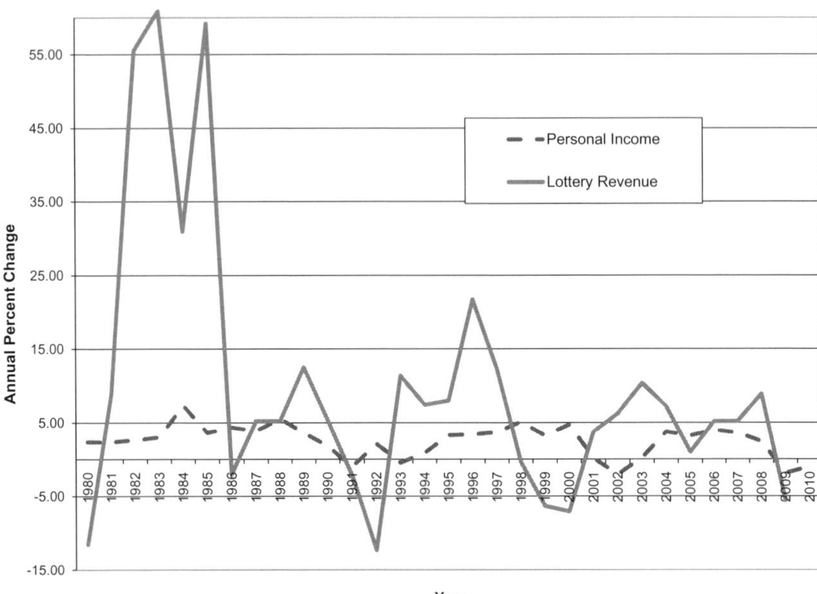

Figure 13.1. Comparison of volatility of lottery revenue and personal income in New York state (inflation adjusted dollars).

Source: Office of New York State Comptroller, 2010. https://www.osc.state.ny.us/.

attract customers. Five common types of lotteries include (Hansen, 2004):

(1) *Instant*: involves a customer "scratching" off the seal on a ticket to see if they won. This was the form of most lotteries in the second wave of their adoption. They are popular with customers because of their "instant gratification."
(2) *Numbers*: this is just a form of the illegal game with the same name. The players select some three or four digit number, with a daily drawing of winners and fixed prizes.
(3) *Lotto*: involves player selection of a set of numbers (6) from some larger group of numbers (40). Drawings are held weekly and the prizes rolled over if there is no winner. This has become probably the most popular game

presently and has received a lot of attention due to the very large potential prizes from multi-state lotto games.

(4) *Keno*: this is similar in many respects to Lotto, the player selecting more numbers from a larger set of potential numbers. Payoff is based on the number of correct selections.

(5) *Video lottery terminals (VLT)*: this is a relatively new lottery innovation available in a few states, which allows individuals to play electronic versions of casino games (blackjack, slots, and poker). Adoption of VLT was a recommendation of some governors (New York, Pennsylvania, Maryland) as a tool for balancing state budgets in the last few years.

(b) *Administrative costs*: One of the most frequent criticisms of lotteries is that they are expensive to administer compared to a conventional tax. Administrative costs involve both expenditures by the government and compliance costs by taxpayers. Looking first at compliance costs, it is difficult to judge lotteries since they are done voluntarily. Clearly, people spend time and money playing lotteries but they do it willingly. The potential compliance costs involve those by vendors who sell the tickets. Since states typically pay vendors 7–8% of sales in commissions, this is an indication of what it takes to get vendors to participate in the lottery.

In addition, the state has to administer the lottery program. This involves finding and monitoring vendors, selling the tickets to vendors, advertising and promoting the games, etc. As Mikesell and Zorn indicate, the typical revenue pattern for a lottery involves rapid initial sales after a particular game is introduced, which tapers off as the game matures. This implies that the state has to continually promote its existing games and search for new games to increase revenue. Unlike most taxes, there does not appear to be a drop-off in lottery administrative costs over time!!

In addition, these administrative costs are quite high!! As indicated in Table 13.3, administrative costs as a percent of sales averages close to 3%, with these costs exceeding 10% in six states. On average in 2008, 3.1% of ticket sales and 11.6% of net proceeds (sales minus prizes) went toward administrative costs. This compares to administrative costs of 1–2% for most general purpose taxes.

(3) *Equity*: Another controversial area concerning lotteries is their equity impact.

(a) *Horizontal equity*: As with excise taxes, lotteries do not tax people with the same ability to pay equally. Only those who use a lottery will bear the tax. While they may do this voluntarily, this does not change the fact that the state is choosing to tax one segment of its population much more heavily than another.

Several studies have shown that lottery sales are not evenly spread out among most individuals, even with the same income. Roughly, 80% of lottery sales are made to 20% of the adult population. These are the heavy players that purchase over 15 tickets every two months. As research suggests, these heavy players are predominantly black males with low educational achievement.

(b) *Vertical equity*: Not surprisingly, lotteries are a regressive form of taxation. Lottery advocates often point to the fact that lottery participation is not limited to just the poor. However, a number of studies find that the Effective Tax Rate (ETR) for lotteries is definitely regressive. The National Gambling Impact Study Commission (NGISC), which was created by the Congress in 1996 to evaluate the impacts of gambling, concluded (Hansen, 2004, p. 28):

> Lotteries, in fact, are highly regressive sources of income. Players with household income under $10,000 bet nearly three times as much on lotteries as those with incomes over $50,000.

To sell lotteries, many states have tied their lotteries to popular public programs such as education. The idea is that the lottery revenue will be used to improve primary education (and who is against better education?). There are two relevant issues with regard to this proposal. First, does the imposition of a lottery increase education funding? The findings of most studies examining this issue are that in most states, lottery finance has not led to increased education funding. Instead, it has allowed other sources of revenue to either be reduced or diverted to other programs.

One exception was the state of Georgia, which used lottery proceeds to fund college scholarships (Hope Scholarships), and pre-kindergarten education. Rubenstein and Scafidi, Jr. (2002)[5] investigated whether the net benefits from the lottery (benefits minus lottery spending) are regressive or progressive. They found that,

> Consistent with numerous other studies, we find that spending on lottery products is highly regressive. We also find that higher income households tend to receive a higher level of benefits from lottery-funded programs than do lower-income households. Taken together, we find a highly regressive pattern of net benefits . . . White households tend to spend less on playing the lottery than nonwhite households but receive substantially higher benefits from lottery funded programs, on average. (p. 236)

(4) *Efficiency*: Evaluating the efficiency effects for a lottery is similar to evaluating the efficiency of an excise tax.

The price that is distorted is the price of a lottery ticket. Because of the government's monopoly power, the price a person pays for a given chance of winning a lottery prize is higher than it would be if lotteries were offered through competitive markets.

The amount of distortion or efficiency loss from this tax depends on the tax rate and how responsive consumers are to price increases (price elasticity). As we already went over, the excise tax rates from lotteries are very high, well above that for

[5]Ross Rubenstein and Benjamin Scafidi. 2002. "Who Pays and Who Benefits? Examining the Distributional Consequences of the Georgia Lottery for Education." *National Tax Journal* 55(2): 223–238.

other excise taxes. This would suggest the definite potential for efficiency losses. If lotteries are treated like other "sin goods" such as alcohol and tobacco, then the demand is likely to be inelastic.

There is one crucial difference between a lottery and other forms of "sin taxes." It is possible that the efficiency losses from an alcohol or tobacco tax may be partially offset by the reductions in the harmful effects from smoking and drinking. This is clearly not the case for lotteries. If lotteries are going to be sizeable sources of revenue, then states have to aggressively market them. As Fisher (1987)[6] states,

> The curious difference about lotteries, of course, is that states promote and encourage consumption of this service so that additional revenue can be generated. Would the public be equally tolerant of state advertising to encourage cigarette smoking so that state tobacco taxes would generate more revenue? As Daniel Suits argued in 1975 regarding state-run gambling, "the government has become a pusher. And they're not pushing fire or police protection — only dreams." (p. 275)

Summary: Based on tax evaluation of lotteries, how do they stack up compared to general taxes and other types of excise taxes? Hansen (2004) summarizes the views of most tax policy experts on the lottery:

> For all of these reasons, the lottery is an example of poor tax policy. Most non-lottery states are currently considering or have recently considered starting lotteries, which is ill-advised from a tax policy standpoint. State-run lotteries make state tax systems more regressive, less transparent, and less economically neutral. Legislators seeking to increase tax revenue would do well to consider other sources. (p. 3)

---

[6]Ronald C. Fisher. 1987. *State and Local Public Finance*, 1st Edition (Glen view, Illinois: Foresman).